PORTRAIT OF CHESTER

Portrait of

CHESTER

by

DAVID BETHELL

ROBERT HALE · LONDON

© *David Bethell 1980*
First published in Great Britain 1980
ISBN 0 7091 8359 3

Robert Hale Limited
Clerkenwell House
Clerkenwell Green
London EC1

Photoset by Photobooks (Bristol) Ltd.,
printed in Great Britain by
Lowe & Brydone Ltd., Thetford
and bound by Weatherby Woolnough Ltd.,

CONTENTS

ILLUSTRATIONS

Water Tower
Constabulary Headquarters
Stanley Place
A house in Park Street

All photographs by the author

1

CITY on the DEE

IN ENGLAND, at the mouth of a wooded vale where the waters of the wide Dee meet the tides of the Irish Sea, stands the old walled city of Chester, the Roman fortress of Deva Victrix, a stronghold of the earls of Mercia, the seat of the palatine earldom, the gateway to Ireland, the cathedral city of the diocese, the county town of Cheshire.

On Christmas Eve, when the gable tenants with helmet and halberd prepared the Watch, the Recorder would tell of times gone by, how the city was founded by giants – giants who had built the great tunnels and cellars under the streets, the crypts and the walls, knit together from great blocks of sandstone. Effigies of the giants were carried at the head of the Midsummer Show.

The chroniclers, compiling their parchment histories in Latin or English or Welsh, said that the city was built by the ancient kings of the Britons. Some said that Ebraucus (Effrawc Cadarn, 'the strong') great-great-grandson of Brutus, first king of the Britons (great-grandson of Aeneas who fled from Troy), built Chester. Ebraucus founded York (Eboracum), Alclud in Albany, the Maidens' Castle on the Dolorous Mountain, and, in 827 BC, when King David was reigning in Judea, Chester. He had twenty wives, twenty sons and thirty daughters, and reigned for forty years. In 1589 a play about 'King Ebrauke with all his sonnes' was performed at the High Cross in the city; in 1563 the history of Aeneas and Dido was acted out on the Roodee.

But other chroniclers related that the city had an earlier existence. Samothes, a son of Japheth (third son of Noah) not recorded in the Bible, settled in Britain after the Flood, and his son Magus founded a city here called Neomagus.

Deva Victrix
The giant who built, or rebuilt, Chester was a relative newcomer, Leon Gawer, the conqueror of the Picts,

9

... a mighty strong giant:
Which builded caves and dungeons many a one,
No goodly buildings, ne proper, ne pleasant.

According to this story, King Leil of Loegria (Effrawc's grandson) founded the city – but this is just a confusion with the legend of the origin of Carlisle. Marius, King of Britain (grandson of King Cymbeline or Cunobelinus), is then said to have walled the city in the early second century and after reigning fifty-three years was buried at Chester.

In a sense the giant Leon Gawer did construct Chester, for he is but a personification of the real builder, the Great Legion. The first Roman penetration into north-west England took place during their second expedition, under the Emperor Claudius, which started in AD 43. Four legions were sent, with one in reserve, and after the initial thrusts a comprehensive treaty was arranged with eleven British kings, bringing the whole lowland area into alliance with Rome; but Wales remained hostile.

Caius Suetonius Paullinus, governor from AD 59, tackled the northern Welsh with an attack on Anglesey by the 14th and 20th Legions. He had prepared a fleet of flat-bottomed transport-ships which were probably assembled in the Dee estuary, and the earliest Roman relics from Chester are of this period. Almost immediately after the conquest of the island, Suetonius had to put down the rebellion of Boudicca (Boadicea) in what is now East Anglia, and it was probably on this occasion that the 20th Legion won the title 'Victrix'.

The next major move against the Welsh was under Sextus Julius Frontinus, who became governor in 74 or 75 and was succeeded in 77 or 78 by Gnaeus Julius Agricola (the Agricola of Tacitus), the legate of the 20th Legion. The earliest Chester inscription is on a lead waterpipe from Eastgate Street: "IMP . VESP VIIII T . IMP . VII COS . CN . IVLIO . AGRICOLA LEG AVG PR . PR" ("Emperor Vespasian nine times, Emperor Titus seven times consul (1st January – 23rd June 79), Agricola legate of Augustus *pro praetore*"). Pigs of lead and coins of earlier dates have been found at Chester, but the waterpipe is the earliest dated fixture.

Chester was the northernmost of the four legionary fortresses built against Wales – Isca (Caerleon-on-Usk), Glevum (Gloucester), Viroconium (Wroxeter) and Deva (Chester). The Dee estuary is the first major inlet at the east end of the coast of North Wales, and most of the river valley was low and marshy.

However, there are two sandstone outcrops above the river where a fortress could ideally be situated – the sites of Farndon and Chester, of which the latter held the strategic position at the head of the estuary. The 2nd Legion Adiutrix built the Agricolan fortress, but was sent to reinforce the Danube defences in 86 and was replaced at Chester by the 20th Legion Valeria Victrix from Inchtuthil. Watling Street runs up from London to Chester, where it swings north-west into Brigantia.

Chester became the permanent home of the 20th Legion until the fourth century. The legion was probably among the troops led to the Continent by Magnus Maximus, proclaimed emperor in Britain in 383 and remembered in Welsh legend as the great King Maxen Wledic.

The earliest surviving detailed description of British topography is the *Geographia* of Claudius Ptolemy. He recorded that Deva, held by the 20th Legion Victrix, was, with Viroconium, one of the two *oppida* of a British tribe called the Cornavii. To the north, extending from sea to sea, lay the Brigantes, whose towns included Vinovium, Camulodunum and Rigodunum on the borders of what is now Lancashire.

Close to Deva was the estuary of the Seteia, presumably the Dee or Mersey, from which the sub-tribe of the Setantii (in modern Lancashire) took their name. The Welsh tribe of the Ordovices (including the sub-tribe of the Ceangi) extended from the Llŷn peninsula to the very borders of modern Cheshire, and their towns included Mediolanum, generally identified with Whitchurch in Shropshire. On the east were the Coritani of Leicester and Lincoln.

The Roman fort was sited on a slight incline, highest at the north, with the river not far from the southern wall. The quay was west of the fortress. The greater part of Deva was barrack blocks, with the headquarters buildings, the *principia* and *praetorium*, at the centre. The site was defended by strong stone walls with an outer ditch, with gates to east, west, north and south (to a bridge over the Dee), and interval towers along each side. The stone walls replaced the earliest defences which were timber palisades on a bank and ditch.

The walls enclosed about sixty acres, a little larger than the other legionary forts in Britain. It was over a third of a mile from the north gate to the south, rather less from east to west. A legion in full strength was about 5,300 men. Outside the walls were the parade-ground, the amphitheatre, baths, cemeteries and quarries, and an attendant Romano-British settlement forming a suburb by the east gate. Further up the Dee was a works depot at Heronbridge, and then the crossing of the river at Farndon was defended by a camp at Holt.

We do not know what happened to Chester immediately after the Romans withdrew – whether it continued as part of the territory of the Cornavii, about whose history very little is known, or whether it had already a substantial occupation of Saxons or Irish. The land of the Cornavii became the kingdom of Powys (probably named from the Latin '*pagenses*', 'provincials'), whose rulers claimed direct descent from Magnus Maximus. Although the classic story of the creation of England is of a long westward push by conquering Anglo-Saxon tribes, it is highly likely that in Cheshire the movement was eastwards, that Chester was the earliest recipient of the new culture, and that the change was very slow, with Britannic or Old Welsh still spoken in the area until a late date.

The mediaeval chroniclers say that when Vortigern, King of the Britons, was deposed in favour of his son Vortimer, he was held at Chester, and that King Arthur received homage from Irish kings there. The attempts to make Chester one of the seats of the legendary Arthur's Court rest almost entirely, however, on deliberate confusion with Caerleon, the legionary fort on the Usk.

Legacaestir
Chester re-enters the realm of written history in 616 when a major battle took place there between Aethelfrith, King of Northumbria, and Solomon (Seluf ap Cynan Garwyn ap Brochfael), King of Powys. Solomon was killed in the battle, and there was a great defeat for Powys. Bede relates that more than two thousand monks from the British monastery of Bangor-is-y-Coed attended the battle to pray for a British victory, and that of these twelve hundred were killed and only fifty escaped by flight; and that Solomon's grandfather, Brochfael, was present at the conflict but fled with all his men.

Bede was writing in about 730 and was born in 673; his is the first surviving record of Chester after the Romans, and he states that the place was called in English 'Legacaestir', in British 'Carlegion' – both derive from the Latin '*castra legionum*', 'camp of the legions'.

By the eleventh century the English name had been shortened to 'Cestre', the modern 'Chester'.

Aethelfrith was descended from the royal House of Bernicia, but the heir to the kingdom of Deira (which had been joined with Bernicia in Northumbria) was Edwin, who lived in exile in East Anglia. Shortly after the Battle of Chester Edwin attacked Aethelfrith and took Northumbria. He reduced the British kingdom of Elmet in the Pennines and attacked North Wales, seized Anglesey and the Isle of Man and besieged Cadwallon, King of Venedotia, in Priestholm Island off the Anglesey coast.

Venedotia (Gwynedd) was the North Welsh kingdom roughly corresponding with the area of the Ordovices conquered by Rome. In alliance with Penda of Mercia, the growing English kingdom of the Marches, Cadwallon retaliated with a major expedition against Edwin, in which the latter and his son Osfrith were killed and Northumbria was devastated, falling apart again into the constituent kingdoms of Deira and Bernicia. The chroniclers say that it was at Chester that Cadwallon was acknowledged King of the Britons.

In the reign of Offa (757–96) the kingdom of Mercia expanded westwards by a series of assaults on North Wales. Earthworks called 'Wat's Dyke' and 'Offa's Dyke' were established from near Prestatyn on the north coast to the British Channel, and running several miles west of Chester, "But now in either side bothe of yond half and on this half the diche, and specialliche in the schires of Chestre, of Schrouysbury, and of Herford in meny places beeth Englische men and Walsche men i-medled to gidres."

In 821 Cenwulf, King of Mercia, died at Basingwerk (Flintshire), and the following year Ceolwulf, his brother, destroyed Deganwy at the mouth of the Conway and brought Powys under his control. Later writers claimed that the Welsh held Chester until 830 when King Egbert subdued North Wales, but both banks of the Dee estuary were probably settled by the English from the eighth century, and the adjoining areas of Wales were part of Cheshire until the creation of Flintshire in 1284 and Denbighshire in 1535. Many Flintshire place-names are Welsh versions of earlier English names.

King Egbert of Wessex conquered Mercia in 829, but the Mercian throne was retaken by Wiglaf in the following year. If Egbert did take Chester, the event may not have been of lasting significance. He is said to have destroyed brazen images set up by King Cadwallon in the city. Egbert's son Aethelwulf, who reigned in Wessex from 839 to 855, is said, without any apparent foundation, to have been crowned here.

In 835 the first Viking raid on England took place, when Danish raiders attacked Sheppey in Kent. From then until the late-eleventh century the country was plagued by these invasions, which led to the seizing of the English crown by Cnut, Harold Harefoot and Harthacnut from 1016 to 1042, and the settlement of the north-east of the country, the Danelaw, by Scandinavians, with the establishment of Viking kingdoms at York from 875 to 954 and in East Anglia from 880 to 902.

The Vikings were most successful in the coastal areas where there were islands and long inlets, and the estuaries of the Mersey and Dee on either side of Wirral would have been most attractive. At that time Wirral was effectively twice as long as today, with the sea washing at Chester's walls, and Ince an island in the salt-marshes of the Gowy. Wallasey was an island, virtually detached from Wirral. Chester was considered to be a Wirral town.

All along the peninsula the Vikings have left their traces in Norse place-names such as Frankby and Greasby, and here we find a distinctive form of stone wheel cross cognate with stones from Norse settlements in Ireland and the Isle of Man. In 894, in the reign of King Alfred, when the country was suffering one of the worst Viking attacks, the English army besieged the Danish host. The Vikings gathered together their women, ships and property for safety in East Anglia, and marched overland to the deserted Roman fortress at Chester,. where they held out against the Mercian levies. The Danes were forced by hunger to eat their horses but, having wintered at Chester, returned to Essex. One chronicle states that Chester was attacked again in 896, and it is likely that Wirral was occupied by Scandinavians in the ninth century. Watling Street to the south formed the boundary between English and Danes.

In 907 Earl Aethelred of Mercia, who was married to Aethelflaed, sister of King Edward the Elder of Wessex, refortified Chester and was probably responsible for laying out the city walls on the lines they follow today. The Roman fortress wall was sufficiently substantial on the north and east to be incorporated, but on the south and west the new walls were taken further towards the river, and in the south-west corner of this area the stronghold of the new defences was constructed.

At about this time north-west Mercia was divided into shires, and the area around Legeceaster became 'Legeceaster scir', Cheshire. After Aethelred's death Aethelflaed was styled 'Lady of the Mercians'; she constructed or refortified numerous positions against the Danes and Welsh in this area. Three of her ten new forts cannot be precisely identified (one may have been at Bromborough on Wirral, one across the Mersey at Warrington), but they included Runcorn on the Mersey, the Iron Age site at Eddisbury in central Cheshire, and Chirbury to the south. Edward built a new fort at Thelwall near Runcorn in 919 and rebuilt the defences at Manchester.

It was by no means an easy job to hold down the north-west or to protect it from invasion. In 920 a Dane called Sihtric, cousin of Raegnald, King of York, brought an army in from Dublin, broke through the defences and annihilated the little town of Davenport (near Congleton). When, in 924, the Welsh and the Mercians of Chester revolted, Edward marched north and put down the uprising but died on 17th July at Farndon. Higden's *Polychronicon* talks of Chester's being again lost to the Danes and recovered by King Edmund of Wessex in about 946.

Edgar, who was consecrated King of England on 11th May 972 at Bath, shortly afterwards took his fleet to Chester, where he received the submission of eight kings. The later chroniclers said that his fleet had first circumnavigated Scotland, and the kings were Kenneth, King of the Scots; Malcolm, King of the Cumbrians; Maccus, King of the Many Isles; Dunmail, King of Strathclyde; Siferth and Hywel (Welsh princes); Iago, King of Venedotia, and Nichil or Juchil, King of Westmorland. The kings went down to the Dee from Edgar's palace (on the western shore) and rowed him in a skiff to St John's Minster (chapter 4) and back again.

In 980, shortly after Edgar's death, a Viking host from the north sailed up the Dee and harried Cheshire. His son, Aethelred Unraed, used Chester in 1000 as a base for his fleet when he attacked Cumberland. The ships failed to make contact with his army and so sailed off and attacked the Isle of Man, while he laid waste Cumbria. Lancashire south of the Ribble was assigned to the earls of Mercia, one of whose seats was at Chester, but only the most tenuous control of Westmorland and Cumberland could be exercised until the late eleventh century.

Palatine Earldom
At the Norman Conquest, Earl Edwin of Mercia joined the

resistance to William the Conqueror, and he and his brother Morcar, Earl of the North, were put to death. In 1069 William sent a major force against the Welsh and the Mercians who were holding Chester. The troops besieged Shrewsbury and seized Chester, which was refortified by the Normans, bringing the whole of Mercia into their grasp.

When Mercia was divided by William into smaller earldoms based on the shires, Cheshire was first assigned to a Flemish noble called Gherbod, but the latter shortly afterwards returned to Flanders, where he was imprisoned, and the earldom of Chester was assigned in 1171 to Hugh of Avranches, son of Richard Goz, Viscount of Avranches and of the Hiemois. This Hugh, who became generally known as 'Hugh Lupus' ('Hugh the wolf'), was effectively the first Norman Earl of Chester, and the local earldom continued in his family until its extinction. Hugh's mother was King William's half-sister; his stepmother was Eormenhild, sister of Leofric the Great, Earl of Mercia, who died in 1057 and was grandfather of Edwin and Morcar.

Cheshire was one of the more difficult areas to suppress, but William gave it to Hugh to hold as freely by the sword as he himself held England by the crown. The actual ceremonial sword of Hugh Lupus (or perhaps of Hugh Cyveliok, a twelfth-century earl of Chester) is in the British Museum; it has the words '*HVGO COMES CESTRIAE*' on the great pointed blade. Hugh extended English power into Wales, captured Gruffydd ap Cynan, King of Gwynedd, and penetrated as far as Anglesey, but permanent gains were elusive.

The Domesday survey of 1086 gives us a considerable amount of information about the city. In the time of King Edward the Confessor (1042–66) it was taxed for fifty hides, assessed from 431 taxable houses, besides fifty-six taxable houses owned by the bishop. The citizens were protected by a system of customary fines for various crimes. A person who committed murder indoors lost all his property and was declared an outlaw. Bloodwites (attacks causing bloodshed) varied, according to the day on which they were made, from 10 shillings to £1. Manslaughter on holy days cost £4, otherwise £2; heinfare (breach of peace indoors) and forestalling (preventing goods reaching the market) cost £4 on holy days, £2 otherwise. Hangewith (wrongfully hanging a thief) would cost the eager citizen 10 shillings, but wrongful hanging by the sheriffs cost £1. Theft, robbery or rape cost the citizens 40 shillings.

Unlawful sex by a widow required a £1 fine; by a girl, 10 shillings. Anyone caught using a false measure in the city was fined 4 shillings; for making bad ale the penalty was 4 shillings or a ride in the cuckstool, an elegant contraption which ducked the offender in a pond or cesspool. Chester was governed by *xii iudices* (twelve judges), a typical Scandinavian form of government – the Vikings were known in Ireland as 'the people of twelve judges'.

Domesday Book records that there were seven moneyers in the city before the Conquest. Many Old English silver pennies from the Chester mint have been found, and in this period every coin bore the name of the moneyer and the mint; about 150 moneyers from Chester have been identified, from the reign of Aethelstan (925–40). Hywel Dda, King of Dyfed, also had his coins struck at Chester in the mid-tenth century.

Every hide in the shire contributed towards the maintenance of the city walls and the Dee bridge one workman or a fine of £2. When Hugh Lupus took the city, it had been almost devastated and was worth only £30; 205 houses had been destroyed. Hugh created eight baronies in his earldom, at Halton, Montalt (Mold), Nantwich, Shipbrook, Malpas, Dunham, Kinderton and Rhuddlan. The barons and the abbots of the monasteries in his earldom formed the earl's parliament held in Chester Castle. Most of these baronies did not survive more than a couple of generations, for lack of male heirs.

Hugh Lupus, to whom the heralds assigned the arms of a white wolf's head on a blue shield, was noted for his rapacity and his obesity – the Welsh called him '*Vras*', 'gross'. He died on 27th July 1101 and was buried in the graveyard of the Benedictine abbey of St Werburgh which he founded in the city, and of which he became a monk four days before he died. His son Richard, aged seven, succeeded to the earldom but was drowned on 25th November 1120 in the English Channel, crossing from France with the two sons of Henry I in the ill-fated *Blanche Nef (White Ship)*. The earldom was inherited by Richard's first cousin, Randle Meschines, Lord of Cumberland, who was forced by Henry I to surrender Cumberland when he took Chester.

Perhaps the earliest traveller's account of Chester survives from this period, that of William of Malmesbury, who wrote: "The natives greatly enjoy milk and butter; those who are richer live on meat. . . . Goods are exchanged between Chester and Ireland, so that what the nature of the soil lacks is supplied by the toil of the merchants."

Randle Meschines died in about 1128 and was succeeded by his son Randle II, de Gernon, who married Matilda, daughter of Robert, Earl of Gloucester. He became perhaps the most important of the Norman Earls of Chester, one of the most powerful of the English barons in the troubled reign of King Stephen. Certainly Chester had been transformed from being a perilous frontier fortress to a fulcrum of the national power-struggle.

After Stephen seized the throne, when King David of Scotland invaded Cumberland and Northumberland, Stephen arranged a compromise by granting David Doncaster and Carlisle and promising the earldom of Huntingdon to David's son Henry. Earl Randle, who was incensed at this blow to his hereditary claim to Cumberland, left Court in a rage. In 1139 King Stephen gave Prince Henry the earldom of Northumberland, including all Northumberland, Cumberland, Westmorland, Durham and Lancashire north of the Ribble.

The following year (although on 31st May there was a serious fire in Chester) Earl Randle and his half-brother William de Romara seized Lincoln Castle. Stephen first made William earl of Lincoln but shortly afterwards attacked them, and Randle retired to Chester and declared for Stephen's rival, Henry I's daughter, the Empress Matilda. Earl Randle and his father-in-law Robert, Earl of Gloucester, (Matilda's half-brother) marched on Stephen at Lincoln with a confused mass of Welsh supporters and captured the King. The earl supported the Empress at the Battle of Winchester against Stephen's remaining forces brought together by the Queen, but this help was late and ineffectual, and the battle became a rout in which the Earl of Gloucester was captured. When Earl Randle was seized by King Stephen at Northampton on 29th August 1146, there was a serious attack on Cheshire by a large horde of Welshmen, but Robert de Montalt, the Earl's *dapifer*, massacred most of them with a small force of armed men at Nantwich a few days later.

In 1149 Randle came to an agreement with King David of Scotland in which he surrendered his claim to Cumberland and David gave him the honour of Lancaster, including all Lancashire north of the Ribble. Lancashire south of the Ribble was still considered an appendage of Cheshire, as were the lowland coastal areas of North Wales, and this significantly increased the power of the earldom. In 1153 Duke Henry (to be Henry II), Empress Matilda's son, granted Stafford and Staffordshire to the earl, but on 16th December Randle died, said to have been poisoned by his wife in league with William Peverell, an old enemy. He was succeeded by his son Hugh Cyveliok (born in 1147 in the commote of Cyveliok, Merionethshire) who married the daughter of Simon, Count of Montfort and Evreux.

During these civil wars in England, Owain Gwynedd (son of Gruffydd ap Cynan) captured the seats of two Cheshire baronies, Mold and Rhuddlan. In 1157 Henry II mounted an expedition into North Wales, and the royal army camped at Saltney, below Chester. Henry received the homage of Malcolm IV (son of David), the new King of Scotland, at Chester for the earldom of Huntingdon, and Malcolm surrendered Cumberland and Northumberland to Henry. The Welsh expedition ended in a compromise which left Owain on the far side of the River Clwyd and Henry recognized as his overlord.

In 1172 Earl Hugh joined with William the Lion, the next King of Scotland, and Robert, Earl of Leicester, in an alliance against King Henry. Hugh and Ralph de Fougères led a rising in Brittany, but Henry put down the revolt and seized Earl Hugh in the castle of Dol. Hugh's lands were confiscated for treason but restored by the Northampton Parliament of 1177.

Chester's earliest surviving charters dates from about 1175, when Henry II notified his bailiffs at Dublin that the burgesses of Chester should have the same merchant rights there as they had in the time of Henry I, his grandfather. Chester was the gateway to Ireland, and the English community in Dublin and the Pale consisted largely of Cheshire men. (Equally, there were foreign merchants, including Germans, in Chester.) A church in Dublin was dedicated to St Werburgh, and was frequented by Cheshire men. In 1183 the secular canons of Downpatrick were dismissed and a convent of Benedictine monks from St Werburgh's in Chester was established.

One Sunday afternoon in March 1181, Chester was almost completely burned down. The following September Earl Hugh died at Leek in Staffordshire and was succeeded by his son Randle III, de Blundeville. On New Year's Day 1188 Henry II knighted Randle at Caen and married him to Constance, widow of the King's own son Geoffrey, niece of William the Lion, daughter and heiress of Conan IV, Duke of Brittany and Earl of Richmond, in whose right Randle held those titles.

The chronicler Giraldus Cambrensis arrived in Chester on 14th

April 1188, made a cursory description of the city and noted these objects of interest:

The inhabitants assert that the Dee changes its course every month; and to whichever of the banks, i.e. of England or Wales, it should incline, they have the very certain prophecy that that race shall go under in that year, and the other prevail.

We saw here what seemed to us a strange thing, that is, deer's cheese. For the Countess and the Earl's mother, having domesticated deer, have presented to the Archbishop three cheeses made of deer's milk and moulded in a little basket.

Also in this same region, in our own time, a deer cow was seen; for a deer had fertilized a cow; . . . it was a cow in all the front part as far as the groin, and then having hip bones, tail, hindlegs and feet distinctively with the hair and colour of a deer. But because it was more domesticated than wild, it remained with the herd.

It happened in the same district, also in our time, that a bitch made pregnant by a monkey produced a litter, the foreparts being all monkey, but the hind quarters dog. When the warder of the soldier's hall, a peasant, saw these animals, he was so stupified by the strangeness of the prodigies, and horrified by such deformities of dual nature, that he killed them all immediately with the stick he was carrying in his hand; not without the appropriate condemnation and indignation of his lord when he found out about the matter.

There was also seen in Chester in our times a crippled woman, lacking hands from birth; to whom, however, nature gave such a remedy against that defect, that she had such flexible feet, so delicately articulated, that she used to sew with a needle as fast, as dexterously and not less subtly, as other women. And despite this disability, she could do with her feet whatever is normally done with scissor and thread by hand, to the admiration of spectators.

So much for the sights of Chester in 1188. About that time a monk called Lucian wrote a little treatise in praise of Chester which is an elaborate exercise in vagueness. The gates, he says, look out upon India to the east, Ireland to the west, Norway to the north and Wales to the south. There is a city wall. There is a fine river full of fish. There is a wharf at which arrive boats from Aquitaine, Spain, Ireland and Germany. Travellers from Ireland stay at St Werburgh's Abbey.

On 2nd July 1189 Henry II died; Richard *Cœur de Lion*, his son, became king and in December went off to the Crusade. When Richard was captured by the Holy Roman Emperor Henry VI, and

John his brother rebelled, the Earl of Chester helped to restore Nottingham to the King's control.

At Richard's second coronation, on 17th April 1194, Earl Randle carried Curtana, one of the three swords of state. Randle's exploits made him a legendary figure, and he is spoken of in English ballads in the same breath as Robin Hood. One of the tales was about an expedition into Wales when Randle, besieged at Rhuddlan, summoned his constable Roger de Lacy from Chester to help. Roger brought together all the minstrels of the city and marched with a great throng of dissolutes against the Welsh, who, seeing the oncoming mass in the distance, abandoned the siege. About 1201 Randle confirmed to the city all the privileges enjoyed in the time of his predecessors, and also confirmed the guild merchant.

Randle III's coat-of-arms is of particular interest, for the heralds attributed to him three golden wheatsheaves (garbs) on a blue shield, the arms which, with the sword of the earldom, are used by the shire today. Randle's father, Hugh II, is said to have had six golden garbs on a blue shield. Wheatsheaves were borne by many persons with names such as White and Whiteley; 'wheat' is cognate with 'white' and just means 'white corn'. Randle III was named after the Norman-French Blundeville, Latin Album Monasterium, English Whitminster, i.e. Oswestry. There is thus a good case for tracing the Cheshire wheatsheaf to a pun on an old name for a Shropshire town.

King John visited Chester in May 1206, and again in 1212, but was prevented from a Welsh expedition because of the unrest among the English magnates. Randle III was in a position of great power, with effective control during John's reign over Cheshire, Lancashire, north Yorkshire, Shropshire, Staffordshire, the Peak in Derbyshire, and North Wales. When John died, Randle was the greatest baron of the realm. In 1214 he founded the monastery of Dieulacresse near Leek, with the monks from Poulton Abbey.

Shortly after Henry III was crowned, the earldom of Lincoln was granted to Randle, on the suppression of a rebellion by Gilbert de Gant, the previous earl. Randle resigned this earldom to his son-in-law John de Lacy in 1232. He made his peace with Llywelyn the Great in Snowdonia, and left England for the Crusade. After a glorious campaign, Randle returned safe and well two years later and set about fortifying his castles at Chartley and Beeston, and building a new abbey at Dieulacresse.

Earl Randle's one failure, which soon proved fatal to the local earldom, was to provide heirs. He divorced his first wife, Constance, and married Clemence, daughter of William de Fougères, widow, but left no legitimate children; nor did he have any brothers. He died at Wallingford in October 1232 and was buried in the chapter house of St Werburgh's Abbey in Chester; his heart was buried at Dieulacresse.

The male heir was John the Scot, Earl of Huntingdon and Cambridge, son of Randle's sister Matilda by David, Earl of Huntingdon, brother of William the Lion. He immediately allied himself with Llywelyn ab Iorwerth, marrying his daughter Helen, who is said to have poisoned him. John died at Darnhall near Winsford in June 1237. The natural heir was William, Count of Aumale, husband of the senior co-heiress, but Henry III annexed the earldom "lest so fair a dominion should be divided among women". The King granted it to his son, Prince Edward, in 1254.

The Gift of the Firstborn Son

When Edward moved into Chester on 17th July 1256, he was met by the citizens and clergy and for three days received the homage of the nobility of Cheshire and Wales. He then went into Wales, inspected his lands, the four cantrefs (Perfeddwlad) adjoining Cheshire, returned to Chester and then proceeded south. In November Llywelyn ap Gruffydd, grandson of Llywelyn ab Iorwerth, attacked and overran the four cantrefs in a week. In the next two years Llywelyn subdued the various princes of North and South Wales and proclaimed himself Prince of Wales. Henry assembled armies at Chester and Bristol in 1257 but could not dislodge Llywelyn. In June 1258 the army was reassembled at Chester for a second campaign, but a truce was arranged on 17th June.

By 1264 the citizens were beginning seriously to fear an attack by the Welsh or by the barons and started to re-dig the fosse by the Northgate. On Christmas Eve Prince Edward granted the earldom, together with the castles of Newcastle in Staffordshire and the Peak, to Earl Simon de Montfort of Leicestershire, whose son Henry arrived in the city on 4th January. Llywelyn came to Hawarden and met Henry, and peace was arranged. At that time Simon was holding Prince Edward as a hostage, but on 28th May Edward escaped while out riding. When the news reached Cheshire, the Prince's allies seized Beeston Castle and besieged Simon's lieutenants in Chester Castle. After the Battle of

Evesham, on 4th August, when Simon was killed, the garrison at Chester surrendered. It so happened that a new abbot of St Werburgh's, Simon de Whitchurch, had been elected during Simon's brief spell as earl, but Prince Edward, who resumed the title, agreed to the appointment. Already the power and privileges of the earldom were being reduced; a statute was enacted requiring the Chester justices henceforth to make account to the royal exchequer. At Michaelmas in 1267 Henry and Llywelyn signed a peace treaty in which Llywelyn was formally allowed the title Prince of Wales.

Henry III died on 16th November 1272, and Prince Edward became Edward I. In 1275 he came to Chester to receive homage from Llywelyn, and when the Welshman did not arrive, Edward refortified his North Wales strongholds. He appointed the Earl of Warwick commander at Chester. In 1277 the King returned, leading an army of over fifteen thousand men into North Wales, and quickly forced the issue, clearing all resistance as far as the Conway, taking Anglesey and preparing new castles at Flint and Rhuddlan. In November Llywelyn submitted to the treaty of Conway, by which he again surrendered the four cantrefs.

Although Chester had been so quickly relieved from the Welsh threat, the levies for the war had been burdensome; worse still, on 15th May 1278 the whole of the town within the walls burned down. The Rows (chapter 4) were then planned, and the city was reconstructed, complete with those convenient inner walkways. When, on 3rd February 1279, a high tide broke down the Dee Bridge, Edward not only insisted that the citizens bear the whole cost of the rebuilding but introduced the Common Law of England to the earldom, something unheard-of.

On 21st March 1282 Llywelyn's brother, David, revolted and seized Hawarden Castle; Ruthin, Hope and Dinas Bran quickly fell to the Welsh. Edward summoned the host to Chester, and it moved out into North Wales in June. Llywelyn was killed on 11th December, and in the following year David was captured. On 19th March 1284 Edward issued the Statute of Rhuddlan which created the new county of Flint. On 25th April Queen Eleanor gave birth to a son, Edward, whose elder brother, Alphonso, had been designated Earl of Chester but died on 19th August. Edward became the heir-apparent and in 1301 was created Prince of Wales and Earl of Chester.

In 1300, at the age of sixteen, Prince Edward came to Chester and received homage from the men of Cheshire and Wales. He ascended the throne on 8th July 1307 as Edward II, and in November 1312 his son Edward was born and created earl. He became Edward III in 1327; his son Edward (the Black Prince) was created earl in 1333.

For most of the fourteenth century the city and shire remained undisturbed and prosperous, despite the horrific episode of the Black Death, which swept through Cheshire in 1349 and undermined the rural economy for a decade. On 9th March 1354 Edward III confirmed the ancient charter of Earl Randle to the city and made the Mayor Admiral of the Dee from Chester to Arnold's Eye, and Escheator within the city. Trade was good:

> Fisch, flesche, and corn low
> This cite toun hath i-now
> Schippes and chaffare
> See water bringeth i-now thare.

"This citee hath plente of lyflode, of corn, flesche, and of fische, and specialliche of pris salmoun."

The tradespeople formed groups called 'guilds' or 'companies', which enforced a certain amount of regulation within each trade. There were more than two dozen guilds; some, like the Fletmakers' Company, are found for only a small period, but others survived in their original form into the eighteenth century. The guilds were responsible for the various pageants of the Mystery or Miracle Plays which were presented at Whitsun (chapter 2), and of the Midsummer Shows on Roodee (chapter 12).

Edward the Black Prince died in 1376, and his son Richard became earl seven months before he succeeded to the throne in 1377. In 1379 there was such abundance in the land that a fat pig could be bought for a penny, and a gallon of claret for fourpence. Two years later came the Peasants' Revolt: on 29th July 1381, after Richard II's proclamation to suppress illegal associations had been recited at the High Cross and at Eastham Church, a group of villeins of St Werburgh's Abbey revolted at Backford, but the rising was quickly suppressed, and sixteen of the peasants were committed to the castle gaol. In 1394 the earl's sheriff was ordered to arrest all disturbers of the peace, because bodies of armed men had been gathering and intolerable felonies had been committed.

Richard II visited Chester in September 1394 on his way to Ireland, the local historians record, and presented the sword of state to the Mayor. The royal party was entertained by the corporation. John Brughill, the new Bishop of Lichfield, was installed at the old cathedral church of St John in Chester in the presence of Richard II in 1398. Richard was so gratified by the loyalty of his Cheshire militia who assembled at Shrewsbury that he elevated Cheshire from a county into a principality and annexed to it Flintshire, Shropshire and the northern Welsh Marches forfeited from Richard, Earl of Arundel. Moreover, Richard confirmed to this principality the ancient liberties of the earldom; these must have been sweet words in the ears of the men of Cheshire.

Richard put a great deal of reliance on his bodyguard of archers from the principality, and their misdemeanours were a principal charge against him when he was overthrown. In 1398 he sent 4,000 marks of gold to Chester for distribution among his supporters who had suffered for him at Redcote Bridge in 1387. The Parliament of 1398 was adjourned to Shrewsbury (the nearest town to Chester outside the shire) and thoroughly consolidated his position, overthrowing all the acts of the Merciless Parliament.

While Richard was in Ireland the following year, his cousin Henry Bolingbroke returned from exile and marched to Chester, where he beheaded Sir Piers Legh of Lyme and fixed his head on a turret of the castle. Henry marched out to Flint on 19th August and seized Richard as soon as he landed. The King was brought back to the city with the Earl of Salisbury, "mounted on two little nagges not worth 40 francs", and was imprisoned in the castle gateway (chapter 8) before being taken on to London and death.

Henry, now Henry IV, abolished the principality of Chester and granted the principality of Wales and earldom of Chester to his eldest son, Henry.

There had been an immediate rising in Chester in favour of Richard: a group of loyalists attacked the Castle, took the keys of the Eastgate, beheaded a Lancastrian and denounced the new King. In North Wales Owain Glyndŵr, who had been squire of the body to Richard, raised a rebellion and was proclaimed Prince of Wales on 20th September 1400. Cheshire men started to commit robberies in the adjoining counties of Shropshire, Staffordshire and Derbyshire.

It proved impossible to put down the Cheshire rising through Cheshire men, and strangers from outside the shire were brought in to hold the principal offices. When Henry IV and his son came to Chester to put down the Welsh rebellion, a body of twenty archers had to be raised merely to guard their provisions. The King's difficulties were compounded by the silting of the Dee and the destruction of the port by the Welsh, which made it very difficult to get supplies to the city by sea. (The decline of the sea-trade itself caused discontent in Chester.) Henry abolished the immunity that Cheshire men had previously had from prosecution for murder and felonies committed outside the shire in other shire courts.

In 1402 the city was still vulnerable, and licences were issued to persons entering to buy food. The shire was summoned to defend the city, and efforts were made to prevent food reaching the rebels. In September 1403 Prince Henry arrived in Chester and ordered the Mayor to expel all the Welsh; no Welshman could "enter into the city before sunrise on any day, on any excuse, nor tarry in the same after sunset, under pain of cutting off of his head". Welshmen entering Chester during the day were forbidden to enter wine- or beer-taverns, to assemble more than two together, or to bear any weapon except for one little knife for eating dinner.

Henry Percy, son of the Earl of Northumberland, allied with the Scots and the Welsh, and Cheshire rose in revolt. Percy had been constable of the castle in 1399 and was a popular figure, and he was joined by many Cheshire men as he marched south. He issued a proclamation at the High Cross that Richard was alive, in custody, and marched south to Shrewsbury. Battle was joined with the royal forces there, and Henry Percy was killed and his army smashed.

In November a fine of 3,000 marks was imposed on Cheshire, and Chester was forced, on pain of 300 marks, to provide shipping to raise the siege of Beaumaris, but the merchants continued to provide food for Glyndŵr's rebels, and the Welsh were able with impunity to assemble at Malpas within the shire. The Prince of Wales issued numerous mandates to Cheshire land-owners to protect their estates in the Marches, but many remained discreetly absent. In 1409 the mayor of Chester was removed from office and a military governor appointed. Three years later Prince Henry appointed commissioners to elect a mayor because the citizens had banded together "forcibly to disturb the free election".

On 20th March 1413 Henry IV died, and the prince became Henry V. Nine years later he died of dysentery at war in France, leaving his son Henry VI, a baby of nine months, who was never created Earl of Chester.

The first half of the fifteenth century saw a rapid decay at Chester. The river was no longer navigable to the city – less than a dozen merchant vessels visited in fifty years. The population fell, and houses and land were unoccupied. Wheat, which had cost 6d a bushel in the heady days of 1379, rose in price to 10½d in 1412, a shilling in 1414, 1s 9d in 1438; the poor were forced to make bread from peas, vetches and fern-roots. The Irish trade continued, but the boats now offloaded downstream:

> Hides and fish, salmon, hake, herringe,
> Irish wooll, and linnen cloth, faldinge,
> And marterns good be her marchandie,
> Hertes hides and other of venerie,
> Skinnes of otter, squirrel, and Irish hare,
> Of sheepe, lambe, and foxe, is her chaffare,
> Felles of kiddes and conies great plenty.

In 1445 Henry VI married Margaret of Anjou; their son Edward, born on 13th October 1453, became the new earl. In 1455, when the unpopular queen visited the city, there was a general uprising which was suppressed with the imprisonment of many citizens in Northgate and the Castle; but when Margaret returned in 1459, she won the citizens over with her courtesy and hospitality, and many Cheshire men fought for the King, and several were slain, at Bloreheath.

It was said that each day before the battle three mermaids arose on the field and combed their hair, singing,

> Ere yet the hawberry assumes its deep red
> Embrued shall this heath be with blood nobly shed.

Bloreheath is stamped on local tradition as a conflict in which the blossom of Cheshire manhood was fruitlessly cut down in civil strife:

> There Dutton Dutton kills, a Done doth kill a Done,
> A Booth a Booth, and Leigh by Leigh is overthrown;
> A Venables against a Venables doth stand,
> A Troutbeck fighteth with a Troutbeck hand to hand;
> There Molineux doth make a Molineux to die,
> And Egerton the strength of Egerton doth try.
> Oh Cheshire, wert thou mad? of thine own native gore

So much until this day thou never shed'st before;
Above two thousand men upon the earth were thrown,
Of which the greatest part were naturally thy own.

On 4th March 1461 Edward, the nineteen-year-old son of the Duke of York, seized the throne as Edward IV. Henry VI was briefly restored in 1470, but on 4th May 1471 Edward's forces defeated the Lancastrians at the Battle of Tewkesbury, and Henry's son Edward, killed. King Edward made his own son, another Edward, less than a year old, Earl of Chester in August. The new earl was received in triumph at Chester; the sword of state borne before him on that occasion is thought to be the same weapon later attributed to Sir William Wallace and exhibited as such at Dumbarton Castle. Prince Edward died shortly after his accession in April 1483, apparently at the hands of his Uncle Richard, who became Richard III. Richard made his son Edward the new earl, but the boy died within the year, before Richard's overthrow by Henry Tudor, Henry VII. In 1489 Henry's son Arthur was created Earl of Chester. The King visited Chester in July 1495, and Prince Arthur in 1499 when he was entertained by a performance of the Assumption of the Blessed Virgin Mary before the abbey gate (chapter 2). Arthur died three years later, and his eleven-year-old brother Henry, Duke of York, became earl; in 1509 he succeeded to the throne as Henry VIII.

In 1503 the Corporation ordered that innkeepers and past mayors and sheriffs should hang lanterns at their doors from nightfall to eight o'clock from 1st November to 2nd February, providing a little rudimentary street-lighting. It was also ordered that every wine-tavern, cellar and ale-bower be shut at nine.

City and County
On 6th April 1506 the city received its Great Charter from Henry VII elevating it to the rank of a county. The Corporation was the Mayor, twenty-four aldermen (including the Recorder), forty councillors and two sheriffs, two coroners and two murengers (to maintain the walls). All the arrears of the fee-farm due to the Crown were remitted, and henceforth the city paid yearly £20 in silver.

Sanitation remained almost non-existent, and in 1507 there was an outbreak of sweating sickness in which ninety-one householders died. "The remark of this destroying angel's respect for the fair sex, was here verified, only four perished." This was an epidemic of a dangerous disease which caused a rapid fever and profuse sweating, and from which the sufferers often died within two or three hours. The plague recurred in 1517, and the city was for a while shuttered and seemed deserted, with grass growing at the High Cross. The same sickness hit England again in 1528, and in 1550 had its last major epidemic, when many more citizens died. Wheat was in great scarcity, the price rising to 16 shillings a bushel.

From the beginning of the sixteenth century the strong new feelings of Puritanism started to stir in Chester. There was conflict between the citizens and the abbot in 1511, and in 1519 the Corporation forbade various Popish customs, "priest's offerings, first mass, gospel ales and Welsh-weddings". In 1540 Henry Gee the Mayor intervened in female fashion: "No manar Single or vnmryed woman Shall were vpon hur hede eny Whyte cap, or of other Colour, vnder payne of ijs for euery tyme so offendinge; nor . . . any hatt of blacke or other Coloure oneles it be when she Rydes, or els goith on Walking Abrode in the feldes or Country."

Henry Gee also ordered that no woman between the ages of fourteen and forty should keep any tavern or alehouse in the city; apparently, it was a common scandal among travellers how young women kept inns in Chester. In 1542 William Beswick, the Mayor, suppressed the brothels in the city, which had previously been licensed by the corporation.

Chester suffered a slight in 1541 when the sanctuary for criminals at Manchester, created the year before, was removed to the city, "forasmuch as the town of Manchester is not walled, whereby the sanctuary men may or can safely be kept in the night season, but that they may and do continually escape out of the town by night, and commit sundry great robberies and felonies upon the King's loving and obedient subjects repairing to the town." The Corporation was incensed, and the Mayor and an alderman rode in person to see the King, and persuaded him to remove the sanctuarymen to Stafford.

Henry VIII had created a new diocese on the dissolution of the monasteries, with the cathedral in the old abbey church of St Werburgh's in Chester. This diocese was based on the Chester archdeaconry of Lichfield diocese, to which was added the Richmond archdeaconry of York. In 1542 the new see was transferred from the province of Canterbury to that of York.

It was in 1543 that Cheshire was further assimilated into the

English administration when Henry summoned two knights from the county and two burgesses from the city to represent them in Parliament. There may have been some reluctance to return MPs, for the first pair from Chester were not sent until 1553.

In 1556 John Webster, the Mayor, attacked the custom of serving Christmas breakfasts, because "dysorderid persons haue vsed themselues Rayther all the daye after idillie in vyse and wantonnes". The following year the Corporation started work on a new harbour at Parkgate, 13 miles downstream from the city, called 'the New Quay'. Nevertheless, the trade was lost irrevocably to the Mersey. In 1586 fifteen ships belonged to Chester as against twenty-eight to Liverpool, and the trend continued thereafter in Liverpool's favour.

Plague again troubled Chester in 1558, with little loss of life, but many fled the city; again in 1574 there was another outbreak "but God of his mercy staid his rod with the death of some few in the Crofts". In the 1560s it was ordered that each citizen should repair the street in front of his property – previously it had been done by the murengers, and ironshod wheeled vehicles were banned. In 1604 a pavier was appointed.

In 1580, when the shire was waiting for a Spanish invasion, Queen Elizabeth ordered the Bishop of Chester to provide men, horse and armour for light horsemen against the enemy. In a moment of panic one night in 1586 false rumours flashed round the city that the Spaniards had landed at the New Quay and that London and Bristol had been put to the torch. The news of the Armada in 1588 winked out from beacon to beacon north from Alderley Edge and Delamere into Lancashire. On 11th November the Bishop proclaimed a thanksgiving for the defeat of the invasion.

The year 1596 saw a famine so terrible that the poor of the city were in a desperate condition. The Mayor cancelled the toll on corn to try to attract grain into the city; wheat cost 40 shillings a bushel, good ale as much as 2d a pint. To try to clear away the poor from the city, in 1598 the Corporation issued an order against the building of cottages; sturdy beggars were put in the stocks for a day and a night. In September 1603 the great plague struck, starting in the house of a 'Musissioner' called Glover in St John's Lane; 650 citizens died by the middle of October, and the Michaelmas fair was abandoned. There was further legislation against cottages; houses were not to be divided into separate households, and citizens were not to have more than one lodger. The Mayor in 1604, Edward Dutton, stayed in the city, although some of this children and servants died of the plague, and many of the citizens fled into the countryside, some carrying the infection with them.

There was the problem of people in the suburbs lying within city parishes having to bury their dead within the walls, whereas the citizens wanted to eschew all contact with their infected neighbours. The townshipmen of Upton were allowed to bury the plague dead at St Oswald's, but they were to do it at six o'clock in the evening, to carry white sticks coming and going, and not to converse with any citizen or go into any house.

When plague broke out in the house of a shoemaker called Richard Bennet, he and his family left for the suburbs abandoning two of his children with two infected servants. The rumour spread that a servant called John Ellis had brought the disease from London, and he was expelled from Chester. The Assizes were moved out to Nantwich on one day; the Exchequer Court was held at Tarvin.

Over thirteen hundred people died in the city before the plague petered out in the spring of 1605, having held sway for eighteen months. Although in modern terms hygiene was rudimentary, and the nature of infection poorly understood, it was already well appreciated that the sufferers should be isolated from the healthy, and cabins were built for them below the city walls by the Dee.

It was not until July 1606, when the plague had passed, that practical efforts at street-cleaning were introduced. A scavenger was appointed "to carry, Convey, take and bringe away all dunnge, mucke, and other filthe and duste out of the streetes". The householders were to sweep their rubbish into piles in front of each house for the scavenger to remove, and were ordered not to block the gutters with filth. Each householder paid him 2d a year, besides his wage from the town of 4d a month. In 1608 the plague started again, but Bishop Lloyd and the Mayor held a day of prayer and preaching, and this seemed to halt the disease.

On 23rd August 1617 King James arrived in Chester. His son Henry had been created Earl of Chester in 1610, but this boy, who would otherwise have become Henry IX, died two years later. On 4th November 1616 Charles, the second son, was made earl.

By then a regular service of carriers had been established from Chester to London, with trips on four days a week to the Castle in Wood Street and the Blossoms at Cheapside. In 1631 the

Corporation was having trouble keeping swine off the streets: Adam Kaine the swineherd was given orders to impound any that he caught in the Northgate ditch, on pain of imprisonment and a shilling fine for each default.

William Prynne, the Puritan pamphleteer, was in Chester in 1631; five years later he was brought to the city to be imprisoned at the Castle. His supporters came out to meet him and fêted him as a hero; they suffered subsequently with fines of as much as £500 and public recantations. Four portraits of Prynne were burned at the High Cross in 1637.

James I died in 1625; Prince Charles became king, and his son Charles was made earl in 1638, at the age of eight.

At the outbreak of the Civil War, in 1642, the Mayor was William Ince, who raised a trained band of two hundred men armed with muskets to defend Chester from any Roundhead attack. He set up an armed watch and collected £500 for the protection of the city. On 8th August Sir William Brereton had a drum beaten in the streets and St Peter's Church bell rung to call the citizens to arms for Parliament. The Royalist Mayor brought the ensuing riot under control, and Brereton was taken to the Pentice (chapter 5). He had a long-standing quarrel with the Corporation over his liability to contribute towards the ship-money tax for his lands in the city.

On 23rd September King Charles arrived at Chester and was given a fine reception. He stayed in the city for five days, lodging at the Bishop's Palace, and was entertained by the Corporation in the Pentice. The city walls and defences were repaired at a cost of £100, and outworks were thrown out to enclose the suburbs. The gentry of the shire made an attempt to declare Cheshire neutral in the oncoming conflict, and concluded a local peace at Bunbury just before Christmas, but it proved impossible to prevent the war's engulfing the county.

Sir William Brereton returned to Chester on 18th July following with a Parliamentary army, but suffered a sharp repulse and withdrew. William Seddon, the vicar of Eastham and a preacher at St Mary's, came to stay in the Bishop's Palace, but Bishop John Bridgeman fled the city. William Seddon ministered to the garrison, and in the subsequent siege his wife bore their ninth child, whom he baptized in the Cathedral font.

Brereton seized Hawarden Castle, about five miles away, and the Chester garrison was busy demolishing buildings outside the defences, including Handbridge on the far side of the Dee. In November Royalist forces from Ireland were besieging the Roundheads at Hawarden, which was taken in early December; Beeston was seized, but the Parliamentary forces could not be cleared from Nantwich.

On 25th January 1644 General Fairfax defeated the Royalists of Lord Byron, and the siege of Chester recommenced in earnest. The first major thrust was on 19th September when the Roundheads broke through the outworks into the eastern suburbs. Five days later King Charles, marching towards Scotland from Hereford, entered the city. He lodged there one night, in the house of Francis Gamul, who had been one of the city's two MPs in Charles's last Parliament, held at Oxford. The following day the King witnessed, from the city walls, the defeat of his army at the Battle of Rowton Heath. He left Chester over the Dee Bridge for Wales with five hundred men, leaving instructions for the garrison to surrender if not relieved within eight days.

But Chester was in no mood to surrender. The Roundheads could not break through the walls, for the defenders repulsed attack after attack and quickly repaired breaches. The cannon-fire, although powerful, was not equal to the Roman and mediaeval masonry. The citizens had all the resources of the Castle armoury, spring-water and stores of grain, which they supplemented with meat from horses, dogs and cats. Brereton determined to starve the city into submission, and his unreasonable demands for unconditional surrender protracted the agonies.

On 3rd February 1646, after twenty weeks, articles of capitulation were agreed, and a dignified surrender took place. Lord Byron, the Royalist commander, was allowed to leave with his retinue and possessions, as were the various city gentry. Looting and desecration of the churches were forbidden, but in 1647 the High Cross was demolished and the fonts were taken from the parish churches. On 19th February a thanksgiving sermon for the surrender was preached before the House of Commons. Parliament replaced the town officers, the justices of the peace and sheriffs with their own appointees.

On 22nd June 1647 plague broke out again in the city; 2,032 persons had died, about a quarter of the population, by 14th October, 209 died in the worst week, the seventh. Parliament had to elect the Mayor and Sheriffs, because it was impossible to hold assemblies; the markets and fairs were stopped, grass grew in the streets, and again the sick were carried out to recover or die in makeshift cabins by the Dee. Families with the means fled the city; the poor stayed, virtually starved because of the collapse in the supply of provisions. Parliament passed an act to provide relief for the city; Norwich sent £20.

"The Plague takes them very strangly, strikes them black of one side and then they run mad, some drowne themselves, others would kill themselves; they dye within few hours, some run up and down streets in their shirts, to the great horrour of those in the City".

In 1654 the county court was moved to Northwich to escape a renewed bout of plague.

King Charles had been executed on 30th January 1649. His son was proclaimed a traitor at the High Cross, and the representations of the royal arms in the city were destroyed. Although there were several Parliamentarians in Chester, there was general dissatisfaction even among them with the King's execution, and it proved difficult to find any subscribers to the Ingagement to serve the Commonwealth without King or Lords which Parliament required be undertaken by all officers of the state. Richard Bradshaw, writing to John Bradshaw, President of the Council of State (and a Cheshire man), complained that only the Mayor, the Recorder and one alderman had acquiesced.

In 1659 Sir George Booth led an uprising for Charles II, then in exile, and took Chester without difficulty. Two regiments were sent from Ireland under Lambert against him. The defences of Chester had been destroyed on orders of Parliament in 1655, and Booth retreated to Northwich, where he was defeated at the Battle of Winnington Bridge on 19th August; Chester surrendered the following day. On 17th September Parliament abolished the city and the Corporation, making Chester part of the shire. The following February, however, the Presbyterian party of Sir George Booth had gained the majority in the House of Commons, and the city's charters were restored.

On 29th May 1660 Charles II arrived in London as king. He planned to institute a new Order of the Royal Oak, to which thirteen Cheshire gentlemen were nominated knights, but was advised that the matter might rekindle faction, so he abandoned the idea. Oak Apple Day remained a popular celebration in Cheshire until recent times.

Bishop Bridgeman died before the Restoration, but the bishopric was revived, and the new man, Brian Walton, was consecrated on 2nd December 1660. When he set out for Chester from London in September 1661, he was met by the first Chester men south of Lichfield. There was a tumultuous welcome in the city, where thousands had gathered to see him. Dr Walton died two months later, and his successor, Dr Henry Ferne, died before he reached Chester. Dr George Hall, parson of Wigan, was next bishop, consecrated in 1662, but he died in 1668 from a wound sustained from a knife in his pocket when he slipped down a hummock in his garden. Dr John Wilkins, the fourth bishop after the Restoration, was married to Oliver Cromwell's sister Robina.

After the Great Fire of London in September 1666, a religious enthusiast, Ann Blow, walked to Chester to proclaim to the Corporation that "the Lord's controversy is great" and to threaten them with fresh evils.

Stage-coaches now appeared on the scene, with regular runs to and from the capital, carrying eighteen passengers a week and taking only four days for the journey in summer (cost £2) and six in winter. Each coach had a total of forty horses and four coachmen, whose drink was paid for by the passengers. To many clear-thinking persons of the time it was obvious that no good would come of such innovations and that the journeys could be made with greater expedition on horseback.

From the Restoration the affairs of Chester became closer and closer entwined with the rising fortunes of the Grosvenor family of Eaton, a township south of the city on the left bank of the Dee. The Grosvenors came from an ancient and distinguished family, but they became unusually wealthy because of the marriage, in 1677, of Sir Thomas Grosvenor with Mary the daughter and heiress of Alexander Davies, who brought the family the amazingly profitable Middlesex estates in the area now known as Belgravia – which takes its name from Belgrave, an otherwise insignificant farm on the Eaton estates near Chester.

Sir Thomas was the first Grosvenor to stand as MP for Chester, elected as a Tory on 17th February 1679. The other city MP was William Williams, the Recorder, who had unsuccessfully challenged a city seat in 1673, when he "engaged himself, if he was chosen, to discharge a debt of forty pounds that the Citty owed to the King. And also promised to lend the Corporation £500 for 7 years gratis; to serve them without salary, and to spend his Estate among them". Having thus acquired the votes of the Mayor and

Sheriffs, he asserted that the freemen were obliged by law to vote as the Corporation directed, and threatened, as Recorder, to disfranchise anyone who voted against him. In the event he lost the poll, despite enlarging his own vote by making new freemen and trying other subtle devices. The other city seat fell vacant two years later, and he was then elected MP.

Religious troubles began to unfold again. In July 1679 a certain William Plessington, who had taken Roman Catholic orders, was condemned to death at the Assizes; he was dragged to the place of execution on a hurdle, and hanged, drawn and quartered.

Because of popular dislike of Charles II's brother, James, Duke of York, and his tendencies towards Catholicism, there was a feeling of affection for the King's illegitimate son, James, Duke of Monmouth, a Protestant. When, on 14th September 1681, the Duke of Monmouth was at Stockton Heath near Warrington, a great many Cheshire gentlemen went to support him. In August two years later he arrived at Chester amid great acclamation, and the mob attacked the Cathedral, and smashed the windows of various gentlemen's houses in the city with stones. Monmouth was exiled shortly afterwards, but after his father died and the Duke of York became James II, Monmouth landed in Dorset to claim the crown – he was quickly defeated and beheaded.

James II was given a warm reception when he arrived at Chester on 27th August 1687, and despite all the claims and counterclaims for the kingship, he clearly seemed to the populace to have the true blood in his veins, for he touched 350 people in the Cathedral quire for the King's Evil, to cure them of their ills. In December James was deposed, and the following February William of Orange became king. (James styled his son James, born on 10th June 1688, Earl of Chester, but the child was attainted in March 1702.) On 4th June 1690 King William arrived in Chester, having stayed the previous night at Colonel Whitley's house at Peel, on his way to Ireland and the Battle of the Boyne.

In 1685 Sir Thomas Grosvenor, then Mayor, won his city seat uncontested, but in 1688 Colonel Roger Whitley was returned. In 1689 he petitioned with George Mainwaring against the return of Sir Thomas; they said that they had been duly elected, as in 1688, but that one of the sheriffs, Edward Partington, had refused to return them and had in fact made false returns in favour of Sir Thomas and of Richard Levinge. Witnesses stated that although the poll had been won by Grosvenor and Levinge, who had fourteen votes more than Whitley, they had paid for the enfranchising of 125 citizens, including apprentices and minors, of whom a hundred or more had voted for them. Parliament divided on this information, and by a majority of one it was decided that Grosvenor and Levinge had been elected properly.

In 1695 Colonel Whitley and Sir Thomas were elected – but the colonel died in July 1697, before this Parliament was dissolved. At the by-election the twenty-six-year-old Thomas Cowper, from a prominent city family, was returned unopposed. Colonel Whitley as mayor had instituted various new rules governing the holding of the election to avoid malpractice, but these were overthrown by his successor, Peter Bennett, who turned out thirty-two members of the council and replaced them with supporters of the Jacobite cause. (Sir Thomas himself had neglected to sign the Association declaring loyalty to King William.) There were clandestine meetings in the Chester area in the eighteenth century called 'The Cycle', at which supporters of the Jacobite cause congregated, but in course of time these degenerated into open social gatherings with virtually no political content.

Sir Henry Bunbury and Peter Shakerley were Chester's MPs from 1701 to 1715, but the latter was replaced by Sir Richard Grosvenor, Sir Thomas's son, mayor of Chester in 1715. Sir Richard represented Chester until his death in July 1732. His brother Thomas Grosvenor was also elected in 1727. Their brother Robert won the by-election on Richard's death, but then Thomas died in 1733. Robert was MP for Chester until his death in 1755.

The Whigs were led by James Mainwaring of Bromborough. In 1746 party feeling was particularly inflamed because of the recent Jacobite invasion, and a parson Parry libelled Mainwaring, who in reply pulled him by the nose.

Celia Fiennes described Chester in 1698:

The streetes are of a great breadth from the houses, but there is one thing takes much from their appeareing so and from their beauty, for on each side in most places they have made penthouses so broad set on pillars which persons walk under covert, and is made up and down steps under which are ware houses; . . . this does darken the streetes and hinder the light of the houses in many places to the streete ward below; . . . the town is mostly timber buildings

By then the Irish trade was suffering from the war with France. In May 1702 the Corporation petitioned Queen Anne: "The Irish

Channell is greatly infested with Privatiers, invited thither by the Prospect of intercepting the Coale Fleetes, and other ships with persons of great Quality and very valuable goods, passing to and from that kingdome".

The Jacobite Rebellion of 1715 did not directly affect Chester – the city had been prepared for an attack with cannon planted at each gate – except that more than 450 prisoners were brought to the Castle. The prisoners had to lie on straw and had no blankets in the worst of the winter, and soon sickness spread with ease; they died "in droves like rotten sheep", and each night four or five bodies were thrown into the castle ditch. The prisoners and the two regiments of soldiers were a burden to the city, and provisions became dear.

Meanwhile the steady march of technology was dragging Chester into the eighteenth century. Tobacco- and snuff-manufactories were established at the far end of the Dee bridge under the aegis of the Tanners Company. As early as 1633 there were thirty-one licensed tobacco-dealers in Chester, of whom twenty-two were ironmongers. On 20th April 1733 work began on the New Cut, a deep channel to Chester which both provided better access for boats and allowed the enclosure and reclamation of the White Sands, which today form the dry pastures of Sealand in Clwyd. When a water-engine on wheels was built to help put out fires, the Mayor ordered that it be brought out every three months to ensure that it still worked, and be tried in his presence.

The manufacture of clay pipes and tobacco became by the 1750s the principal industry in Chester, and the pipes were made from clay brought from the Isle of Wight, Poole and Bideford. Chester clay pipes were reputed the best in Europe.

Daniel Defoe came to Chester:

Nor do the Rows add anything, in my opinion, to the beauty of the city; but just the contrary, they serve to make the city look both old and ugly.

When I was formerly at this city, about the year 1690, they had no water to supply their ordinary occasions, but what was carried from the River Dee upon horses, in great leather vessels, like a pair of bakers panyers. But at my coming there this time, I found a very good water-house in the river, and the city plentifully supply'd by pipes.

'Bonnie Prince Charlie' entered Cheshire on 1st December 1745 in the second major Jacobite attempt to recapture the throne.

Chester was fortified in advance, and householders were ordered to lay in a fortnight's supplies, but the great Scottish army struck across the east of the county, through Alderley and Macclesfield. The area around Chester Castle was cleared, with the tower of St Mary's Church half demolished, the churchyard walls pulled down, and the warehouses between the Castle and the Dee removed. The officer of the Engineers was about to start on an extensive outer perimeter of flankers and outworks, but the rapid collapse of the invasion rendered that unnecessary.

On 18th June 1750 a service of stage-chaises was started from 'The Three Pigeons' in Bridge Street to 'The Castle and Falcon' in Aldergate, London, with three journeys a week, starting at six in the morning, and costing 3 guineas. On 4th May 1771 the first sod was cut of a new canal, to connect Chester with Nantwich, running directly outside the north wall, joining the Dee by a set of locks. The first flat (barge) passed from the canal to the river on 11th December 1776.

It became customary for Chester to be illuminated in honour of great and exciting news, the streets festooned with lanterns and banners, and lamps and candles in every window. On 13th February 1780 Admiral Rodney's victory at Cape St Vincent was so celebrated; in 1789 there were illuminations for George III's recovery from illness; in 1797 for Admiral Duncan's victory at Camperdown; in 1798 for Nelson's victory of the Nile; in October 1801 for Peace. It happened that the news of Cape St Vincent arrived when the first stone of the new Bridgegate (chapter 9) had just been laid, and this addition was made to the brass plate on the foundations:

The great and joyful news was announced this day of the British fleet, under the command of the Admirals Rodney, Hood and Drake, having defeated the French fleet in the West Indies, taking the French Admiral De Graffe and five ships of the line, and sunk one. The battle continued close and bloody for eleven hours.

Georgian Chester
What was Chester like at the beginning of the nineteenth century? The streets were narrow but paved or cobbled, with great numbers of little alleys and entries running off to the backs of houses, cutting through to other streets and passageways. Some of the area within the city walls was pastureland, but the now

deserted areas at the back of the main streets were clustered with dwellings, many of them cramped and insanitary.

Although much of the half-timbering of the sixteenth- and seventeenth-century city survived, a great deal was replaced by high brick houses, some ornamented with stone quoins and pillars. The Rows were cramped, nowhere more than about ten feet wide, with low ceilings about six feet above the floor. The shops did not have large windows but opened like market-stalls directly onto street or row. The streets were dusty or muddy according to the weather, and many of the houses were decrepit.

At night there was barely any lighting in the streets, but for lamps consisting of crude posts formed of branches of oak, on each of which were mounted two rush-lights. The peace was kept by the 'charlies', night-watchmen who carried horn lanterns in tin frames and patrolled the streets, shouting "Past twelve o'clock, and a fine night!", "Past two o'clock, and a cloudy morning!".

The better-off travelled by sedan-chair, of which there were several in the city, and some new houses were built with large porches to enable the householder to step into the sedan without having to face the elements. There were rows of sedans standing at the Cross, the bearers leaning against St Peter's Church wall, each with a bundle of twigs, from which they whittled vent-pegs for beer-barrels, strewing the footpath with their chippings. The sedan-chairs were eventually replaced by private carriages and the horse-drawn cabs which plied the streets in the nineteenth century.

The city was a natural rendezvous for beggars, augmented by the locals at various times of the year. At Easter the girls would bar access to the city through the gates, insisting on 'lifting' the traveller and demanding money before he should be released. Spring brought demands from housewives and urchins for 'pennies for the Maypole'. From three weeks before Christmas to Christmas Eve Welsh women flooded into the city to beg for money from house to house, and the poor would beg corn from the local farmers, usually being allotted a quarter for each member of the family.

Although the houses were heated by fires, fed with coal brought in panniers from Flintshire, and later by canal-barge, and though there were brewhouses and factories close to the city centre, the prevailing south-west wind from the sea and the Welsh mountains kept the air clear, with virtually no fog and occasional hazy mornings. Visitors walking the walls were charmed not only by the sights of Chester but by extensive views to the sea, the mountains and inland to the Bickerton Hills.

The average life-expectancy of the inhabitants was fifty-eight years. In 1774 the population was 14,713; in that year there had been a bad outbreak of smallpox in which 202 had died; 1,183 had recovered from the disease. Generally speaking, the situation was regarded as one of the healthiest in the country, and there was no great working-class population in poverty as in the nearby manufacturing towns of Cheshire and Lancashire. The women were remarkably beautiful, but many were unmarried, and the families were small, less than three children per couple.

Mail-coaches were introduced in 1784. Hitherto the post had been carried in saddle-bags by relays of horses, travelling between postmasters' stables on the main roads, and these continued until 1837, when the last relay, that to Northwich, was replaced. A letter which left by the horse-mail on Monday evening from London would arrive at Chester on Thursday morning; a letter for Glasgow took five days. "The Mail is generally intrusted to some idle boy without character, mounted on a worn-out hack, and who, so far from being able to defend himself or escape from robbers, is much more likely to be in league with them". The new mail-coaches dashed to Chester from London at an average 8 mph, and the post took 22 hours 45 minutes.

The first stirrings of workers' unions had already troubled Chester. In 1788 the journeymen tailors had demanded a rise from 12 shillings to 14 shillings a week, claiming that in fact through lack of work their average wage had been 8 shillings to 8s 6d. The master tailors were affronted and prepared to indict the workers at the next Quarter Sessions for illegally conspiring, reminding the journeymen in an advertisement in a Chester newspaper that the penalty for the first offence was a £10 fine, or twenty days' imprisonment on bread and water; £20 for the second offence, or the pillory; £40 for the third offence, or the pillory and loss of one ear.

The city had two newspapers, rather slim affairs, mainly carrying national news from London and local advertisements at this period. The *Chester Courant* originated as *Adams' Weekly Courant* in 1732; the *Chester Chronicle* started in 1775. The *Courant* survived to 1891, when it was amalgamated with a newcomer, the *Cheshire Observer*; the *Observer* and *Chronicle* are both still in production. Other newspapers appeared on occasion, such as the

Chester Herald of 1810–13. The earliest news-sheet was the *Weekly Journal*, published in 1721.

Travel to and from Chester was increasingly by stagecoach; of the twenty-six regular services introduced by 1831, twenty were from the Feathers Inn in Bridge Street, six from 'The White Lion' in Northgate Street. Goods were carried by packhorses which were loaded and unloaded in Upper Northgate Street and Liverpool Road, and by market-boats on the canal. These barges took passengers and goods to Ellesmere Port, the terminus of the canal on the Mersey, from which they were ferried to Liverpool. One-horse flies were not introduced into Chester until the late 1820s.

The General Public Library was established in 1817, but there had been small private lending-libraries used by the more cultivated citizens from the early eighteenth century.

The port was virtually dead, although the boats of the salmon-fishermen still lined the banks at Handbridge, and wooden and iron vessels were built on the Chester bank at the Crane. The Irish trade and the Irish travellers were now handled through Parkgate, and increasingly through Liverpool and then Holyhead, but in each case the goods and the people still passed through Chester.

The Snuff Mills at the far end of the Dee Bridge still produced snuff and tobacco, and lead-shot was manufactured at Boughton. There were several breweries and tanneries, ropewalks by the walls, and glove- and boot-manufactories.

Life in the city was greatly affected by the to-ings and fro-ings of the soldiers at the Castle, and those *en route* to Ireland. The Cheshire Militia were busy elsewhere most of the time, but when they returned there were parties, reunions, brawls and general festivities. Chester was patriotic, and every victory of the nineteenth century as the Empire was constructed and successive European wars were won was greeted with enthusiasm.

On 27th July 1803 we find the city preparing to meet the threatened invasion by Napoleon. The colours of the Volunteers were planted on the Roodee, where several hundred enthusiasts enrolled at the drumhead. In the evening they assembled at the Abbey Court and marched with pipe and drum behind the Mayor and the commander to the Roodee, and more were enrolled, nearly a thousand men in all, many of whom were drawn from the Royal Cheshire Militia which had returned from active service in Liverpool the previous year.

At Christmas the naval press-gang operating in Chester discovered that one of the Volunteers had been at sea, and carried him off to the gaol. After parade the Volunteers went to the gaol, but their commander, Major Wilmot, intervened, saying that he would put to death the first man to attack the building. The Volunteers were unimpressed and suggested that they would break his sword over his head. It was the work of moments to smash in the windows and the door of the prison, and the gaoler, unwilling to risk a general break-out, handed over the miscreant. The Volunteers chaired him through the streets, before smashing the windows and doors of the Naval Rendezvous House. The press-gang thought it wise to absent themselves during the proceedings, and their colours were torn down and dragged in the gutter. When order had been restored, the press-gang was withdrawn from Chester, and four companies of the Shropshire Supplementary Militia were brought in from Liverpool. An inquiry was held and retribution ordered the following month.

The great influx of Irish labourers into Chester, Birkenhead and Liverpool, and the difficulties of the British administration in Ireland, stimulated a rising tide of nationalist Protestant feeling in Chester. On Friday 27th April 1827 a No-Popery meeting was held at the Town Hall to petition Parliament against granting political power to Catholics. Richard Tyrwhitt, the Recorder, proposed the motion. After reciting the history of Catholic emancipation, and the havoc wreaked on behalf of past popes, he turned to the present:

It was only necessary to advert to the present state of Spain, wherein the weakness and despotism of the Government, the luxury and profligacy of the priesthood, and the misery of the subject, were notorious to all Europe. The re-establishment of the Inquisition too clearly proved that the Catholic religion was unchangeable, and always the same; and even within the last six months a man had been burnt at the stake for not going to mass!

The motion was carried by an immense majority. The Catholic priest in charge of the Queen Street mission, the Reverend John Briggs, then rose and, amid hisses and applause, castigated the Recorder for whipping up old hatreds, and opposed the petition. The meeting grew disorderly as the arguments became more heated, with charges of disloyalty being thrown at the Catholics. The meeting ended at four o'clock "after one of the most crowded and uproarious meetings witnessed in the Town-hall".

On Monday evening, 27th October 1862, after there had been serious Irish disturbances in Birkenhead, a large crowd of Friends of Garibaldi, some armed with staves, assembled at the Castle gates. A bottle was thrown at the leader and hit a boy full in the face, badly wounding him. The Garibaldians marched on Boughton, "a locality inhabited almost exclusively by Irish labourers", many of whom stood ready for battle in knots on the street corners. Their appearance dissuaded the Cestrian mob, who retired to the High Cross, where an effigy of the Pope was exhibited, and the crowd chanted "To Hell with the Pope!"

On Sunday 10th February 1867 Fenians (Irish Republicans) held a meeting in Liverpool and resolved to attack Chester Castle the following day, to seize the arms deposited there, attack the banks and jewellers' shops, cut the telegraph wires, tear up the rails and make good their escape by rail to Holyhead, from which to pass to Ireland. There were on that day 10,100 stand of arms, 4,000 swords and 900,000 rounds of ammunition in the Castle, and 5,040 barrels of gunpowder, guarded by six soldiers. The Fenians also believed the 54th Regiment to be disaffected and to have Irish sympathizers.

One of the Fenians, an ex-officer called Corydon, who was one of fifty American-Irish who had come to Britain to foment violence, had been captured in Liverpool on the Monday morning and revealed the plot to his interrogators. The news and consequent instructions buzzed along the telegraphs to Manchester, Chester, Holyhead and London.

From noon on the Monday about seven hundred young Irishmen arrived in Chester on trains from Liverpool, Preston, Manchester and Halifax. The unusual numbers of Irishmen leaving from Liverpool attracted attention, and fresh warnings were telegraphed. The Chester magistrates met immediately, and special constables were sworn in. The 230 Chester Volunteers (enrolled only seven years previously) were called up, and the police stood by.

Matters went quietly until four o'clock, when a train from Manchester and Stalybridge brought a reinforcement of four hundred Irishmen in one batch. Forty arrived from Halifax, seventy from Leeds. By five o'clock there were about fifteen hundred Irishmen in the city, and their leaders gathered for battle-orders.

The railway authorities prepared to pull up the lines. At eleven o'clock two companies of the 54th Regiment and the Volunteers mustered in the Castle. About one o'clock another company of the 54th arrived from Manchester. A gunboat left the Mersey for Holyhead. Extra police were assembled in Liverpool. At 2.30 in the morning the 1st Battalion of Scots Fusiliers, five hundred men, left in a special twenty-seven-carriage train from Euston for Chester.

Through the night five hundred special constables sworn in during the day paraded the streets. The Fenians formed into columns on the main roads out of the city. The Cheshire Yeomanry were summoned. Before the Scots Fusiliers arrived, the Irishmen started to melt away, and by morning they had gone. Some ammunition was found abandoned on waste ground. The citizens of Chester crowded to the railway station and gave the Fusiliers a rapturous welcome.

On the night of Friday 18th October Fenians threw a bottle of phosphorus at the police office. It landed on the roof of the police court and exploded; a wooden ventilator caught fire, but a fire-engine had extinguished the flames within fifteen minutes; no one was injured. Meanwhile a group of Irishmen gathered behind the Castle, hoping (in vain) that the troops would be drawn away by the incident. The Volunteers were warned, the 18th Royal Irish put on standby, and special constables sworn in. A £100 reward was offered for the arrest of the arsonist.

Grosvenor Chester

During the nineteenth century the immensely wealthy Grosvenors of Eaton, who distributed lavish patronage on the city and its institutions, had a large faction of supporters who were strongly opposed by a larger but less influential mass of citizens, whose fortunes were championed by the Egerton family of Oulton. It is an old Chester game to guess at the wealth of the Grosvenors: in 1829 their income was reckoned at 2d a second.

Sir Richard Grosvenor, MP for Chester in 1754, succeeded to the estates on his father's death in 1755 and was created Baron Grosvenor of Eaton in 1761 and Earl Grosvenor and Viscount Belgrave in 1784.

The citizens had had a long litigation with the Corporation, which was controlled by the Grosvenor interest, until 1790, when the case was abandoned and one of the city MPs, Wilbraham Bootle, resigned. Sir Richard's son Robert took the seat and held it until 1802, when his father died and he inherited the peerage.

Richard Drax Grosvenor, Robert's first cousin, took over his seat. The election was in the hands of the freemen; the freedom was in the hands of the Corporation; and the Corporation was in the pockets of the Grosvenors.

When Drax Grosvenor resigned his seat in 1807, the Ègertons entered the fray. Sir John Grey-Egerton stood, and won, and the day of his victory became a day of triumph for his supporters, remembered in a song, 'The Glorious Sixth of May'.

In 1809 there were disturbances on the election of the Mayor, when the contestants were Thomas Evans, the Grosvenor choice, and William Seller, the popular candidate. Evans was elected by a majority of the Corporation. But the election of the people's Sheriff, which did not rest with the Corporation, was strongly contested, with extensive canvassing by the Egerton side. The Grosvenor party opened sixty-eight public houses and gave away thousands of blue and gold ribbons. Despite this largesse, the Corporation had great difficulty in holding the election, and the mob burst into the Town Hall, chanting and shouting so as to prevent the business proceeding. The weight of the crowd was so great that the bar, the wooden fence at the side of the court, was broken down, and the citizens proceeded to smash up the tables, benches and other furnishings, persuading the Corporation to adjourn the election.

The result of the 1818 election caused so much jubilation that a dinner was held, to which all the freemen were invited, and a tea was given for their wives; a song, 'Mrs Freeman's Tea-party', was specially composed.

The Mayor in 1819, John Williamson, furthered the Grosvenor interest by hiding in a bedroom of a doctor's house in Watergate Street, so that freemen could not be enrolled. Williamson was fined £1,000 in consequence and was ordered to reside in the King's Bench prison in London for six months. He married shortly before leaving Chester, and the honeymoon was completed in gaol. The cook at Eaton sent him a large game-pie and other luxuries at Christmas.

In 1820 William Seller, an Egerton man, became Mayor. The Duke of Wellington, a member of the government, visited the city on 27th December, and had a poor reception from both Corporation and citizenry. When he was insulted in Castle Street, he naïvely asked "Is this Grosvenor Street?" That year General Grosvenor's carriage was waylaid after an election meeting, near the Dee

Bridge: the horses' harness was cut, and the carriage was thrown into the river; the General escaped uninjured. The elections in 1821 ended in another fracas, with the Town Clerk and his clerks assaulted, the city sword and mace seized by the mob (but soon recovered), and the aldermen fleeing into the council chamber.

By 1828 the Grosvenor faction was losing the struggle for power. John Parry stood for Sheriff against the popular candidate, George Allender, but met with such overwhelming opposition that he withdrew from the contest. Other gentry in the neighbourhood opposed the Grosvenors; Sir Thomas Stanley threatened to build a brick-kiln on his land immediately opposite Eaton to disfigure the view for them. In 1835 the Municipal Corporations Act reformed the elections, giving the vote to the rate payers, and reducing the sheriffs to one.

Perhaps as an expression of the citizens' political impotence in the early days, there was a mock Corporation, the Mayor and Council of Duan, with sword and mace, formed by the skinners, who marched through the streets on the day of the election of the real Mayor. A room at the 'King's Arms' near the Eastgate was set up as a council chamber where a drinking and gambling club called 'the Honourable Incorporation' met in burlesque imitation of the city dignitaries.

There is a story, perhaps apocryphal, that a handbill was distributed in Chester in 1815, announcing that the Government needed cats for despatch to St Helena to deal with a plague of rats, and offering 16 shillings per tom, 10 shillings per female, and 2s 6d per kitten, brought to the city for purchase on a certain day; and that in consequence of this hoax no less than three thousand cats were brought to Chester by a crowd of hopeful vendors.

Tourism was increasing, and the American Washington Irving visited the "quaint little city" in 1830: "I had been carried back into former days by the antiquities of that venerable place, the examination of which is equal to turning over the pages of a black-letter volume, or gazing on the pictures of Froissart". Perhaps the city was too quaint; in April 1832 cholera broke out, and there was another outbreak as late as 1865.

The Grosvenors of Eaton were prominent in the restructuring of the city which produced the Chester we have today. Their largesse was immense, and the effects were far-reaching. They paid for the demolition of the mediaeval north and east gates, and all the gates were replaced with simple Classical arches at the period when Classical architecture was in vogue.

The Grosvenors built a large handsome single arch, the Grosvenor Bridge, across the Dee, by which direct access to the city could be had from the south-west, and from the new lodge built at their northern gate at the end of the Chester Approach from Eaton Hall. The bridge was opened in 1832 by Princess Victoria, the future queen. From it a wide a new road, Grosvenor Street, was driven into the town centre, cutting diagonally across the ancient street-pattern, with the demolition of a swathe of buildings, including the parish church of St Bridget, opposite St Michael's.

Around their estates almost every farmhouse was rebuilt in a variety of pseudo-Elizabethan or pseudo-Jacobean styles, distinguishable by their diapered blue-and-red brickwork and barley-stick chimneys. Great approaches were laid out to the hall in each direction, and a vast park was constructed, into which were thrown the lands of adjoining farms. Three parish churches were demolished, at Pulford, Aldford and Eccleston, and rebuilt in mediaeval styles.

The centrepiece of the Grosvenor fantasy was Eaton Hall. The red-brick and stone hall of about 1700 was replaced in 1803–12 with a three-storey Gothic mansion, to which wings were added in 1823–5. It was restructured in 1845–54 and rebuilt in 1870–83 by Alfred Waterhouse, at a cost of £600,000, as a 'Wagnerian palace' in a thirteenth-century style, with a 175-foot clock-tower like the tower of Big Ben.

The Grosvenor coat-of-arms, a golden wheatsheaf on a blue shield, glinted out from great hall, city centre, farmhouse and church, carved, painted and gilded, like a fragment of the Cheshire arms. When the Marquis of Westminster's eldest son was born in 1825, he was called Hugh Lupus, after the first Norman earl. In the courtyard of Eaton Hall was erected a huge equestrian statue of Hugh the Gross, cast in bronze, and weighing over seven tons. Hugh Lupus was created Duke of Westminster; the family had reached the highest rank of the British peerage less than two hundred years after their ancestor, the son of a country squire, had married into the wealth of London.

The Royal Hotel near the Eastgate was renamed 'The Grosvenor'; across the road the Grosvenor Club was built. The Grosvenor Museum was built in Grosvenor Street. The Grosvenor-

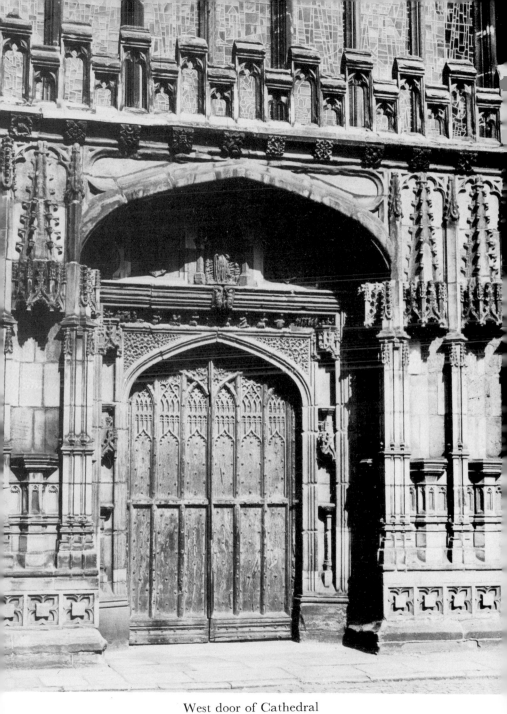

West door of Cathedral

(Overleaf) St Werburgh and St Giles

St John's ruins

Nunnery arch

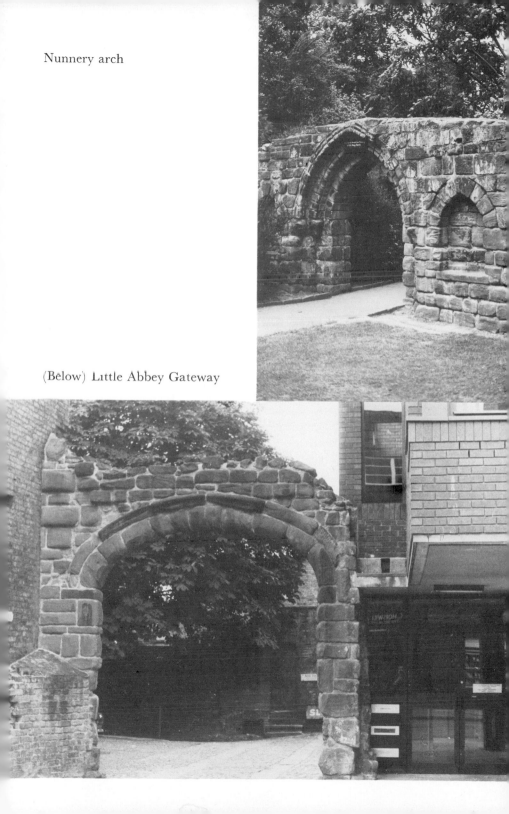

(Below) Little Abbey Gateway

Roman Gardens: (above) pillars;
(below) reconstructed hypocaust

Eastern entrance to amphitheatre

(Overleaf) Cathedral Tower

Laing shopping precinct leads back from by the Grosvenor Hotel. The Grosvenor Park was laid out by the Groves, with a large statue of the second marquis.

The greatest construction and destruction committed by the Grosvenors in Chester was in the rebuilding of the city centre. When we go to Chester and smile at the half-timbering and admire and photograph it, we are looking not at a mediaeval or even a seventeenth-century city but at an elaborate fantasy of a wealthy Victorian family. The most striking buildings, the rich concoctions of Shoemakers' Row, at the High Cross, and in St Werburgh Street, are fictions. And how much ancient Chester can we find in Eastgate Street, or Watergate Street, or Bridge Street? Building after building flowed from the pens of the Eaton architects to charm with their picturesque and horrify with their grotesque. Chester is a Victorian city, interspersed with some fine Georgian houses and the occasional Jacobean survivor.

Shortly after the opening of the first railway line in 1840, mailbags were sent by train; indeed, earlier, when the London to Liverpool line was completed, mailbags were taken to Hartford Station by cart. When the line to Holyhead was opened, this was used for the mail to and from Ireland, and the post-train, which left Chester at one o'clock in the morning and arrived at Holyhead just after three, was nicknamed 'The Wild Irishman'.

When King William IV died at 2.30 a.m. on 20th June 1838, and Princess Victoria became queen, there was still neither train nor telegraph. It took a little over a day for the news to arrive in Chester, and the proclamation was read at the High Cross on the 22nd, when the populace had their first chance to shout "Long live Queen Victoria!"

The telegraph was established, and it was by this that the news of the fall of Sebastopol arrived in 1855. Electric light was first used in the city on 6th November 1879, at the Hydraulic Engineering Works in Charles Street. The devastation of the city centre by the 'vandal restorer' was becoming so obtrusive that 'restoration', earlier championed by the intelligentsia, was developing into a term of abuse. On the other hand, some of the new black-and-white architecture was replacing nondescript brick houses and local eyesores, and was welcomed as a genuine attempt to beautify.

Electioneering was still subject to abuse. In 1880 the independent candidate, Mr Malgerini, appeared to have been unwelcome to the mob, for the most extraordinary violence was used towards him. Alderman Littler, trustee of the Grosvenor property in the city, tried to influence the tenantry. The manager of Messrs Wood's large chain and anchor works sought to influence his workers. The candidates' agents took large numbers of voters, without any disguise, into various public houses in Saltney and Handbridge and treated all round, canvassing at the same time. At 'The Birmingham Arms' and the Red Lion Inn the tap was kept flowing for the whole of the election day at the expense of an undoubted agent of the Liberal candidates. The bill for drinks were not shown in the candidates' accounts; that at 'The Birmingham Arms' was £29 10s 11½d.

In a committee room a resolution was passed that the canvassers (the 'drink captains') should give the voters drinks as they brought them to the poll. In lieu of good old honest bribery many prospective voters were 'employed' for three weeks before the election, and their costs were entered in the accounts as billposters or messengers. Circulars sent to persons with a vote in Chester but living in distant towns said, "Please come to the committee rooms, and I shall happy to pay you your day's wages and expenses before voting". Free bread was distributed to some voters; others were given liquor, tobacco, a coat, money. The scandal was such that a Royal Commission was appointed and an inquiry held, and this was the last election in which any serious malpractice occurred.

The population of Chester increased gently throughout the nineteenth century; 15,052 in 1801, 21,363 in 1831, 35,257 in 1871. In 1888 it became a county borough, with wider boundaries including the suburbs which had spread out well beyond the city. In 1921 the population was 40,802; in 1961 58,950.

A glance at the Census returns shows how rapidly the whole nature of Chester has changed. In 1841, for instance, the major occupations were general labourers (998), boot- and shoemakers (353), tailors (242), domestic servants (241) and army half-pay (228). By 1921 the balance was quite different: 1263 domestic servants, 1209 railwaymen, 1,118 hoteliers and lodging-house keepers, 998 professionals and 937 builders. The impact of tourism on employment was dramatic.

In 1961 there is a thorough change again: 3,090 clerks, 1,200 fitters, 1,050 salesmen and sales girls, 790 cleaners, 780 labourers, 780 shopkeepers. Chester had come into its own as an administrative centre, with a vast increase in bureaucracy. This is not to belittle the continuing growth in tourism; more than half a million visitors come to Chester each year, more than to any other place in England, outside London.

Henry James in *The Ambassadors*, in 1903, summarized part of the charm that still attaches to the city:

> The tortuous wall – girdle, long since snapped, of the little swollen city, half held in place by careful civic hands – wanders in narrow file between parapets smoothed by peaceful generations, pausing here and there for a dismantled gate or a bridged gap, with rises and drops, steps up and steps down, queer twists, queer contacts, peeps into homely streets and under the brows of gables, views of cathedral tower and waterside fields, of huddled English town and ordered English country.

The spasm of activity reshaping the city centre began to lose its impetus by the time of the Great War. One of the last old houses to be demolished was the Old Toyshop on the north side of Eastgate Street, dated 1679, pulled down in 1913. The restoration of the Cathedral, which continued fitfully from the 1840s to the 1920s, had transfigured it from a sombre church of crumbling red sandstone into the dull, crisp, odd-looking confection we have today.

To see how Chester and Cheshire suffered in the two World Wars, it is necessary only to see the long rolls of honour in the south transept of the Cathedral. In the Great War Chester functioned more or less as normal, though women were drafted in as postmen and lamplighters. In physical terms Chester was practically unscathed, almost untouched by bombs in the last war, despite the devastating raids on Birkenhead, Liverpool and Manchester.

Antiqui colant antiquum dierum

In summer 1919 a consortium bought a site of 52 acres in Curzon Park, facing the city across the Dee, for £17,000, and proposed to spend £1¼ million on establishing an engineering works which would have employed five to six thousand workers. There was no town-planning scheme then, but the council hastily adopted one, which excluded Curzon Park from industrial development. A new town-planning scheme was introduced in 1927. In 1929 preparations were made for the destruction of Newgate, the one remaining gateway of any antiquity: the city proposed a Gothic archway with posterns; the Society for the Protection of Ancient Buildings suggested an unpretentious bridge of iron. In 1930 the council purchased the fifteenth-century Blue Bell Inn in Northgate Street with a view to demolishing it for road-widening, but there was a public outcry which stayed their hand.

In 1937 the Newgate was built in what was then considered to be a mediaeval style, and the old Newgate (now called by its older name, Wolfgate) to the north was reprieved at the last moment.

An inner ring-road was proposed in the new development plan adopted in 1950 under the Town and County Planning Act, with the intention at the same time to "clear outworn [sic] property from either side of the city walls and to lay out the land as ornamental gardens or car-parks". Much of the housing in the back streets was written off as slums, and large areas were demolished and the citizens rehoused in the suburbs, increasing the need for traffic into the city centre, and the pressure on car-parking. The Ancient Monuments Society protested at the destruction of historic buildings, including St Martin's Church, but the ring-road system proceeded and was completed in the 1960s.

A bomb attack on the Inland Revenue offices at Hamilton Place in April 1969 smashed two hundred windows, split walls and blew doors off hinges. The following August a time-bomb was found on the steps of the city health offices at St Martin's House, Princess Street; a loose wire had prevented it from exploding. These incidents were blamed on Welsh extremists.

On 5th October 1970 Humber Airways opened an air service from Chester airport at Hawarden to London; the trip took seventy minutes in the air, two hours in all, at a cost of £7, with two services a week.

In 1972, when the inner ring-road had been completed, the High Cross was 'cut' – that is, all traffic except buses was forbidden to cross the area, and the four main streets became part of a new one-way system. The citizens could now see the full fruits of the transport policy: the city-centre congestion had been more or less eliminated, at the expense of "knocking down Chester to make roads to bring people to see the Chester you've been knocking down to make roads". The ring-road formed a *cordon sanitaire* into which relatively few wheeled vehicles could enter, and having entered were caught in a maze which at every point led them outwards again.

In 1975 work began on the Chester by-pass from Great

Boughton to Broughton, taking traffic from Manchester to North Wales across the Dee and away from the city centre. The local government changes of 1974 saw the survival of Cheshire in a truncated form but the addition of Chester and Tarvin Rural Districts to the old county borough to form the new Chester District.

In judging the additions to the Chester townscape in this century, we might ask ourselves whether the demolition of any one of them would cause the slightest regret. The most pleasing newcomers are the Northgate Arena, a handsome recreation-centre built close to part of the new ring-road called St Oswald's Way, and the Cathedral *campanile*. Egerton House, one of the best Georgian buildings in the city, was demolished for the construction of one section of the new road. The roundabout on St Oswald's Way is the most prominent feature of Chester from the air and consumes about as much space as the Cathedral.

Chester is now well into the television age, and the increasing hordes of tourists are fed audio-visual pap at the Heritage Centre, St Mary's and the British Heritage Centre. The authorities have assembled in the city centre one of the most elaborate displays of street-furniture in the country – posts, notices, no-waiting signs, parking signs, white lines, yellow lines, arrows and stripes, further disfiguring one of the most viewed and photographed town centres in the world.

The city is becoming like a large film-set with elaborate and convincing façades behind which there is nothing worth seeing; the main streets are a historic ghetto; the back streets are gutted. Whereas conservation is pointed directly at buildings of Architectural Importance, the townscape as a whole has gone hang. The population does not live in the city but in great sprawling featureless suburbs. Local government has attracted to the county town a large new mass of civil servants who then worry about the congestion of the streets and the lack of parking-space.

But we can still hope that, just as Chester gives a great deal of pleasure to millions of visitors and attracts an immense affection from its citizens and the people of Cheshire and England in general, present disappointments will prove superficial and the city will regenerate, not as a museum-piece, nor destroyed in the cause of modernity, but as a living city for as many centuries to come.

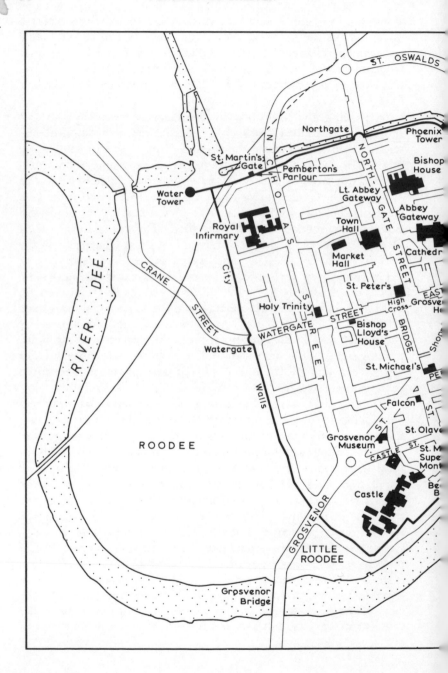

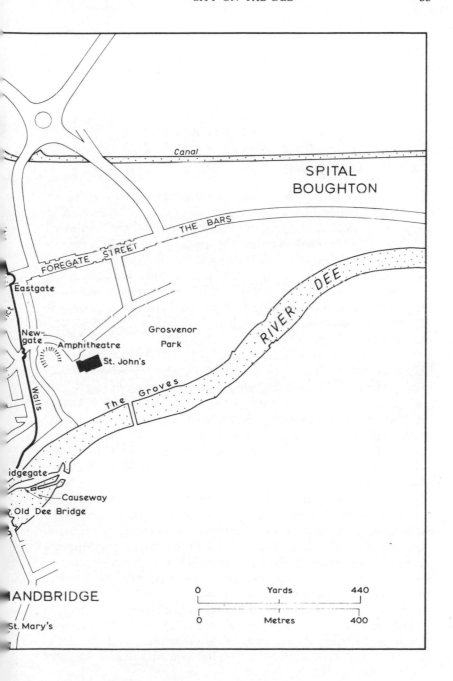

Canal

SPITAL
BOUGHTON

THE BARS

FOREGATE STREET

Eastgate

Grosvenor
Park

New-
gate   Amphitheatre

St. John's

The Groves

RIVER DEE

Walls

idgegate

Causeway

Old Dee Bridge

ANDBRIDGE

St. Mary's

| 0 | Yards | 440 |
| 0 | Metres | 400 |

2

SAINT WERBURGH's CATHEDRAL
Benedictine Abbey and City Walls

ACCORDING to Henry Bradshaw, a sixteenth-century monk of Chester, Christianity was introduced to the city in the reign of King Lucius in about AD 140, and the first church there, dedicated to St Peter and St Paul, stood on the site of the present Cathedral church and was the mother-church and burial-place for a parish including all Chester and the countryside within a radius of seven miles. What basis is there to this story? Lucius did exist and was a king of the Britons, according to Bede, and wrote to the Pope, St Eleutherius, in about 180, asking to be made a Christian. The chroniclers reckoned that Lucius was grandson of King Marius, whom Bradshaw recorded as having fortified Chester and having been buried there. The twelfth-century *History of the Kings of Britain* by Geoffrey of Monmouth, who elaborated the old chronicles with a great deal of apparently fictional detail, says that Lucius established three archbishops in England, one at London, one at York and the third at the City of the Legions. But Geoffrey specifically states (and Bradshaw ignores) that the City of the Legions in question was Caerleon-on-Usk, close to his own Monmouth.

Bradshaw then stated that King Alfred's daughter Aethelflaed, wife of Aethelred, Earl of Mercia, changed the dedication to the Holy Trinity and St Oswald and had the present St Peter's Church built, to which the old dedication was transferred. Earl Aethelred died in 911, and from then to 919 Aethelflaed continued his work in fortifying Cheshire, but we have no evidence to support Bradshaw's ideas about the dedication.

The certain history of the abbey starts in 875 when the remains of St Werburgh the Virgin, buried at Hanbury in Staffordshire in 690, were transferred to Chester as the safest place available in the face of a Danish army advancing on Repton. Although it was later

56

claimed that St Werburgh was responsible for founding a nunnery in Chester, it may well be that she had little or no connection with the city during her lifetime; indeed, the city at that period may have been waste.

St Werburgh (Waerburh) was daughter of Wulfhere, King of Mercia from 657 to 674, who encouraged Christianity in his lands. She became a nun at Ely and later had direction of several Mercian monasteries. St Werburgh is particularly remembered for the miracle of the wild geese, which occurred on her father's estates at Weedon in Northamptonshire. A large flock of these *gantae* had descended on the fields and were ravaging the King's crops, but St Werburgh, being equal to the situation, instructed a manservant to collect the birds. Despite the apparent absurdity of the request, the man went out to the flock and told the geese to go to his mistress; meekly they did. The following morning Werburgh allowed them to fly away, on strict instructions not to return to Weedon, and they rose into the air. But when the flock realized that there was one goose missing, they flew round and round the house, almost darkening the sky, clamouring for its return. St Werburgh discovered that one of her servants had retained a goose for his personal consumption, and when the bird had been freed and rejoined the flock, all was well, and the lands of the kings of Mercia were thereafter shunned by wild geese. St Werburgh's feast-day is 3rd February; her translation is celebrated on 21st June.

St Werburgh died about 690, but nine years later, by popular demand, she was disinterred. Her *Life* states that this was done on the instructions of King Ceolred of Mercia (709–16), although he is elsewhere recorded as a dissolute youth who suppressed monasteries and died insane. Her body and clothes were found to be in perfect condition, and she was transferred to a special display coffin, but alas, as the Danes began to threaten the land, her body disintegrated and on 'translation' to Chester was no more than dust and bones.

The remains were placed in a casket at Chester, which was in about 1300 put into a beautiful new carved stone shrine. The shrine was broken up at the Reformation and parts were incorporated in the *cathedra* the bishop's throne, but in 1876 these and other pieces were gathered together, and the stonework was reconstructed.

The shrine is a nice piece of Decorated masonry, with a feretory for the saint's remains above the aumbrys in which pilgrims placed their offerings. The top of the shrine, decorated with pinnacles, was particularly fine and was ornamented with thirty-four figures of Mercian saints and kings from Werburgh's family, each of which held a scroll with his name. These included King Crieda (c.584), founder of the Mercian kingdom; King Penda (632-54) Werburgh's grandfather; King Wulfhere; King Ceolred, and King Offa (757-96). The figures have lost their paint and are mutilated, most having been decapitated, presumably during the iconoclasms of the sixteenth century.

Bradshaw claimed that the remains were responsible for various miracles which had saved Chester in times of danger: when the Welsh under King Gruffydd besieged the city, the shrine was lifted up onto the battlements; as soon as the King looked upon it, he was struck blind, and the siege was abandoned.

The earliest document recorded in the abbey cartulary is a grant of seventeen houses by King Edgar (959-75) to the house of St Werburgh, but doubts have been cast on the authenticity of this charter. In the time of King Aethelstan (925-39), the chronicles say, the monastery was founded and dedicated to St Werburgh and St Oswald. In 1057 Leofric, Earl of Mercia, enlarged and endowed the foundation.

After the Norman Conquest, Hugh Lupus, the first Norman earl, and Ermetrude his wife restored the possessions of the pre-Conquest canons to a convent of Benedictine monks which they established here in 1093, with the consent of King William Rufus, to pray for the souls of the King and his parents (William the Conqueror and Queen Matilda), and of King Edward the Confessor, among others. Anselm, then Abbot of Bec, visited the earl, who was ill, and laid the foundation-stone of the new abbey buildings. Anselm made Richard, his own chaplain, the first abbot and on his return south was himself made Archbishop of Canterbury. Randle II granted the monks a tenth of his rents from the city, and one in ten of all fish caught in the Dee.

The precincts of the abbey included the whole north-east quarter of the city between the walls and Eastgate and Northgate Streets. The Earls of Chester gave the abbots equal rights within their jurisdiction to their own, which were themselves equal to those of the Crown elsewhere in the country. The mediaeval trials by fire, water and combat were practised in the abbot's courts; prisoners were held over the abbey gates, and convicts hanged by the abbot's officers. In the fourteenth century the abbey also gained from the

Pope, in return for a large payment, exemption from control by the episcopal authorities of Lichfield Diocese.

The abbey had a hard time at first. In the twelfth century its lands on the Wirral and Ince coasts were badly damaged by high tides and flooding, and other estates were destroyed by the Welsh. The church was in ruins, and the monks started the rebuilding with a new quire. However, the abbey had wide estates including much of the land around Chester, and many manors in Wirral and elsewhere in the shire. The monks carried on extensive trade from Chester: among their charters was one from the King of the Isles (the western islands of Scotland) granting their vessels toll-free right of passage and fishing along his coasts.

When Roger de Montalt became Justice of Chester in 1258, he attempted to recover the estates which his ancestors had given to the abbey by seizing them with armed men. A compromise was eventually reached with Roger by which a small part of the estates was surrendered to him; the chroniclers noted that Roger's eldest son died within a fortnight and that Roger died in want, his burial-place unknown to the masses. Roger Venables, Baron of Kinderton, tried to wrest Astbury from the monks but died the following year. In 1263 William de la Zouche, Justice of Chester, brought his soldiers into the abbey and defiled its sanctity; in response all the churches in the city were closed. A similar incident occurred in 1493 when a brawl in the quire before the high altar nearly ended in the death of one man, a certain Patrick Kelling; the abbey church was closed until St Werburgh's Day, St Oswald's Church until St Oswald's Day.

By the fourteenth century the thirty or so monks at the abbey were living a life of relative ease, discarding their habits in favour of fashionable clothes with ornamental belts and knives, hunting in the forests and feasting noisily. Scraps which might have been given to the poor were used to feed greyhounds and hunting-dogs. The abbot was free of all superiors but the Pope and the Bishop, and indulged in numerous petty misdeeds; equally, on one occasion the monks beat up a new abbot. In 1377 the abbot obtained a licence to embattle the abbey walls.

In the sixteenth century the abbots built fine new halls on their manors and laid out a thousand-acre park at their main country estate, Saighton. Henry VIII granted them free warren in all their lands in Cheshire.

Simon Ripley, the twenty-third abbot, was responsible for

major rebuilding in the fifteenth century and left the church in much the state in which the Victorians found it. He was depicted in a painting of the Transfiguration on the north side of the north-east pillar of the crossing. Simon's initials are visible in the north arcade, R on the third pillar from the west, SR on the western respond.

In 1540 the monastery was dissolved, and the church became the Cathedral of the new Diocese of Chester. John Clarke, the twenty-fifth and last abbot, became the first Dean. It was at first planned to convert St Werburgh's Abbey with Wenlock Abbey into a collegiate chapter, but this idea was abandoned. At first the church was treated with almost as little respect as the other dissolved abbeys; by 1580 it was "in great dekay and the glasse thereof carryed to their pryvate benefices" by the Dean and Chapter.

The Cathedral suffered during the Civil War, and more during the Monmouth Rebellion. When the Duke came to Chester in August 1683, the mob

> furiously forced the doors of the cathedral church and destroyed most of the painted glass, burst open the little vestrys and cupboards, wherein were the surplices and hoods belonging to the clergy, which they rent to rags and carried away: they beat to pieces the baptismal font, pulled down some monuments, attempted to demolish the organ and committed other most enormous outrages.

A brief was issued by William III to raise £7,000 for repairs; Daniel Defoe, who visited the Cathedral at that time, said: " 'Tis built of a red, sandy, ill looking stone, which takes much from the beauty of it, and which yielding to the weather, seems to crumble, and suffer by time, which much defaces the building."

The major restoration, however, was by Sir George Gilbert Scott in the late-nineteenth century, following piecemeal improvements in the 1840s. Part of this work was structural restoration. It was discovered that the eastern part of the church had no foundations, and it had to be underpinned, with foundations inserted and missing buttresses replaced. In digging the foundations of the east end, various Roman relics, including two coins of Domitian (AD 81–96) and a centurial stone, were found. Apart from this, the gist of the restoration was an attempt to restore or improve upon the mediaeval appearance of the Cathedral, and the result is more or less the Cathedral that we have today. From the mid-nineteenth century the diocese has been pared down by the creation of sees at Liverpool, Blackburn and Manchester.

The shrine of St Werburgh stands at the west end of the chancel, the Lady Chapel of the Cathedral, behind the high altar in the quire. The chapel, dedicated to St Mary and now appropriated to the various women's organizations of the diocese, has the dimensions of a small church in itself, complete with side aisles. It is thought that the chapel of St Werburgh, in which the shrine originally stood, was at the east end of the Norman quire and was consumed when the quire was lengthened in the thirteenth century and the Lady Chapel added.

The great east window was filled with mediaeval stained glass which showed the genealogy of the Virgin Mary from Jesse of the line of David, i.e. a 'Jesse tree'; the glass was already imperfect before the siege, and the last surviving piece, showing Mary's head, in the very apex of the window, was destroyed when the present east window was inserted in 1859.

The chapel is of three bays with a vaulted stone roof, in which are three carved bosses, representing the Holy Trinity, the Madonna and Child, and the Martyrdom of St Thomas à Becket, whose girdle was preserved in the abbey until the Reformation. There are three pointed arches in the side walls of the chapel, in one of which there are two piscinas. The deans and prebends of the Cathedral were usually buried in the Lady Chapel.

Until the base of the unfinished south-west tower was fitted out, in 1635, the Consistory Court was held in the Lady Chapel. It was here in 1554 that George Coates, the Bishop of Chester, pronounced sentence on George Marsh to be burned to ashes as a heretic (chapter 4).

The next five bays to the west form the quire, which is screened off from the side aisles. At the east end is the High Altar; the three western bays are occupied by the magnificent wooden quire-stalls. On the right-hand side of the altar are four sedilia, removed here from St John's Church by Dean Walker in the sixteenth century; on the left are two aumbrys. Work was in progress on the quire in 1194, but it may not have been completed until considerably later. There are five pointed arches on each side, below a triforium and large clerestory. The wooden vaulting of the roof dates from the Victorian restoration.

Thomas de Byrchehylles, the fourteenth abbot, was buried on the south side of the quire in 1323, beneath a brass engraved with his likeness. In 1787 the grave was opened and his body found to be almost completely undecayed. A wand of hazel, reckoned to be proof against witchcraft and the Devil, had been put in the grave with him.

The High Altar is made from woods brought from the Holy Land, and there is a seventeenth-century eagle lectern.

The first six stalls from the west were reserved for the six prebends of the Cathedral; the stalls by the entrance belong to the Dean and Vice-Dean; the Vice-Dean's seat was formerly used by the Mayor. The quire-stalls date from the time of the abbey and were carved about 1380. There are forty-eight seats, each with a misericord; above each seat is a magnificently carved wooden tabernacle, covered with crockets and pinnacles. These tabernacles were supported by slender wooden columns, which were cut away during the Victorian restoration, and angels added to the pendants. At the same time five of the mediaeval misericords were destroyed as being vulgar; various alterations and replacements were made, and the woodwork was not reassembled in the original position, so that carvings related by the same theme are scattered.

There are numerous allegorical and mythical figures in the carving of the misericords, corbels and bench-ends, and they are generally well-preserved and repay close attention. Of the forty-three surviving misericords only a few have specifically religious subjects: a Madonna and Child, the Coronation of the Virgin, and St Werburgh. The last shows three scenes from the legend of the geese: on the left are the geese in the pen, on the right the repentant servant, and the centrepiece is the missing goose being released by St Werburgh to the flock flying above.

Many of the carvings are of gargoyle-like grotesques, but others refer to characters popular in fourteenth-century literature – Sir Gawain, Tristram and Iseult, and incidents from Aesop's fables and the Bestiaries – and to contemporary scenes, such as the hen-pecked husband, the wrestlers, and pigs running in the forest.

The dean's stall is thought to have been originally the seat of the abbot and has a marvellous carved bench-end with a Jesse tree, the Coronation of the Virgin Mary by the Holy Ghost, above a sleeping Jacob, and a little figure of a pilgrim. The vice-dean's stall opposite has the pelican feeding her young with blood pecked from her own breast. The Jesse tree also appears on the far bench-end on the north side of the quire.

Until the nineteenth century there were galleries around the quire, hidden by the tabernacles, and over the entry was a large gallery containing "a very deep and tuneable organ", upon a stone screen. This screen was removed by the Victorians, and the present organ on a screen across the north transept was built, and the present rood screen was placed across the entrance to the quire. The organ-loft and screens were designed by Scott and are beautiful pieces of restrained decorative Gothic.

The north aisle by the quire, now used by the girls' associations of the diocese, has a Tudor chapel at the east end dedicated to St Werburgh. There is a piscina in the south wall where the original altar was, but the aisle was extended to the east during the thirteenth-century reconstruction, and the eastern end is Perpendicular in style. At the west end of the aisle the restorers have exposed the base and capital of a Norman column which were used as part of the foundations when the quire was extended. Part of the *pulpitum* has also been preserved here, together with some mediaeval tiles.

The north side of any church was looked on with some disfavour, and the burying-space here was relegated to petty canons and other minor members of the Cathedral.

The great tower of the Cathedral, which stands 127 feet high, is supported on the four pillars of the crossing. The tower is said to have been completed in 1210. Until the new concrete *canpanile* faced with Bethesda slate was built to the south-east of the Cathedral, the bells hung in the great tower. The *campanile* was opened in 1975. Before the Victorian restorations, the tower was a picturesque, if crumbling, pile of soft sandstone, inhabited by jackdaws. The curfew was rung each evening at nine o'clock, a custom originating in William the Conqueror's order that the bell of the church of Stratford-le-Bow in London be rung at eight each night to warn the inhabitants to *couvre feu*, put out their lights: in Chester the curfew was called 'the Bow Bell'. When the bishop or dean was to preach, the event was preceded by the tolling of the big bell.

The tower was refaced and restored in the 1860s for £6,700, and Scott added four octagonal corner turrets, which, together with the general pinnacling and the addition of further turrets over the east end of the quire and the west end of the nave, radically altered the appearance of the exterior. Scott 'restored' to the east end of the south quire aisle not only the hexagonal apse but also an ugly triangular slab of stonework, postulating that a similar embellishment had been present in the mediaeval design.

This aisle is now dedicated to St Erasmus. In the south wall are two low wide arches for tombs. One of these had a gravestone of Purbeck marble on which was a monumental brass with the effigy of the twenty-first abbot, John de Salghall, buried there in about 1452. The coffin was opened in 1827:

> His body was enveloped in folds of cerecloth, and an illegible writing on parchment lay upon his breast. His gold ring of office, containing a large sapphire, was on the forefinger of his right hand. This was not interred again with the rest of the contents of the coffin but is now preserved among the treasures of the Chapter.

William de Bebington and William de Mershton, the fifteenth and eighteenth abbots, were also buried nearby in the fourteenth century.

In the second bay of the south wall from the west a small doorway (marked in about 1540 as "door into green churchyard") was found during the restorations and beneath it a coffin in which was a shrunken body wrapped in very coarse reddish-brown hempen cerecloth, which "a few seconds after exposure, crumbled into dust". It has been assumed that these were the mortal remains of Ranulph Higden, a monk of this abbey, who compiled the *Polychronicon*, a long history of the world from the Creation to 1352. A copy of the manuscript is in the Chapter Library.

A mystery surrounds the large sarcophagus in the south aisle. The tomb is of black alabaster, with a plain marble slab on the top, the sides decorated with quatrefoil-headed arches and roses and leopards' heads. Until the seventeenth century the top of the tomb was painted in oils with the figure of an emperor in his robes and crown. In 1355 Godstall Lane south of the abbey was described thus: "Sant goddestall Lane . . . goithe out of [Estgate Street] into the Sade Church yarde. This Goddstall lieth Buried within the abbay Churche in Chester, and he was An Emperoure and a vertuose disposed man in his Lyuynge". St Werburgh's Chronicle records that in 1110 King Henry gave his daughter to an emperor of Germany, "who now lies at Chester". It is true that in 1109 Henry I's daughter Matilda was betrothed to Henry V, Emperor of Germany, who died at Utrecht in 1125, but the chroniclers claimed that he retired to live as a monk at Chester under the name Godstall and died here:

This Henry, after that he hadde punesched his flescheliche fader, and his goostliche fader the pope, and the cardynales, at the laste also hym repentede, and went away, unwetynge his wyf Molde of Engelond, and excilede hymself by his good wille, and lyvede at Chestre ten yere as an heremyte; and for he wolde note be knowe there while he was on lyve, he cleped hym self Godeschal, that is Goddis cleping.

The tradition is, moreover, related (*ut creditur*) by Giraldus Cambrensis who was living in the twelfth century, only a few decades after the event; Giraldus's emperor is an unspecified *"Imperatorem Romanum Henricum"*.

At the head of the tomb there was, before the Reformation, an image of the Blessed Virgin Mary. The Black Friars recorded that on one occasion when they were processing past the image, it raised itself and, with its finger pointing to them, said "Lo! my brothers beloved and forechosen".

There is general agreement that the tomb in the south quire aisle is of about 1300, and clearly whether Henry or Godstall was buried at Chester or not, is too late for him, unless erected in his honour at a much later date. The tomb had a sliding lid and contains a lead coffin.

As late as the seventeenth century it was common to continue burying within the church; the cost to those not privileged to free access was £5 for burying in the 'side alleys', £10 in the body of the quire. But it became clear that such interments helped to undermine the Cathedral fabric. The side walls of the eastern end were leaning feet out of true by the nineteenth century.

The nave, the body of the church, extends for 145 feet from the west door to the crossing. There are seven bays, including the bases of the uncompleted south-west and north-west towers. Six pointed arches on clustered columns with foliated capitals divide the nave from its side-aisles or arcades. The south side of the nave dates from the fourteenth century; the north side was completed a hundred years later, and the clerestory in the sixteenth century, at the close of the abbey's life. The wooden vaulting in the roof was introduced in Scott's restoration.

The stone *pulpitum*, removed during the restorations, came across the nave at the end of the sixth bay, and below the clerestory is a carved stone imp to ward off evil spirits from the quire.

The west end of the church partly adjoins the old King's School, on the site of part of the abbey buildings, and there is no clear west front to the Cathedral. The beautiful west door has been attributed to Simon Ripley or his successor John Birchenshaw, the twenty-fourth abbot. The doorway is a Tudor arch flanked by narrow niches, beneath a frieze of small carved angels. On the tympanum is a small statue, perhaps of St Werburgh, between the arms of England quartering France Ancient (the royal arms) and the same with a label (for the Earl of Chester). On each side of the doorway are three empty niches with crocketed stone tabernacles, and above is the great west window. In 1506 the old steeple, perhaps the south-west tower, was dismantled, and in 1508 John laid the foundation for the new steeple in the presence of Thomas Harwarden the Mayor.

The south-west porch (the 'singing-school porch') was built at the same period but is a much more modest piece of work than the west front. Over the porch is a little room in which the Cathedral muniments were stored – these are now at the Diocesan Record Office in the Castle.

The south-west tower, which was not completed or was pulled down after only a few years, was fitted out as the Consistory Court in 1635 and has the original furnishings, complete with the canopied throne of the Chancellor of the diocese. There is a bracket for the Bishop's silver mace surmounted with a mitre, which was borne by the apparitor of the court in the procession from the Chapter House on the enthroning of each new bishop.

Below the throne is a large wooden table and benches surrounded by a low panelled enclosure, with doors at the far end. Close to the west door is the old Cathedral font, perhaps dating from after 1683 when the Monmouth rioters smashed the previous one.

The north-west tower has been used as the baptistry since 1885, in which year the sixth-century stone chest font from Venice, ornamented with chi-rho and peacocks, was brought here. The tower, which does not rise above the level of the nave clerestory, contains some of the older surviving stonework of the Cathedral. There is a high Norman arch blocked in with masonry and supported by slim round pillars in the west wall. The north wall has a high, round-headed window above the level of the adjoining cloisters. In the north-west corner is a spiral staircase which led to the upper storey. The monks used the bottom of the tower as their wine-cellar.

The oldest major stonework in the Cathedral is in the north

transept, which has a fine Norman archway below the seven small arches of a triforium. This remains from a double arcade of such small arches, which faced a similar triforium on the west wall. The archways leads through to the sacristy or vestry and has been partly blocked off with an ugly wooden partition. The north transept is of just one bay, adjoining the chapter house to the north and the cloisters to the west.

At the entrance to the sacristy is a seventeenth-century carved unicorn horn (perhaps from a narwhal). One of the misericords in the quire shows the capture of a unicorn by the time-honoured method of trading on the beast's fatal attraction to virgins.

In the centre of the north transept is the ornamental sarcophagus of Bishop John Pearson, who died in 1688, with his effigy attended by two angels. The tomb was constructed in 1863, when his remains were removed here from the quire, within the altar-rails, where he had been buried without memorial. On the sides and ends of the sarcophagus are carved the heads of the twelve Apostles, with the parts of the Apostles' Creed attributed to each written below. Pearson wrote An Exposition of the Creed ("one of the glories of our theology"), The Golden Remains of John Hales, Vindiciae Epistolarum Sancti Ignatii and Annales Cyprianici; he was described as the greatest divine of his age, "his very dross was gold".

From the north transept is the entrance to the cloisters. During morning service on New Year's Day 1784 a hare suddenly appeared in the cloisters and ran through the body of the church and out at the west door, with some of the citizens in pursuit. It struck off down Northgate Street and left by the Milk Stoups towards Eastgate where it was brought down by the racing throng.

On 22nd December 1887 Joseph Crawford, who was accustomed to smoke his pipe when entering the Cathedral, was approached by the Precentor. Crawford cursed and swore at him and was brought before the magistrates and bound over to keep the peace. That same day he went back into the Cathedral, started shouting during the afternoon service and went up to the quire screen, gesticulating at the officials and waving his hat. He was imprisoned for a month in consequence.

The cloisters formed a quadrangle, with the church on the south, the great hall and the green hall on the west, the chapter house on the east, and the monks' hall or refectory on the north. The quadrangle surrounded the sprise garden, in which was the sprise, a fountain fed with fresh water piped in from Christleton outside the city walls. Edward I granted the monks a licence to drive this pipeline through any intervening property and to puncture the walls near the Kaleyard to bring the water through.

In the south and west cloisters were more than a dozen carrels, small studies divided by pillars. The cloisters have Norman stonework surviving but were rebuilt in the 1520s and then fell into disuse after the Dissolution. The south walk collapsed completely and was rebuilt by the Victorians. There are large obtusely-pointed windows looking into the garden, and the cloisters were vaulted throughout in stone. Over the east walk was a monks' dormitory, destroyed about 1800. The cloisters have been glazed with stained glass representing the festivals of the Church calendar.

In the south walk, in the church wall, are two Norman arcades of six semi-circular arches, three on the east with ornamental pillars, where four of the early abbots were buried – Richard, the first abbot, in 1117; William, the second abbot, in 1140; Ralph, the third abbot, in 1157, and Robert de Hastings, the sixth abbot, in 1193. When the Victorian restoration was in progress, three tombstones were found here, one inscribed 'RADVLPHS ABBAS III', another 'ROBERTVS NOVI . . . ABBAS QVARTVS'.

At the south-west angle of the cloisters is the Norman doorway into the church and, on the west, one into the vaulted abbot's passage. The latter was blocked at the Tudor reconstruction, when a stone shaft was built in the middle of the arch.

Above the passage is St Anselm's Chapel, the Norman abbot's chapel, now used by the bishop. The stucco ceiling and the screen and altar-rails are all Jacobean, as is the bay added for a chancel. The conventual buildings to which the passage led are now destroyed, on the right was a chamber containing the abbot's well; in front was a long gallery from which doors led off to the abbot's pantry, the strong-beer-cellar and the serving-men's hall.

Along the west side of the cloisters is the six-bay great cellar with beautiful stone vaulting; part of this undercroft is now used for the Cathedral bookshop. The upper floor, which contained the green hall and the great hall, is now destroyed – there is a flat roof. A spiral staircase led up to the halls by the entrance to the cellar.

In the north-west corner of the cloisters is a doorway leading to the refectory kitchens and Abbey Square. Outside this doorway was the monks' cellar and the passage to the abbey court.

The north cloisters are flanked by the refectory, a fine hall which from the seventeenth century to 1876 was used as part of the King's School and divided by a passageway. The entrance from the cloisters is through a fine antique stone doorway, of the early-thirteenth century; on its right the ribs of the cloister vaulting spring from a carved shield of Henry VIII. The refectory has been restored to its former glory, with a great new hammer-beam roof. The refectory, or 'fratry', was built about 1290 and has a beautiful stone pulpit at the eastern end, above the dais for the high table. A little door in the south-east corner leads to steps set in the wall leading up by a pillared arcade to the projecting pulpit.

From the north-west corner a doorway led into the pantry and kitchens. On a flag at the north-east corner of the cloisters was a mark called 'the Devil's footprint'; it was said that if the flag was taken up and replaced, the footprint would reappear on the new stone. At the north end of the east cloister is a doorway to the stairway which led up to the monks' dormitory. Behind this is the ancient priests' cellar, now used as a parlour or warming-room, a vaulted two-bay chamber with octagonal pillars. A passageway called 'the Maiden's Isle' or 'Slype' separated them from the Chapter House. The passage led to the vaulted kitchens and offices, long since gone, and to the Green.

Earl Hugh Lupus, the founder of the Benedictine abbey, was buried in the graveyard, but when Randle Meschines, his nephew, the third Norman Earl of Chester (1119–28), granted a charter of confirmation to the monks, he mentions that he has had the remains transferred into the chapter house, where he himself was to be buried. Many of the Norman Earls of Chester were buried there, but there is no monument to them; as also the seventh, eighth, eleventh, twelfth, thirteenth and seventeenth abbots.

The chapter house has an outer vestibule, with a vaulted roof supported on four free-standing stone pillars. On the right-hand side are three arches beneath which the abbots were buried. The chapter room is also vaulted and lit by large lancet windows. Its construction has been ascribed to Simon de Whitchurch, the thirteenth abbot (1265–89). At the east end, set in the wall under the east window, is a thirteenth-century cupboard, overlaid with wrought iron. Part of the Cathedral Library, including a twelfth-century Bible and a fifteenth-century Book of Hours, is kept in the chapter house.

In June 1723 remains ascribed to Hugh Lupus were found beneath the chapter house:

in a stone coffin, wrapt in gilt leather, with a cross on the breast, and at
the head of the coffin a stone in the shape of a T, with the wolf's head,
in allusion to his name, engraved on it. Immediately over his head was
a very singular covering, made of paper, nicely platted, so as to form
most elegant little squares of black and white.

  The Scull and all the Bones were very fresh, and in the right
Position . . . the String which ty'd the Ancles together was whole and
entire.

Beneath the wolf's head on the stone is a monogram, which may be
SR, the initials of the twenty-third abbot, Simon Ripley – but we
know that Simon died at Warwick and is buried at St Mary's there.
The wolf's head was also borne on the arms of Earl Richard,
Hugh's son, who died in 1120 in the *White Ship*.

  Because of the loss of Cathedral plate and records from before
the Civil War, there has been a strong suspicion among anti-
quarians that, although these might have been destroyed, they
might equally yet be found. This theory is reinforced by the
tradition of a lost chamber within the walls, sealed up during the
siege and never re-opened. Scott, during the restorations, searched
eagerly for the lost room, but in vain.

  Sir Peter Leycester, the great Cheshire historian, who was alive
at the time of the siege, records that the original charter of the
foundation (which disappeared at that time, but of which he made
a copy) was among the records of the Cathedral which were
removed in 1648 to "a certain room within St Werburgh's
Church". The treasurers' accounts from 1573 to 1623 have several
references to "the Treasure house", but its location has never been
found. To some extent this search was resolved, unspectacularly:
in 1924 Canon May, the honorary librarian at the Cathedral,
discovered a quantity of the lost pre-siege documents in the library
muniment room.

  West of the cloisters and the refectory is the Abbey Square,
mostly now enclosed with handsome Georgian town-houses but
entered from Northgate Street under a large mediaeval gateway,
the Great Abbey Gate. This dates from the thirteenth century and
was rebuilt in 1591. A spiral staircase led up to the room above the
arch in which the Pleas of the Abbey were held, and this was later
used as the registry. It is said that a room over the gateway was
used as a prison and that George Marsh, the Puritan, who was
afterwards burned at the stake in Spital Boughton, was held there

for four months. Once or twice sympathizers cast money in to him through a hole in the wall.

The courts of St Thomas were held in the room on the north side of the gateway and later removed to the refectory. They were held before the seneschal (the clerk of the chapter) and a jury of abbey or cathedral tenants. The presentiments generally related to petty misdemeanours and the upkeep of property. In 1693, for instance:

We present Richard Thomason, for not removing his midding and cleansing his watercourse in the Northgate-street, and doe Amerce him in the sum of 3s 4d. . . .

We present the Deane and Chapter for not repairing the Courthouse; and also for a Dunghill before the Regester office, and we do Amerce them in 13s 4d.

The chapter maintained a pair of stocks and a cuckstool to keep malefactors and scolds in order.

On the south side of the gateway is the old porter's lodge; the gateway continued in use after the Dissolution, and provision was made for "ij porters to kepe the gates and shave the company xij£ per annum".

The outside and inside of the sandstone gateway are formed by two large arches, but the semicircular outer archway is constructed over a thick stone wall in which is the pointed arch for the main gate, and a small postern doorway. The gateway is ribbed and vaulted, with carved keystones, one of which is thought to represent St Werburgh. On either side of the front arch are two plain pointed windows or niches.

On 22nd October 1651, in the recriminations of the Civil War, Sir Timothy Featherstonhaugh was beheaded in front of the Abbey Gates. He had seven sons and seven daughters by his wife Bridget; two of his sons were killed fighting for the King at Worcester, two others were in Charles II's Life Guards. Sir Timothy raised £700 and troops for Charles I and himself fought against the Roundheads. He was actually tried and condemned for corresponding with the Royalists.

His last letter to his wife survives:

My dearest
it is a sad farewell I now must take and my greifes doe sup'abound for you and my poore children
    this fatall sentence is irreuocable . . .
    thou hast beene to me an unparalleld wife and a mother to thy children

though my death be fatall and some will make it scandalous yet
posteritie truth another generation may not call it soe nor would our
age have cald soe some yeares since
   I hope in the eyes of God and good people itt will be esteemed little
lesse than A maytirdome and I hope since no remedie I must die (and
soe must all) I shall die a good Christian . . . I leaue you all to God and
them to the[e]
   if I had the Indies I would leave itt to the[e] . . .
   without salt teares itt is time my thoughts and Actions be wholy
taken upp with the contemplation of heaven where with comforte I
hope wee shall meete And till then God blesse my children and the[e]
and comfort the[e] and thy poore unfortunate dying husband
          Ty: Fetherston.

The Abbot's Fair was held for three days from the feast of 21st
June, the translation of St Werburgh, during which period he
claimed the tolls, and all business had to be transacted (as during
the Midsummer Fair) in front of the abbey gateway. Booths were
placed there for the merchants, thatched with reeds cut by the
monks on Stanlow Marsh. During the fair, jurisdiction in the city
was by the abbot's court of Pie Powder: the monks arrested
malefactors, and felons were hanged on the earl's gallows. During
the fair the liberties of the city were proclaimed a sanctuary for
criminals, who could pass undisturbed as long as they committed
no fresh crimes.

At Whitsun each year the Mystery Plays, performed by the
members of twenty-five city companies, were shown before the
gates. The date of the composition of these plays, of which we
have an entire copy, is uncertain. Various dates were suggested in
the seventeenth century, varying from 1268 to 1339. They were
attributed to a monk called Randle, later equated with Randle
Higden, the author of the *Polychronicon*. The earliest record of a
performance is 1566 or 1567. Certainly, other plays are recorded in
Chester earlier, and in 1499 Prince Arthur watched one from the
gateway. The prologue to the plays, written about 1533, declared
that they were written by a monk called Sir Henry Frances, who is
in fact found in abbey records in about 1380. It is stated that Henry
obtained from the Pope (Clement VI?) a grant of a thousand days
of pardon, plus forty days of pardon from their sins (that is, less
time in Purgatory after death) from the Bishop of Chester (i.e. of
Lichfield) to every person watching the plays peacefully, and that
anyone disturbing them would be accursed.

The pageants took three days to perform, the Monday, Tuesday and Wednesday in Whit week, first before the Abbey Gates, then at the High Cross before the Mayor in the Pentice, and then in each of the main streets. On the Monday nine pageants were performed, from the Fall of Lucifer to the Three Kings at the Nativity. Tuesday covered the life and death of Christ to the Harrowing of Hell, in another nine pageants; and seven pageants on Wednesday dealt with the Resurrection through to Doomsday. Thus in the three days the twenty-five companies, each of which had a play to perform, covered the religious history of the world.

Each company performed on "a highe scafolde with 2 rowmes, a higher and a lower, upon 4 wheeles. In the lower they apparelled them selves, and in the higher rowme they played, being all open on the tope, that all beholders mighte heare and see them." These scaffolds, which were called 'pageants', were built by the Company of Joiners, Carvers and Turners, who did not have a play of their own.

The surviving texts are, of course, of great interest, although to us, as indeed to the more puritanical of the sixteenth-century citizens, they often seem to be grotesque burlesques, more of an affront to Christianity than a religious devotion. There was a reluctance even to print an edition of the text in the nineteenth century because of its crudities, "an almost insurmountable obstacle to presenting the entire series to the eye of the public at large". There were strong moves to ban the Whitsun plays in the reign of Elizabeth, and in 1571 the Archbishop of York sent an order stopping them, but it arrived too late to have any effect. They were revived in 1600 but did not continue for long.

The first play was that of the Tanners, the Fall of Lucifer. God enters: "*Ego sum alpha et oo, primus et novissimus. It is my will it shoulde be soe; hit is, yt was, it shalbe thus. I ame greate God gracious which never had begyninge*". The angel Lucifer, abetted by Lightborne, sits on God's throne during His absence, expressly disobeying His instructions. God is angry and says: "I charge you to fall till I byd 'Whoo', into the deepe pitt of hell ever to bee". The Drapers then presented the Creation. Minstrels play as Adam is led by God into Paradise. God makes the woman from Adam's rib. The stage directions add: "Then Adam and Eve shall stand naked and shall not bee ashamed. Then the sepente shall come up out of a hole". They eat the forbidden fruit, "Then Adam and Eve shall cover ther members with leaves, hydinge themselves under the trees. Then God shall speake [minstrelles playe] 'Adam, Adam, where arte thou?'." Unconvinced by their excuses, God drives Adam and Eve out of Paradise. The action moves on thirty years: Abel lumbers in with a plough, only to be killed by Cain. God reappears ("minstrelles playe"), and Cain is banished.

The Waterleaders and Drawers of Dee (fishermen) present the pageant of Noyes Fludd. "And firste in some high place – or in the clowdes, if it may bee – God speaketh unto Noe standinge without the arke with all his familye." After some minor altercations, "Noe with all his familye shall make a signe as though the wrought upon the shippe with divers instruements." The animals are gathered for the ark. To overcome the logistical problems of assembling pairs of lions, leopards, horses, oxen, swine, goats, calves, sheep, kine, camels, asses, deer, cats, dogs, otters, foxes, fulmars, hares, bears, wolves, apes, owls, marmosets, weasels, squirrels, ferrets, rats, mice, herons, cranes, bitterns, swans, peacocks, cocks, kites, crows, rooks, ravens, ducks, curlews, doves and redshanks on the stage, they are painted on the boards of the ark. Noah's wife is reluctant to leave, enjoying the convivial company of the good gossips, who are broaching a bottle of malmsey, but her sons carry her off to the ark.

The Barbers presented Abraham and Isaac, and then the Cappers the history of Moses, and the Wrights dealt with the Annunciation of the Blessed Virgin Mary and the Nativity. The play proceeds in English, but Mary sings a *Magnificat*, and the Emperor Octavian (Augustus) breaks into Norman-French.

Joseph brings two midwives, Tebell and Salome, to deliver Mary's child, but Mary says they will be unnecessary. Jesus, is born, and a star appears. Salome tries to touch Mary *in sexu secreto*, and her hand is paralysed, but Jesus cures her. The Painters deal with the Shepherds. The first Shepherd is a Cheshire man, called Hankyn, familiar with the district from Conway to Clyde. He is busy with his herbs for his sheep,

> Henbane and horehounde,
> tybbe, radishe, and egermonde, . . .
> fynter, fanter and fetterfowe,
> and alsoe penyewrytte
> Here is tarre in a pott
> to heale them from the rott;
> well I can and well I wott
> the talgh from them take.

The second Shepherd is called Harvey, the third Tudd Tybbys-sonne, who has some supper, prepared by his wife:

> And here ale of Halton I have
> and whot meate I had to my hyer;
> a puddinge may noe man deprave,
> and a jannock of Lancastershyre.
> Loe, here a sheepes head sowsed in ale,
> and a grayne to laye on the greene,
> and sowre milke.

The first shepherd produces a pig's foot from his pocket; Tudd Tybbyssonne has

> gambonns and other good meate in fere,
> a puddinge with a pricke in the ende.

Much of the action is spent in coarse wrangling with another shepherd called Trowle, who is seen on a nearby knoll with his dog, Dottynolle. They see the star and wend forth to Bethlehem. Hankyn brings Jesus a bell: "I praye thee save me from hell". Harvey has a flackett: "Therby hanges a spoone for to eat thy pottage with at noone, as I myselfe full oftetymes have donne". Tudd Tybbyssonne brings a cap, "for I have nothinge elles", and Trowle offers Him "a payre of my wyves ould hose".

Four boys next appear, with more presents. The first says,

> But thoe hit lacke a stopple
> take thee here my well fayre bottle,
> for yt will hold a good pottle.

The second gives his hood, the third "my pype that soundeth so royallye", the fourth his nuthook, so that Joseph need not hurt his hands pulling down apples, pears and plums for his little boy.

The Vintners presented the Three Kings from the East; the Mercers dealt with their arrival at the stable, and the Goldsmiths did the Slaughter of the Innocents. Herod, who is constantly swearing by Mohammed, is attended by two knights called Sir Grymball and Sir Lancherdeepe.

The Ironmongers presented the Crucifixion. After a great deal of time has been spent by the four Jews dicing for Jesus's seamless garments, Caiaphas, the High Priest, breaks in:

> Men, for cockes face,
> howe longe shall pewee-ars
> stand naked in that place?
> Goe nayle him on the tree!

The Cooks' play was the Harrowing of Hell, drawing largely from the Apocryphal New Testament. Jesus is met by Adam, the prophet Isaiah, Simeon Justus, John the Baptist, Seth and David. Satan from his throne invites the hellhounds to partake of this "noble morsell", but Jesus summons the Archangel Michael to lead all the good dead forth from the Gates of Hell. The play ends with a vignette in which an alewife tells how she blended ashes and herbs into the ale she brewed, and kept false measures, and so is condemned to stay in Hell; she points out the moral:

> Tavernes, tapsters of this cittye
> shalbe promoted here with mee
> for breakinge statutes of this contrye,
> hurtinge the commonwealth,
> with all typpers-tappers that are cunninge,
> mispendinge much malt, bruynge so thinne,
> sellinge smale cuppes money to wynne,
> agaynst all trueth to deale.

The Skinners show the Resurrection: Pilate introduces himself, being an aristocrat and a foreigner to boot, in Norman-French. The Websters presented the twenty-fifth and last pageant of the cycle, the Last Judgment, which closes with Jesus condemning a pope and an emperor to eternal fire, and their being dragged off by two demons.

Inside the Abbey Gates was a pond called 'the Horse Pool', used for watering the monks' steeds. On New Year's Eve 1523 Roger Ledsham, the gatekeeper, fell into this pool and was drowned. In 1584 the courtyard was levelled and the pond filled in. There is now an oval green in which stands a column from the old Exchange, surmounted with a cross. The square is cobbled, with flags for carriages.

The abbot's house stood on the south side of the courtyard, now called Abbey Square; only the vaulted beer-cellar survives. After the Dissolution the courtyard fell into disrepair. Parts of the buildings were let out to citizens, and a malthouse was erected on one side of the square, a brewhouse on another. In 1637 William Laud, the Archbishop of Canterbury, was scandalized to hear of the state of the precincts, complaining of the noise and filth and smoke from the brewhouse, and wrote about it in strong terms to the Dean and Chapter.

The abbot's house became the Bishop's Palace when the new

diocese was created. When Charles I was in the city in May 1642, he and his train were lodged there. After the siege and the destruction of the bishopric, the palace was sold for £1,059 but on the Restoration was given back to the diocese. On the night of 27th August 1687 James II lodged there; the following morning he walked through the city to the Castle, the Mayor, bareheaded, carrying the sword before him. The Mayor of Chester had the ancient and peculiar privilege of bearing a sword unsheathed and erect in the presence of anyone but the monarch.

Bishop Keene (1752–71) rebuilt the Palace in 1753 in sandstone; Bishop Jacobson (1865–84) removed to a new palace near St John's Church (chapter 4), and the old palace was sold to the Dean and Chapter for £3,000. The King's School, established by Henry VIII in 1541 at the dissolution of the abbey, was conducted in the old refectory and removed in 1876 to the site of the Bishop's House. The School's motto is *"Rex dedit, benedicat Deus"* ("May God bless [what] the King has given"), and the scholars' straw hats had blue-and-gold ribbons with the monogram HR. The same monogram and motto were carved below the oriel window at the west end of the school; the building now belongs to Barclay's Bank, for the school was moved in 1960 to new premises in Wrexham Road.

The present Bishop's House, in the north-east corner of the square, is the late-eighteenth-century Deanery, built on the site of the Chapel of St Thomas the Apostle which stood there before the Reformation. Near the north-west corner of the square is a single old sandstone arch called 'the Little Abbey Gate'. On the north side of the square were the abbot's storehouse and brewhouse, and a bakehouse with two ovens, one 19 feet across. The great well, which was used by the householders until relatively recent times, stood immediately in front of the brewhouse. Along the west side, from this corner, ran the great kiln and drying-floors.

Dean William Smith, on moving into the Deanery in 1767, wrote:

> Within this pile of mould'ring stones,
> The Dean hath laid his weary bones –
> In hope to end his days in quiet
> Exempt from nonsense, noise, and riot:
> And pass, nor teiz'd by fool nor knave,
> From this still mansion to his grave.
> Such there, like richer men's, his lot,
> To be in four days' time forgot.

He died in 1787, aged seventy-six, and was buried in the Cathedral, where his widow erected a monument to his memory.

The Cathedral precinct extended to the city walls from Eastgate to Northgate via the north-east corner. Chester has a complete circuit of walls, which may be walked in their entirety without a gap, except where they are crossed by Grosvenor Street. On the west and south there are stretches where the wall is no more than a stretch of pavement. This circuit is mostly the line of the mediaeval walls, which encompass a considerably larger area than the Roman fortress walls.

The northern and eastern Roman walls form part of the circuit, but the mediaeval north wall continues westwards to the old Dee bank at the Water Tower, and southwards as far as the Castle, which it encloses, and the Old Dee Bridge. On the outside of the wall was a deep fosse, which is almost entirely filled in, but which greatly facilitated the cutting of the Shropshire Union Canal running alongside the north wall.

It has been a principal delight of visitors to Chester to walk the walls, and in the eighteenth century efforts were made to repair the walks and complete the circuit. The walls had been repaired throughout the Middle Ages by the murengers, whose expenses were met by a tax on imports called 'murage'.

The walls are flagged and rise in some places to 20 feet or more, with rails on the inside and the battlements on the outside. Most of the material of the walks dates from repairs from the eighteenth century to the present day, but the mediaeval and Roman stonework in the lower courses can easily be recognized as being much more worn and imperfect. The most ancient fabric was put together in dressed stone without mortar.

William Webb, in about 1615, talks of the walls as "a very delectable walk, feeding the eye, on the one side, with the sweet gardens and fine buildings of the city; and on the other side with a prospect of many miles into the county of Chester, into Wales, and into the sea". Even before the rebuilding of the four gates, it was possible to walk across each in the circuit of the walls.

When Dr Johnson came to Chester in 1774, he walked the walls with Mr and Mrs Thrale and their daughter. He insisted on completing the full circuit, and they did not get back until an hour after Miss Thrale's bedtime. Johnson wrote: "I have known my mistress fifteen years and never saw her fairly out of humour, but on Chester walls."

John Wesley walked the walls in June 1752. Jonathan Swift, who had to pass through Chester on the way to and from Ireland, but who did not enjoy the experience, wrote:

> The walls of this town
> Are full of renown,
> And strangers delight to walk round 'em;
> But as for the dwellers,
> Both buyers and sellers,
> For me, you may hang 'em or drown 'em.

A variant of this healthy exercise is running round the walls. The circuit is about 1¾ miles but includes various ups and downs. In 1792 a twelve-year-old boy won a small sum by running twice round in twenty-three minutes. On 10th July 1607 a butcher called William Henckes won a wager by riding his horse around the walls. A visitor in 1705 records:

> A Gentleman told us a Story of a Man who was us'd frequently to leap over the Gateway, from one wall to the other, upon discoursing whereof, a Gentleman offer'd to lay him 20 Guineas, he could not doe it, he took up the Bett, but fail'd in the attempt, and broke his Legg. Yet after his Legg was well again, he perform'd it with all the ease imaginable.

The seventeen-year-old Jane Hester Reilly in 1791 commented: "Though it is the public promenade for all the beaux and belles in Chester, it is by no means pretty, only one peep at the Dee and its banks; there are here and there little watch towers which are now converted into resting-places for the Masters and Misses of the town to flirt in."

Opposite the end of Abbey Street on the east wall was the Saddlers' Tower, taken down in 1779. This had been quite a high turret, rising about 20 feet above the walkway, and contained rooms with groined roofs. Over the doorway was a machicolation for pouring boiling water, lead and suchlike on attackers.

The monks of St Werburgh had access to their gardens outside the wall through a small stone archway called 'the Kaleyard Gate'; the simple stone archway there was rebuilt in 1693. The Kaleyard ('cabbage garden') was the convent garden outside the walls. The monks constructed another large arch nearby, but the threat that it posed to the city's security was so great that in 1322 an agreement was reached with the Corporation that the large gateway be replaced with a more modest postern just big enough for a man to lead a horse through, and to put a drawbridge across the fosse at the Kaleyard Gate. The second gateway survived until the seventeenth century but was not replaced when the walls were rebuilt after the Civil Wars.

At the north-east corner of the walls is the Phoenix Tower, from the leads of which Charles I, attended by the Mayor, Sir Francis Gamul, and Alderman Cowper witnessed the defeat of his forces at Rowton Moor in 1645, "and was all the while a sad spectator of most of this tragedy". At this time the tower was used as the meeting-place of the guild of Joyners, Carvers and Turners. The turret was earlier called 'Newton Tower' (it overlooks Newton outside the walls) and was built in 1613 and restored in 1658. It was used by the Company of Painters, Glaziers, Embroiderers and Stationers, whose emblem was a phoenix. The Phoenix Tower has long been used as a museum, now devoted to the Civil War period and containing armour and cannon-balls. When this was a private museum, at the turn of the century, a disgruntled visitor described the contents as "a miscellaneous collection of all sorts of more or less useless articles – badly stuffed birds, snakes' skins and sharks' teeth, bits of doubtful Roman pottery and horn cores of *Bos longifrons*, pottery and savage weapons." He also claimed that one of the city guides had told visitors that King Charles drowned in the canal.

In 1690 Nicholas Cardiffe clandestinely married John Owens, gentleman, to Elizabeth Thropp in the Phoenix Tower (he also married another couple in a private house in Bridge Street). On 15th May he was brought before the Lord Bishop and the Chancellor in the Consistory to explain himself, and he begged them on bended knee for absolution, which was granted.

Until about 1810 there were coats-of-arms of several of the city companies on the south side of the tower, and at the corner of the walls was a recess with a semicircular arch, in which was a raised seat. Above the entrance doorway there is a carving of a phoenix and the date 1613.

The north-east tower of the Roman fortress would have stood at this corner, and in the Deanery Field within the city below have been found traces of the barracks buildings, with many small finds including chain and scale armour fragments, coins, ballista balls and a bronze military badge. In 1925 a small white marble base from an altar was found there, with the inscription:

GENIO . SIGNI(F)
LEG . X̄X̄ . VV
T FL VALERIANVS
COLLEGIS . D . D

("To the genius of the standard-bearers of the Twentieth Legion Valeria Victrix, Titus Flavius Valerianus gave this to his colleagues".)

Two Roman interval-towers projected inwards into the fort between the north-east corner and the Northgate. In the *intervallum*, the area immediately within the walls, were long stone rampart buildings. The city wall east of Northgate has a large section of the original Roman stonework, from a rebuilding in about AD 300, standing up to 16 feet above the old ground-level and topped with a moulded cornice, marking the Roman rampart walk.

The first Roman defences were of turf, soil and loose rock from the outer ditch, resting on timber foundations, and about eight yards thick. The first walls were built at the front of this rampart and were erected in about AD 105. The stonework was set into a foundation cut into the solid rock. The rebuilding in about AD 300 involved a thickening of the fortress wall and a reconstruction of the upper masonry as we can see it today, but with a battlement along the top to protect defenders. There is no evidence that there was ever any major assault on the walls during Roman times, but it is a witness to the skill of the masons that such large sections have withstood not only the ravages of weather over sixteen or seventeen hundred years but also deliberate assaults with cannon during the siege.

3

ST OSWALD, KING and MARTYR
Eastgate, Northgate, and Water Tower

St Oswald's parish church was the south transept of the Cathedral, which was until the nineteenth century walled off from the rest of the building. This curious situation arose from events when the present Cathedral was still the church of St Werburgh's Abbey. The abbey was at first dedicated to the Holy Trinity and St Oswald, and this part of the abbey church was set aside for the use of the parishioners, and was referred to as St Oswald's or St Werburgh's. The area of the abbey precincts adjoining the transept was used as the parish graveyard.

In the fourteenth century St Oswald's congregation was removed to St Nicholas's Chapel nearby, and the south transept of the abbey was enlarged in the general rebuilding by Abbot Simon Ripley. In 1488 the south transept was restored to the parish, on condition that the Mayor and parishioners "Edifie a new Rofe and Three Doores and Halfe a Doore of Timber, and Sett upp upon the new Church of Saint Oswald, and it sufficiently to cover, and the North Syde of the sayd Church to be Batteld with Stone, and Guttured with Lead sufficiently".

St Oswald's was re-opened on Christmas Day 1490 and continued as a separate church, where the Corporation and citizens attended divine service, despite many attempts by successive bishops to have the church reunited with the Cathedral. The Mayor and Corporation, in full ceremonial dress and preceded by a band, would process to the church from the Exchange each New Year's Day for morning service. In 1881 the congregation was assigned to the new church of St Oswald and St Thomas in Parkgate Road. The screen between the south transept and the Cathedral nave had been removed in 1828.

Until 1595 there were no seats other than those for the Mayor and aldermen. The more distinguished citizens were buried within the walls, and the burials or 'lestalls' here were accounted the

82

property of the Dean and Chapter and leased to the vicar of St Oswald's at £5 *per annum*, paid at Easter.

In 1633 the Visitors of the Archbishop of York reported on the state of St Oswald's: "The said Church was very undecent and unsemely, the stalls thereof being patched and peeced and some broken, and some higher than other; and the said Church was much defiled with rushes and other filthiness." In consequence it was ordered that the church be paved with flags and the rushes cleared out. It was a constant trouble to keep the citizens' animals and rubbish out of the churchyard: in 1557 it was reported that the graveyard was defiled with cattle; in 1575 2d was paid to the Bellman "to warne the Citizens not to lay any trees in the Churchyard"; in 1618 6d was paid to a man to keep watch to see who brought muck into the graveyard.

In 1709 a gallery was erected on the west side of the church to accommodate the increasing congregations. The lay-out of the church was very odd, with the nave breadthwise, separated from the sides by four pointed arches on each side, supported by clustered pillars. But the altar was on the east side of the church, and the seating was arranged lengthways along the transept. The eastern side of the church was called 'the quire'. By 1826 St Oswald's was looking decrepit again and was reflagged; new pews, pulpit and reading-desk were put in, and the west gallery was dismantled and replaced by one over the south end. In 1855 gas-lighting was installed.

The north bay of the quire was dedicated to St Mary Magdalene; the second bay was the chancel, and the south bay was dedicated to St Nicholas. The third bay is now the chapel of the Cheshire Regiment, with rolls of honour of men killed in the two World Wars – 8,417 in 1914–18, 715 in 1939–45. Above St Nicholas's Chapel hang the colours of the regiment in which General James Wolfe was wrapped after he was killed in the battle of the Heights of Abraham in 1759, when the British Army secured Quebec. On the wall nearby is an alabaster monument to Sir William Gerard, Lord Chancellor of Ireland, who died in 1581; he was Recorder of the city.

In old St Oswald's stands the sarcophagus with an effigy of Hugh Lupus Grosvenor of Eaton, the first Duke of Westminster, who died in 1899. Behind him is a cluster of small monuments and memorials on the west wall. On one of the pillars of the Cathedral tower is a pretty alabaster monument from St Oswald's with the effigies of "that grave and worthy citizen" Thomas Green, sheriff in 1551, Mayor in 1565, who died in 1602, and of his wives Ellen and Dorothy. In the south transept there are also memorials to Fulk Aldersey, Mayor in 1594, died 1608, son and heir of William Aldersey, Mayor in 1560, who died in 1577, and to a number of members of the Booth families of Woodford and Dunham Massey. These include the Latin inscription to Catherine, daughter of George Booth, wife of James Howard, who died in 1765, aged ninety-three having lived through the reigns of seven monarchs – Charles II, James II (and the Interregnum), William III (and Mary II), Anne, George I, II and III. The inscription records that she lived for a long time among courtiers – on one occasion, to save her husband, she thrust herself between him and an enemy's sword and was wounded in the left breast. "This sad misfortune brought more grief to King William III than to herself, and God quickly restored her to health."

On the south-west pillar of the tower is a white marble monument to George Clarke of Hyde, who died in 1760. His family was from Somerset, but he emigrated to America and became Lieutenant Governor of New York. He retired to Chester and lived near White Friars. The tablet was originally close to the entrance to the Lady Chapel, presumably where he was buried.

On Sunday 24th November 1839 a small portion of St Oswald's fell into the church during a service, with a rumbling noise; pieces fell on the pews and seats. There was an immediate rush for the doors, and the children of the four schools in the congregation panicked. Their screams could be heard as far away as Eastgate Street. At the door leading into the Cathedral, women and Blue Coat boys were knocked over and trampled on by the crowd. One of the Green Cap boys, a cripple, unable to raise himself from the ground, lay there for a long time until his master, who heard his groans, drew him up from under the feet of the crowd.

St Oswald's parish, apart from the Cathedral precincts, included Eastgate Street east of Godstall Lane to the Eastgate, and the north-western segment of the city from Northgate Street to the Water Tower. The parish registers from 1581 and other records from 1575 are now kept at the Cheshire Record Office. St Oswald's Ward consisted solely of the Cornmarket (Northgate Street) south of the Stoops; the Cornmarket Ward extended from the Stoops north to Parson's Lane (Princess Street), including the south side of that street. Eastgate Street, with Fleshmongers' Lane (now lost in the Grosvenor-Laing Shopping Precinct) and St Werburgh Street, formed Eastgate Ward. The parish was right in the heart of the old city, once a very crowded area. A 1619 survey of trades in St Oswald's parish shows that there were fourteen shoemakers, fourteen widows, eleven husbandmen (agricultural labourers), ten weavers and nine inn-holders.

Running off east from Northgate Street is an entry called Music Hall Passage. On the north side of this can be seen mediaeval masonry protruding from the fabric of a men's outfitters. This is what remains of the ancient chapel of St Nicholas which was used as St Oswald's Church in the fifteenth century. When the chapel became vacant in 1490, it was left empty for many years, but in 1545 the citizens bought the building and rebuilt it, putting in a floor above head-level. The basement was then used for storing wool, corn, cloth and other goods sold by strangers in the fairs. The first floor became the new Common Hall, where the courts of the mayor and the county of the city were held, and from 1574 the courts of the sheriffs. The rebuilding of 1545 was partly financed by a gift of three tons of iron (worth £24) from John Walley, the Mayor, Master of the Company of Ironmongers. The windows were decorated with stained glass with the arms of various prominent city families.

Occasionally special assizes were held in the Common Hall under the Chief Justice of the palatinate, who was formally received into the city from the Castle at Gloverstone (chapter 8) and escorted by the Sheriffs and Constables and a guard of freemen carrying halberds.

After 1698, when the new Exchange was built, the chapel was in disuse again and was converted into the city theatre, licensed as the Theatre Royal in 1777 – it had been used for theatrical performances while still the Common Hall. Mrs Siddons, John Kemble, Garrick, Kean and Grimaldi the clown were among the celebrities who played there. In 1855 the building was demolished, except for the more substantial old stonework, and rebuilt as the new Music Hall, the first concert taking place there on 26th November 1855. The hall accommodated about fourteen hundred people, with galleries, orchestra-pit and organ. It is said that the word 'solidarity' was coined in Chester Music Hall by the great comedian Kossuth in the middle of a fervid harangue.

Charles Dickens read there in January 1867:

I have seldom seen a place look more hopelessly frozen up than this place does. The hall is like a Methodist Chapel in low spirits, and with a cold in its head. A few blue people shiver at the corners of the streets.

At Chester we read in a snowstorm and a fall of ice. I think it was the worst weather I ever saw. Nevertheless the people were enthusiastic . . . it was the most tremendous night I ever saw at Chester

By another metamorphosis the Music Hall became the Picture Palace, but it has been empty for much of its recent history. Two doors to the north is the house where a bucketful of Roman bronze coins was found in a rock-cut cellar in 1883. Northgate Street partly overlies the *via decumana* of Deva Victrix, just as Eastgate Street is the Roman *via principalis*.

The Roman *porta principalis sinistra*, the eastern gate, was built bodily into the mediaeval Eastgate, "a goodly great gate, of an antient fair building, with a tower upon it, containing many fair rooms within it". Like the other gates, Eastgate was held by a hereditary sergeant, who exacted tolls for entrance and exit. It was granted to the de Bradford family in 1270 in compensation for their loss of Bradford manor to Vale Royal Abbey. The sergeants had the right of inspecting measures used within the city and held the standard crannock and bushel by which salt was measured. At a later period the Mayor took over this function, which was by no means ceremonial. In 1794 he seized from various shopkeepers 165 weights, all underweight, and eighteen faulty pairs of scales. The wares of three bakers included no less than 255 loaves under weight.

The mediaeval gate was a massive affair, with a single pointed arch supporting a great high square battlement of stone with octagonal corner turrets, arrowslits and crenellations. The Company of Joiners held the rooms in the tower in the sixteenth century. The problem with the gate was the narrowness of the archway. William Cowper, mayor in 1754, railed off a footpath so that pedestrians could get through in safety.

In 1767 the gateway was demolished, and the present plain wide stone archway with small posterns for pedestrians provided by the Grosvenors. On the outside of the gate, picked out in blue and gold, are the Grosvenor arms, and the inscription "ERECTED AT THE EXPENCE OF RICHARD LORD GROSVENOR A:D:

MDCCLXIX". As the mediaeval work was dismantled, the Roman fabric returned to view, only to be destroyed in its turn. There were two barrel-vaulted entrances built of large-cut stones; each entrance had two arches about 20 feet apart, with guard-houses on each side. Over the central pillar on the outside was a statue of a soldier (or Mars).

Although only parts of five letters have survived, fragments of a large slate plaque found in the walls near the east end of the Cathedral (and now preserved in the Grosvenor Museum) have been interpreted, adventurously, as the remains of a dedicatory inscription to Trajan supposed to have been on the gateway below the statue.

The appearance of the new Eastgate was totally transformed in 1897 by the addition of a wrought-iron ornamental clock painted red, blue, white, gold and black, and decorated with the arms of England and Randle Blundeville. Because of the importance of the suburb east of the gate (chapter 4), Eastgate arch and the clock have become the centrepiece of the city and perhaps a more familiar sight to the occasional visitor than the High Cross or the Cathedral.

Opposite the Grosvenor Hotel a passageway led to the Corn Exchange, built in 1859 for farmers attending the corn-market, on the site of the earlier Manchester Hall, which was used by manufacturers from Wigan, Glasgow and Manchester during the fairs. While the premises at the back were being excavated in 1862, a battered altar with this inscription was found, close to the steps from near the Cathedral onto the city walls:

DEAB
MAT
RIB . DO
NVM

("A gift to the mother goddesses".)

A gold torque was discovered in St Werburgh Street nearby, and a tombstone with the inscription

D . M
FESONIE SEVERI
ANE . VIXIT . ANN
XXV . . .

("To the spirits of Fesonia Severiana, who lived twenty-five years.

. . .") In 1896 on the east side of the street another altar was found, with the simple inscription

GENIO

C

("To the genius of the century".)

From the mediaeval Eastgate Street ran several side-alleys:

> On the northe syde of the said strete is a Layne that goithe out of the said strete, By the measeside late William Stannier, and so into the Kirke yorde of sante Oswaldes, caulyd Leen Lane. And Beneathe it, upon the same syde, nere the Estgate, is a Layne caulyd sant goddestall Lane, and so goithe out of the Sade strete into the Sade church yarde. . . . and vppon the syde nere the estgate ther ys A Lane caulyd saint Werburge Lane and it Shoutythe into the forsaide church yarde, and ouer Anendes this Lane on the other Syde ys A Lane caulyd Flesshemongers Lane, And it puttethe upon peper stret.

St Werburgh Street and Godstall Lane remain, although both are greatly altered; Leen Lane is entirely blocked and gone, but Fleshmongers' Lane became Newgate Street, mostly lost beneath the shopping precinct. Eastgate Street is the most lavishly ornamented of the great Victorian creations in Chester, with some Georgian and earlier fabric peeping through.

The ugly tall stone Gothic Browns Crypt Buildings, west of the shopping precinct entrance, stand over a thirteenth-century crypt, now used as a restaurant. Most of the buildings on this side are Victorian, many replacing Georgian town-houses and shops, but No. 22 is a timber building of 1640.

Opposite the Grosvenor Hotel is the Midland Bank, the old Grosvenor Club, a very successful brick and stone 'Flemish-Gothic' affair of 1883 designed by John Douglas, and ornamented on the crowning gable with a little Grosvenor coat-of-arms. The arms above the ground-floor windows are of the twelve Welsh shires, for these were the premises of the North and South Wales Bank.

Along the north side of the street, starting from steps by Moss Bros, is the Dark Row, a narrower, darker and more interesting passageway than the Rows on the south, and continuing round the corner and along the start of the east side of Northgate Street. The Boot Inn, on the north side of the street, has a black-and-white third storey, dated 1643.

St Werburgh Street, joining Eastgate Street with the Cathedral precinct, is the most impressive stretch of revival black-and-white in the city – not a jostling crowd of competing styles and lunatic ornament like Eastgate Street but a finely-detailed but regular course of neat timbering, designed by John Douglas for the Grosvenors. Godstall Lane is now an internal passageway running parallel to the west.

Godstall Lane was at various periods known as Baxters' Row, the Dark Rows, Butter Shops Row, the Dark Entry, London Baker's Entry and Pepper Alley. Several Roman finds have been made here, in the heart of the fortress, including a strip of bronze marked "VTERE FELIX" ("fertile in the womb"), and another altar, actually found buried beneath the street:

GENIO
SANCTO
CENTVRIE
AELIVS
CLAVDIAN
OPT . V S .

("To the sacred genius of the century, Aelius Claudian, the *optio* [centurion's assistant], has fulfilled his vow".)

At the north-western end of Eastgate Street, across from St Peter's Church, were the mediaeval Buttershops, adjoining the Milk Stoops, posts where milk was brought for sale. The property was bought by the Corporation in 1593 for £20, to rebuild them "in suche bewtifull sorte as they shall thinke likeste". The shops were thereafter called 'the New Buildings'.

The Shopping Precinct, which extends back from Eastgate and Upper Bridge Street Rows almost as far as Newgate, was constructed in the nineteenth century and added to recently, communicating with a multi-storey car-park near Thimbleby's Tower on the east wall. The entrance on Eastgate Street is where Welsh honey was brought for sale, at a flight of steps called Honey Stairs.

The present Godstall Lane was opened up rather to the west of the old Dark Entry, which was indeed a dark passageway, the boundary between the parishes of St Oswald and St Peter. In the early-nineteenth century a Miss Sayers had a girls' seminary in the entry; later in life she retired to the house adjoining; in old age she had the misfortune to fall forward onto her fire, and her clothes caught fire: she rushed into the entry in fright, but the draught here turned the smouldering garments into a torch, and she was burned to death.

The Northgate, the *porta decumana* of the Roman fortress, was built up in the Middle Ages into a minor stronghold. There was a narrow archway between two large square castellated towers; above the portcullis were small stone-built chambers; the outer walls were decorated with carved coats-of-arms. Above the towers was erected a great half-timbered house with three projecting gables.

The Northgate housed the city gaol, of which the gatekeeper was the gaoler; he also collected toll at the gate. The gaoler had custody of the gallows and the pillory and was responsible for hanging condemned men, from both the Northgate and the Castle, at Boughton (chapter 4) or from the 'drag' on the south side of the gate. The prisoners were held in the chambers over the arch, but condemned men were held in a "dark stinking chamber called dead men's room", and there was a cavity called 'the Little Ease', only 17 inches across, in which prisoners could be tortured by lowering the boarding of the roof. In front of Northgate was a mediaeval cross, demolished during the Reformatory purge of 1583.

A hundred years later the gaol briefly contained a rather special prize, the O'Brenan gang – Patrick, Tall James, Little James and Daniel O'Brenan. These self-proclaimed Tories (in the original meaning: highwaymen) had held county Kilkenny in terror in the early 1680s. They had stolen about £12,000 during their exploits, been once caught and condemned, and were rescued by force from the hangman. When Ireland was too hot for them, they set sail for Wales, separately shipping their thoroughbred horses on a boat to Mostyn and following themselves in a shallop landed at Beaumaris. Arriving in Chester, in their fine clothes, with their fine horses, they were seized; one drew his sword, injuring a Cestrian who grasped it in his hand, but they were overpowered and taken off to Northgate.

A letter was sent off to the Duke of Ormonde, Lord Lieutenant of Ireland, who was also a benefactor of the city, having paid for the erection of the Engine House, opposite the Exchange, three years before. The Duke was naturally delighted and told the Chief Justice, but the Mayor of Chester refused to send the prisoners over to Ireland without a royal warrant.

About a fortnight later, on Hallowe'en 1683, matters took a new turn. The O'Brenans had been kept in irons day and night, with shackles on both legs during the day and double-ironed and locked in their beds at night. Shortly after Thomas Green, the deputy gaoler, had gone home that night, Little James drew a knife from his pocket and tried to strike the gaoler's throat, catching his left wrist. The gaoler, Richard Wright, started screaming for help, but Little James said: "God damn mee, if thou speak another word I will presently cutt thy throat" and knocked Richard to the floor, thrusting his head under the bed and stamping on him with his knees. After some altercation, Patrick produced a Bible, and the O'Brenans swore that they would not kill Richard, and he swore that he would keep quiet. Meanwhile Tall James tried to cut the throat of another prisoner, Thomas Greene, in hopes of stifling his cries, and badly injured him about the head and face.

The gaoler's wife, Frances, was thrown to the ground and told to keep quiet. Mary Swettenham, a servant-girl, armed herself with a candlestick and a quart jug, which she threw at Little James. He came at her with the knife; she tried to push the other Irishman off her mistress, and he struck at her, but Little James stopped him, saying that she was a devil. Mary retreated and locked herself in the cellar, but the Irishmen came to her afterwards and spoke to her tenderly, one saying, "Sweetheart, you and I it may bee may meet again", to which she replied "It may bee, in another country."

The O'Brenans unlocked the debtors' prison, freed a certain Scot called William Browne and fled. Gaoler Wright hurriedly locked himself in, secured the other prisoners and called for help. The hue and cry was raised, and horsemen were sent in pursuit.

The O'Brenans were not caught, but the youngest brother, Daniel, aged about thirteen remained in custody at Chester. The gang reappeared in Ireland, where they broke into Kilkenny Castle and stole the Duke of Ormonde's plate. Shortly afterwards they treated with the Lord Deputy and were given protection in exchange for their service in rooting out other 'Tories'.

When Bonnie Prince Charlie's troops were advancing south in 1745, Northgate was walled up as part of the precautions. In 1767 four prisoners, led by Evan Thomas, held there for murder and robbery, attacked the turnkey, whom they locked in the dungeon. Gaoler Whitehead, aroused by the noise, was attacked by Thomas, who stabbed him in the throat and killed him. Mrs Whitehead unlocked the outer door and called for help, and three Cestrians in the street ran to her aid and held three of the men, but Evan Thomas escaped, and his irons were found the next day in a field near the city. Again, on 24th August 1806, the City Beadle, Joseph Crofton, was pushed down the steps at the gaol by a runaway apprentice he had apprehended, and was killed. It was felt that the gaol accommodation was unsuitable, and the new city gaol (chapter 12) was built in 1807.

The mediaeval gateway was demolished by the Grosvenors in 1808 and replaced by the present uninteresting single arch with two high postern arches for pedestrians, and four columns on each side. The inscription on the outside is:

PORTAM SEPTENTRIONALEM SVBSTRVCTAM A ROMANIS VETVSTATE IAM DILAPSVRAM / IMPENSIS SVIS AB INTEGRO RESTITVENDAM CVRAVIT ROBERTVS COMES GROSVENOR. / A.R.GEORGII TERTII LI.

("The north gate built by the Romans being now about to disintegrate, Robert Earl Grosvenor has had it entirely restored at his own expense, in the 51st year of the reign of George III.")

In about 1615 Northgate Street, from the Milk Stoops near the Cross to the Northgate, was described by William Webb:

After it hath led you to the common-hall of pleas of the city, it then spaciously opens itself to a goodly corn-market place, situated before the fair gates of the antient and famous abbey . . . having also in the midst of that corn-market, a fine shambles for a flesh-market, lofted with a store-house for corn, and other commodities, as occasion serves. From thence narrows itself again to the North-gate, on the one side with fair houses; and the other with the wall of the abbey.

A great part of the older housing here was burned down on Midsummer Day in 1494 or 1501. The house in the Cornmarket was built in 1557, and the street, which hitherto had been muddy and rutted, was paved in 1568. In 1573 the citizens moved the Cornmarket house over against the old abbey walls, now the Bishop's quarters, so the Dean and Chapter took the matter to the Exchequer Court, claiming the ground to be theirs. In 1575 the Mayor, Henry Hardware, settled the quarrel by removing the house to the ditch outside the Northgate and setting it up as a House of Correction for the poor. There remained the problem of a shambles, so the derelict shire-hall from the Castle ditch was bought in 1580 and rebuilt in 1581 in the cornmarket.

The Market Square, opposite the west end of the Cathedral, is dominated by the Town Hall. Old St Nicholas had served for the Corporation until the seventeenth century, when plans were made for a new building called 'the Exchange'. The long brick building of nine bays and three storeys was completed in 1698 and cost £1,000. Celia Fiennes saw it when it was brand-new:

> There is a new Hall building which is for the assize and it stands on great stone pillars which is to be the Exchange, which will be very convenient and handsome; the Hall is round, its built of bricke and stone coynes, there are leads all round with battlements and in the middle is a tower; there are ballconies on the side and windows quite round the Cupillow that shews the whole town round.

It was supported on four rows of stone arches and pillars, in which several shops were established in 1756. On the main front were a statue of Queen Anne and coats-of-arms of the earldom, the Principality of Wales, the Duchy of Cornwall and Queen Anne, all carved by John Tilston (a local man, who is buried in the south aisle of St John's), painted and gilded.

All the functions of the Common Hall and the Pentice were eventually transferred to the Exchange, with the city records and the portraits of past benefactors. On 30th December 1862 the building took fire and was burned down, but the citizens saved the records, which included the charters and the admissions registers to the freedom of the city dating from 1392, and all but two of the portraits.

The foundation-stone of the present Town Hall, 90 feet further west of the Exchange, was laid on 25th October 1865. The new building cost £40,000 and was opened by the Prince of Wales (and Earl of Chester) on 14th October 1869. The statue of Queen Anne was repainted and set up on the present façade – she originally held an orb and sceptre, but they had been destroyed by election mobs in 1784 and 1812; the statue was later removed to the Water Tower gardens and eventually lost.

The new Town Hall is a Gothic creation, of grey sandstone, with a 160-foot central tower and a massive ten-bay frontage of four storeys. The double grand entrance is on the first floor, reached by flights of steps from the street.

The city archives are kept in the City Record Office in the basement. The Town Hall also houses the civic plate and the fifteenth-century great sword of Chester in a seventeenth-century scabbard, the silver mace of 1668 (given to the city by the Earl of

Derby), and the Mayor's oar. This is a small silver oar dated 1719 carried ceremonially by the Water Bailiff, to symbolize the Mayor's office as Admiral of the Dee.

Next to the Town Hall, on part of the site of the Victorian Market Hall, built in 1863, stood an ancient coaching inn called 'The White Lion'. Until the Town Hall was built after the fire, there was a battered milestone against the front of 'The White Lion' from which (as opposed to the High Cross, used later) the mile-posts of the coach roads were measured.

The coach-service from Shrewsbury via Wrexham and Ellesmere started in March 1788, when the fare was 13s 6d inside, 7s outside. At 'The White Lion' coaches could be taken for Holyhead (1½ guineas), Parkgate (3s 6d, for Dublin by packet), Liverpool (5s to New Ferry), Manchester and the royal mail to London (3 guineas).

Behind the Exchange there was another inn called 'The Saracen's Head', also now demolished. Tiles of the 20th Legion Valeria Victrix and an altar with this Greek inscription were found there in 1851:

. . . HPCIN

(YP)ERMENECIN

EPMOΓENHC

IATROCBωMON

TONΔ ANEΘHKA

("To the mighty saviour gods, I, Hermogenes, a doctor, set up this altar.")

In Northgate Street, in what is now the large open space in front of the Town Hall, were the Fish Market, the site of the Exchange, the Butter Market and the Shambles. Every Saturday a vegetable market was held between the Fish Market and the Exchange. After the Town Hall was built, all these were gradually tidied away. In April 1922 the council called on the tenants in the Fish Market to abandon their old custom of shouting to sell their fish. Shortly before Christmas in 1954 the Improvement Committee decided that the pigeons in the Market Square should be shot.

It is currently thought that the *praetorium*, the commandery in Deva, lay north of the *principia*, in the area now taken by the Market Square and the Town Hall. Remains of a large quad-rangular building have been found in excavations in the market, and the remains of the 'Roman Strong Room' are preserved on display in the Forum shopping precinct. At the back of the Town Hall are the new precinct, Market Hall and the Gateway Theatre, with a prominent cantilevered auditorium butting out towards the inner ring-road, above a miserable semi-crenellated rear wall of stained concrete. The Cattle Market was removed from Northgate Street to the Cow Lane canal bridge in 1849.

A colonnade from the *principia* was found in 1897 when the rows on the west side of Northgate Street (Shoemakers' Row) were being rebuilt. A fragment of an altar to the genius of the 20th Legion and a Roman quern were also discovered. The rows were replaced there by the Grosvenors as a colonnade, and, if the destruction of the old row was inexcusable, the end-product is quite attractive, a glorious black-and-white concoction with a statue of Edward VII and a Latin inscription on the north end. The cellars of No. 23 on this side contain parts of columns of the north wing of the *principia* building *in situ*.

The two mediaeval streets running west from Northgate Street were Parson's Lane, opposite the Abbey Gates, and Barn Lane further north; the loyal citizens renamed these Princess Street and King Street. Most of this area is rather disappointing today, and part is being redeveloped. King Street and Princess Street lead to Nicholas Street, the wide swathe of the inner ring-road.

On Northgate Street north of the Town Hall are the Georgian Pied Bull Hotel and 'The Red Lion' built out on pillars over the pavement. 'The Pied Bull' contains a seventeenth-century staircase and other ancient furnishings. On a pillar at the front is a coaching-sign, dated 1763, giving the distances to London, Worcester, Ludlow, Bristol and Bath. A coach-service to Birkenhead started from 'The Pied Bull' in 1784.

The white rendering of a low building north of 'The Red Lion', Snow White's, conceals the timbering of the old two-gable 'Blue Bell Inn', thought to date from the fifteenth century. The first gable is above a continuation of 'The Red Lion' colonnade. 'The Blue Bell' claimed to have been licensed from 1494, but the name does not appear earlier than the eighteenth century.

When Handel visited Chester in 1741, on his way to Ireland, he stayed at the 'Golden Falcon Inn' near Northgate and would smoke a pipe over a dish of coffee in the Exchange Coffee House.

When John Minshull, Lord Lieutenant of Ireland, stayed in Chester on his way there in 1711, there was an altercation as he departed between his servant and a waiter concerning some sum that had not been paid. The waiter seized the bridle of the servant's horse, whereupon the servant drew a pistol and shot the man dead. The servant was arrested and thrown into Northgate gaol, but Minshull declared that if the man were convicted, he would get a pardon for him from the King. This naturally incensed the Mayor, who declared: "I will take care that the King and the Lord Lieutenant shall not have any further trouble about this matter" and had the servant executed the very morning after the conviction.

A flight of thirty-one steps on the west side of the Northgate connects the street with the city walls. The walls west of Northgate are part of the line of the Roman fortress defences and contain some of the ancient masonry. About a hundred yards west of the gate is the site of a small archway found in 1883. The Roman wall was rebuilt in about 300, perhaps after a barbarian attack in 296, and the core contains pieces of tombstones, many of which have been recovered and are now in the Grosvenor Museum. Dozens of inscriptions, several of particular interest, have been found.

A particularly good tombstone from here shows a lady reclining on a high-backed couch. Above her are doves and tritons; she holds a cup raised in her right hand. The inscription is:

D . M
CVRATIA . DINY
SIA . VIX . AN . XXXX
H . F . C

("To the spirits, Curatia Dinysia lived forty years; her heir had this made.")

Nicholas Street, the inner ring-road, breaks through the walls under St Martin's Gate, a concrete construction of 1966, close to a plain square tower called 'Morgan's Mount'. The location of the north-west corner tower of the Roman fort is marked with cobbles in the pavement by the gate. In 1914 a hoard of old English silver pennies of the late-tenth century was discovered nearby. Morgan's Mount now forms a raised square railed platform from which can be viewed the Welsh hills and the Northgate Locks on the canal below the walls. There is a little room within, with a stone bench and doors and windows fitted with iron bars.

'Morgan's Mount' was originally the name of a hill about a hundred yards to the north, which was fortified as part of the

High Cross

St Michael's Rectory

(Opposite) Gateway Theatre

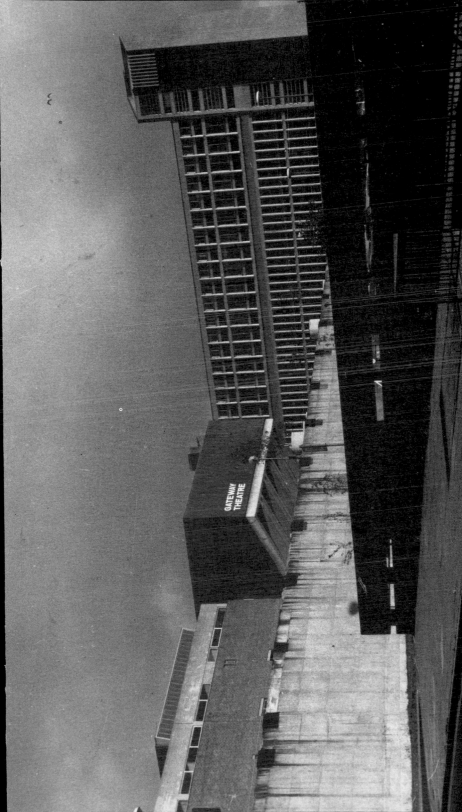

Northgate Row East

(Opposite) Dark Row

St Michael's and St Peter's (background)

(Opposite) Town Hall

Dee Bridge

Queen's School

outworks of the northern suburbs during the Civil War. Morgan's Mount and another fortified mount in a lane leading to Finchet's Stone Bridge were the strongpoints on the western flank of the outworks, beyond which lay the city wall, with a semicircular turret called 'the Alcove', and the Water Tower by the Dee. The defenders placed their cannon on Morgan's Mount.

On Saturday 4th October 1645 the besieging forces of Parliament brought up four large guns on this side of the walls:

> All Sunday the enemy played their artillery so violently, that they beat down some of the battlements, and forced the king's soldiers to retire from the walls: they likewise, by a shot, scattered the carriage of one of the largest cannon, which in the fall had two foot of the muzzle broke off. That night the besieged repaired the damages, and made entrenchments in the Lady Borough Hey, which they found to be very serviceable in the defence of that part of the city.

The next day the Roundheads tried to break down the walls by further battery with their cannon closer to the Water Tower, but the walls proved too solid, and the defenders too tenacious.

The Alcove, Goblin Tower or Pemberton's Parlour, west of St Martin's Gate, was the mediaeval Dille's Tower. It was largely destroyed in the siege but the tower was rebuilt in 1702 when John Pemberton, a local ropemaker, established a ropewalk in the pretty grove inside the north wall from beyond the present Pemberton Road to the west wall. John Pemberton is said to have sat in the alcove watching his men and boys at work below. He was Mayor in 1730 and is named on the tablet on the north side of the Water Tower arch. The royal arms and those of the city, carved in stone by John Tilston, were placed on the tower in 1702 and, when it was rebuilt in 1894, were incorporated in the new fabric; the stonework above the level of the walk is all new. A large crumbling tablet records repairs to the walls in 1701–8 with the names of the mayors and murengers. The semicircular alcove is liberally sprayed with graffiti; at the back are three Victorian arrowslits.

The line of the old wall is broken to the west by the railway line, beyond which is the north-west corner of the walls, with a mediaeval turret called 'Bonewaldesthorne's Tower'. This small rectangular tower has a little pointed doorway and contains a room with a fireplace and a stairway leading up to the roof.

The turret was the protected entrance to an open gallery along an embattled spur wall thrown out westwards to the Water Tower or New Tower. This was built in 1322, in the water of the Dee, to defend the harbour along the west wall by Watergate. The tower was constructed by John de Helpston at a cost of £100. The round tower is built of soft red sandstone, and crenellated, and still stands 75 feet in height above the grass – the River Dee has long since retreated elsewhere. The spur wall is built on two low stone arches (one buried from sight), under which the river once flowed. Beyond the tower was a deeper foundation of stonework reaching out into the Dee. In the seventeenth century there were still large iron mooring-rings on the tower.

A pretty little tablet on the north side of the arch records its repair in 1730, when John Pemberton was mayor, and gives the names of the murengers. The tower is surrounded by a small public park called 'Water Tower Gardens', with a putting-green, bowling-greens and tennis-courts, reached by a flight of steps from the walls near Bonewaldesthorne's Tower. The two octagonal vaulted chambers within the Water Tower have been used in recent years as a museum of mediaeval Chester. A Roman column has been re-erected close to the city wall.

During the plague of 1603 many infected citizens were taken down to cabins built along the riverbank in the Quarrell (quarry) near the Water Tower, in an attempt to stop the disease spreading; in 1648 cabins were put up during the plague of that year, both under the tower and in the adjoining saltmarshes.

This brings us to the limit of St Oswald's parish within the walls, for St Martin's-in-the-Fields adjoins to the south; on the city walls can be seen an inscribed stone set up by the churchwardens of St Martin's:

SO FAR GOETH
THE PARISH OF S. M.
R.H. I.W. C.W.

The area outside the walls on the north of the city lay within St Oswald's parish. The whole of Northgate Street with the lanes on both sides beyond the Northgate was in St Thomas's Ward. The ward took its name from an ancient chapel dedicated to St Thomas à Becket (martyred in 1178) and recorded as a cemetery in 1190. The Chapel was at the north end of Northgate Street. The Dean and Chapter's Court of St Thomas had jurisdiction over the ward and eight townships outside the city.

This area was before the siege part of the city's handsome suburbs: "Without the East and North gates, the city extends herself in her suburbs, with very fair streets, and the same adorned with goodly buildings, both of gentlemen's houses, and fair inns for entertainment of all resorts." As the siege approached, outworks were thrown up to protect these suburbs. They stretched across from near the Water Tower to the Dee at Boughton, cutting the suburbs and city off as a peninsula. Within this area not only was the city cut off from the suburbs by the city walls but the suburbs were separated into three cells with intervening walls. From near Pemberton's Parlour the outworks ran north to the city limits with the two towers mentioned above facing west and Reed's Mount and Phoenix Tower Mount facing east. East of this lay the cell extending to Flookersbrook and protecting Flookersbrook Hall. The perimeter wall continued from near the hall to Boughton.

On 19th September 1644 thirteen hundred men from the Parliamentary forces besieging Beeston were brought to Chester and broke through the outworks into the Boughton cell, which brought them up to the city walls at Foregate, but the northern suburbs remained in the hands of the citizens. By the end of the siege virtually the whole of the suburbs had been destroyed, either laid waste by the besiegers or cleared away by the defenders. On the east of Northgate Street was a large windmill, but the defenders feared that the tower might be used for attacks on the city if it fell into the hands of the besiegers, and it was demolished in 1643. Flookersbrook Hall was destroyed in the siege, and a new octagonal windmill built on the site. In the late-eighteenth century this was converted into a dwelling-house called 'Folly House'.

The dirty waters of the Shropshire Union Canal lie in a deep sandstone cut beneath the north side of the city walls. There is a delicate single-arch footbridge from the Northgate to the far bank, called 'the Bridge of Sighs'. The prisoners from Northgate gaol attended service in the Chapel of St John in the Blue Coat Hospital, and after the canal was cut, a bridge was built but became unsafe and was replaced by the present structure, which cost £20. Debtors in the Northgate were allowed a pound of bread a day, but only on condition that they attended chapel; a minor canon from the Cathedral conducted prayers there twice a week. When the canal was cut, the outer fosse of the Roman fortress was excavated, and the canal runs in the line of that ditch. In the sixteenth and seventeenth centuries the ditch was used for the town Pinfold, in which stray cattle and pigs were penned.

The northern part of the city, from the walls south to the Cornmarket, formed a liberty called 'the Free House'. Convicted debtors imprisoned in Northgate could petition the Corporation to be allowed to live in the Free House, on condition that they did not leave the area or enter any other dwelling-house, and they were to attend service at Little St John's.

The Hospital of St John the Baptist, Little St John's (which was an extra-parochial liberty), was founded by Earl Randle Blundeville for the maintenance of thirteen "poor and sillie, or poor and feeble" citizens, "whereof each shall have for daily allowance, a loaf of bread, a dish of pottage, half a gallon of competent ale, and a piece of fish or flesh, as the day shall require". Edward II granted the mastership of the hospital to Birkenhead Priory.

The hospital and chapel were demolished during the siege but rebuilt after the Restoration. At the front of the site was constructed, in 1717, the Blue Coat School, founded in 1700 by Bishop Nicholas Stratford. Twenty-five boys, dressed in blue, boarded there, while 120 in green, called Green Caps, were taught there as day-scholars. In 1760 it was complained that

> Some years ago it was usual to bind [the scholars] out to the tradesmen and artificers; and consequently, when out of their time they were admitted freemen and had a right to vote in the election of members to represent the town in Parliament; but it having often happened that many of them were too honest, or too obstinate, to receive direction in that material point from any superior but their own consciences, the practice of making them saucy rebellious tradesmen has been discontinued, and they are put out to horse-hirers and jockeys, not free of the city.

The building was restored in 1854. Some Roman bronze articles and an antefix rooftile with the boar of the 20th Legion were found. A statue of a Blue Boy was placed in a niche at the front of the building. The school was closed in 1949 and is now used as a young people's club, and the main entrance is embellished with graffiti. It is a large brick building with stone quoins and a central doorway beneath a pediment, a blue-and-gold clockface and a handsome green cupola. On either side are projecting wings, forming a small courtyard by the street. The almshouses on the site of the hospital were rebuilt in 1854 and face a central cobbled courtyard at the rear of the school.

Upper Northgate Street has been largely destroyed by the construction of a large roundabout, with dingy half-lit vandalized subways and a central fountain, on the inner ring-road. There is very little to tempt a visitor beyond the roundabout. Closer to the walls is the Barclay Art Gallery, on the west of the street, with a little stretch of arcade; across the road, on the corner of George Street, is the large Victorian terracotta Bull and Stirrup Hotel, with a green pyramidal roof on a square corner turret.

There was a maypole at the top of Northgate Street, which was dismantled in about 1800, but for many years afterwards urchins would cadge coppers with the phrase "Remember the maypole."

From the northern suburbs of the old city, let us now turn to the area by the east wall, where the only ancient parish church outside the walls, and the ancient Cathedral of Chester, can be found.

4

SAINT JOHN the BAPTIST
Amphitheatre, Foregate and Spital Boughton

St John's Church stands outside the city walls not far from the south-west corner of the Roman defences. The parish included all the eastern suburbs outside the walls, with a small area south of Eastgate Street within them. St John's Ward included Eastgate Street and the Foregate, but the church and Love Lane, the street on which it stood, formed St Giles's Ward.

The grounds east of the church along the north bank of the Dee were laid out as a park and given to the city by the Marquis of Westminster in 1867. The area is called 'Grosvenor Park' after him, and two years later a large statue of the Marquis was erected there. Two Russian guns which had been captured at Sebastopol and brought in state to the Castle in June 1857 were placed by the monument. The Marquis is represented in a mediaeval garb appropriate to his title, looking rather odd with his Victorian side-whiskers; the large white statue stands at the head of an avenue across the park.

The Shipgate arch, the western arch from St Michael's Church, and one from the Nunnery ruins (chapters 9, 6 and 10) were also re-erected in the park. There is a little stone arch for a drinking-fountain (now dry) called 'Jacob's Well', with the inscription:

> WHOSOEVER
> DRINKETH
> OF THIS
> WATER
> SHALL THIRST
> AGAIN
> JOHN IV.13

The park was constructed on an estate, worth £40 *per annum*, put up for sale in 1725 as "A large well Built House, and large Yard, Court, Orchard and Garden, Stables, and other Conveniences. Also two Messuages and the Herbedge in St John's Church Yard;

102

and five shillings at Midsummer yearly for ever from the Weavers Meeting House in the Church Yard. Likewise a large Field, called the Hadland."

The ornamental gardens include southern terraces which overlook the Dee, and there is easy access to the Groves and the landing-stages along the river. Queen's Park Bridge, built in 1923, leads across the Dee to the leafy suburbs of Queen's Park. The grey-painted suspension bridge is decorated with the colourful arms of the Norman Earls of Chester.

On the far side of the park, on Union Street, is the main entrance facing Grosvenor Park Road, a half-timbered lodge built by the Grosvenors. The lodge is decorated with little painted look-alike figures of the Norman earls with their coats-of-arms. While the park was being prepared, a cholera epidemic broke out in the city, and its first building was a shed used as an isolation ward for the infected.

As the park was laid out, a long line of Roman earthenware water-pipes was discovered close to the lodge. These brought fresh water from Boughton into the *castellum aquae* (reservoir) in the fortress. The continuation of the line has been found much further east, near Old Government House. In the Cherry Orchard north of Cherry Road, further east again, and probably on the site of the spring feeding the water-supply, a beautiful little altar was found in 1821, with this inscription:

NYMPHIS
. ET .
FONTIBUS
LEG . $\overline{XX}$.
V . V

("To the nymphs and fountains; the 20th Legion Valeria Victrix.")

In 1849 another altar was found not far from there, near Bulkeley Street:

GENIO
C A VERIN
IVL QVINTILIANVS

("To the genius of the century of Aurelius Verinus; Julius Quintilianus [set this up].")

An altar found in Chester in the eighteenth century but now lost had the inscription:

DEAE
NYMPHAE
BRIG .

("To the nymph goddess [of Brigantia?].")

The nymphs and fountains altar was placed in a temple specially built for it in the grounds of Eaton Hall by the Marquis of Westminster.

In the lower part of the park, in what had been Billy Hobby's Field, was a well named 'Billy Hobby's Well', which had a great magic reputation. Chester maidens would stand with the right leg immersed in the water wishing for husbands. The Grosvenors' architect John Douglas designed a little mediaeval-style canopy for the well, which is now blocked and dry.

The portion of St John's parish within the walls included what is now the Grosvenor-Laing Shopping Precinct, the walls from Eastgate to Newgate, and the Grosvenor Hotel, certainly the most famous hotel in Chester, and a great favourite of American visitors. The present building is a large five-storey affair of 1866, with a colonnade by the street; there are two central gables, and corner turrets, that on the west being decorated with the Grosvenor arms.

The hotel was built for the Grosvenors of Eaton but incorporated some of the fabric of an ancient inn called 'The White Talbot' or 'The Golden Talbot' (the Grosvenor crest) and later 'The Royal Hotel'. The plague of 1608, in which fourteen people died, started at 'The Talbot'. The old inn was destroyed in the bombardment during the siege:

> The Talbott, an house adjoining to the Eastgate, flames outright . . . another Thunder-crack invites our eye to the most miserable spectacle spite could possibly present us with – two houses in the Watergate skippe joynt from joynt, the main posts josell each other, while the frighted casements fly for feare . . . The grandmother and three children are struck stark dead in the ruins of this humble edifice, a sepulcher well worth the enemies remembrance.

The eighteenth-century inn had its own cockpit: in April 1738 the gentlemen of Flintshire and Cheshire set thirty-one pairs of cocks at each other at 10 guineas a battle, and 200 guineas the main (series), with ten cocks for by-battles. On 17th September 1751 this advertisement appeared in the *Chester Courant*:

"The ancient and well-accustomed inn, known by the name of the Golden-Talbot, is now fitted up in the neatest manner, where all gentlemen, ladies and others, who shall be pleased to make use of the said house, may depend on the best accommodation and most civil usage. N.B.: The house is new-fronted; the Coffee Room fitted up in a grand manner, and the whole made very commodious."

In 1771 a new Assembly Room was opened at 'The Talbot', "everything being conducted with the strictest degree of propriety". The hotel became the principal rendezvous for the sporting aristocracy visiting Chester during the races, with balls and assemblies held during May Week. In 1762 a coach-service to Woodside Ferry (for Liverpool) was started from 'The Golden Talbot', powered by "six able horses".

The walls from Eastgate to Newgate were ordered to be destroyed by Parliament on 4th November 1655 but were rebuilt in the eighteenth century. It is not a particularly interesting stretch of the city walls, hemmed in as it is by the backs of adjoining houses and offices. There is a fourteenth-century turret called 'the Wall Tower', 'Wolf Tower' or 'Thimbleby's Tower', to the north of the Wolf Gate. The semicircular turret, although partly destroyed during the siege, is a good piece of mediaeval sandstone masonry, into which visitors can peer from the wall and drop their rubbish. The remains of the groin-vaulting of the inner rooms can be seen. The tower rose above the parapets, but the top was demolished in the siege. In the eighteenth century the turret was used as a laundry.

From the corner of the Grosvenor Hotel a street led south from Eastgate Street to the Newgate. This was Newgate Street, the old Fleshmongers' Lane, now replaced on the north by the first-floor entry to the warren of the shopping precinct. On this corner a Roman altar was discovered in 1693, with the inscription:

PRO . SAL . DOMIN
(ORV)M . N . INVI
CT(I)SSIMORVM
AVG . GENIO . LOCI
FL(A)VIVS . LONG(VS)
TRIB . MIL . LEG . XX (.V.V.)
(ET .) LONGINVS . FIL
EIVS . DOMO .
SAMOSATA
V . S

("For the welfare of our lords, the most invincible emperors, to the genius of the place, Flavius Longus, military tribune of the 20th Legion Valeria Victrix, and Longinus his son, from Samosata, have fulfilled their vows.")

On the other side of the hotel, between the building and the city walls, another altar was found in 1884:

IO(VI)
OPT(IMO)
MAX(IMO)
V. . .

("To Jupiter, best and greatest . . . .")

In 1738 a sculpture of a *retiarius* (a fighter with trident and net) was found on the east side of Newgate Street, and ten years later a centurial stone marking a portion of the wall built by the first cohort.

Giraldus Cambrensis, writing in about 1200, ascribed the foundation of St John's Church to Aethelred, King of Mercia (uncle of St Werburgh), in 689, "with the help of Wilfric, Bishop of Chester". The Chester abbey chronicler Henry Bradshaw elaborated this: King Aethelred, he said, was told to build the church where he should see a white hind. This explained the effigy of a bishop grasping a hind, in a niche on the west side of the church tower. This appears in fact to be a statue of St Giles, who lived as a hermit fed by the milk of a hind. The statue, now placed over the north porch, survived intact four successive falls of the tower(s) which it decorated.

In the nineteenth century about fifty old English coins dating from the tenth century were found at a depth of 16 feet below the church, and it has been suggested that they were placed there at the foundation. The chroniclers state that in 1057 the church, already collegiate, was repaired by Earl Leofric of Mercia and given further endowments.

St John's Church is the ancient cathedral of Chester. It was a seat of the Bishops of Mercia, and the see was transferred there from Lichfield in 1075 by Bishop Peter, only to be moved in 1095 to Coventry by his successor, Robert de Lindsey. It is said that Bishop Peter was buried there. At that time, of course, the present Cathedral was St Werburgh's Abbey church. Giraldus claimed that the bishoprics of Chester (Coventry), Hereford, Worcester,

Bath and Exeter were all once suffragan to St David's, suggesting that there was a Celtic church on that spot.

The main fabric of St John's dates from about 1120 or earlier, may have been completed about 1250 and survives from what was a massive and handsome edifiçe. The plan is similar to that of the Cathedral, in the form of a cross, with nave and transepts, a central tower, a quire and tiny chancel. The nave was flanked by eight semicircular arches on 66-inch diameter stone pillars, the quire by a further four arches. Above these are triforium arcades of pointed arches, and then a clerestory.

After the great plague of 1348, Sir Piers le Roter granted the church of Thornton-le-Moors to the Dean and Chapter, who erected a chantry in his honour in St John's, served by two chaplains. Three of the stalls in the quire were held by the prebends of the Holy Cross, who were coparceners in the glebe. The court of Chester Archdeaconry was held at St John's, where wills were proved and marriage-licences issued; the archdeaconry comprised, besides some Welsh parishes, the whole of Cheshire, and Lancashire as far as the Ribble. At the Dissolution there were seven prebends at St John's. The Dean was made Dean of the new cathedral.

About 1200 Roger, Baron of Halton, granted to Hugh Dutton of Dutton authority over all the lechers and whores in Cheshire; this became the rather more prosaic right of licensing musicians and minstrels. The lord of Dutton would ride up to the Eastgate each Midsummer Day, preceded by banner, drum and trumpet, and proclaimed a procession. The musicians and minstrels would gather and, playing and singing, proceed to St John's Church, where the Court of Minstrelsy was held. The lord of Dutton's steward issued yearly licences at 2s 2d *per annum*. The jurors wore linen towels over their shoulders for the following year. Musicians were forbidden to play on the Sabbath without special licence from the court.

By the fourteenth century the parish was having difficulty maintaining the great edifice. The Bishop of Lichfield decreed in 1346 that the church be repaired, but two years later it was still in a state of dilapidation, and the tower in danger of falling. It was again ordered that the interior be restored "and that the Statutes and Ordinances and Commandments in the Martyrology" should be carefully set out in plain and legible lettering on the church wall.

The prebends of the Holy Cross were distinguished as east,

north and south, set about a deeply venerated image of the Rood in St John's, which was a popular point of pilgrimage and to which oblations were given. In 1412 the Forester of Delamere was sent a warrant to deliver to the Dean and Chapter eight oaks towards the repairs. The Bishop had complained that the Dean and Canons were non-residents, and the church's revenues had been drained by long leases of their property.

In 1548, during the Reformation, it was reported that St John's was

a paryshe churche of itself, having MCC hoslyng people wthin the same . . .

the bodye of the same churche thowghte suffi'ent to s'ue the said p'ishoners wt the charge of xx£ so that the hole ch'unsell, wth the twoo isles, may be well reserved for the king's matie having vpon them lead to the quantitie of xxxviij Fothers.

Bells belonging to the said college, and as yett hanging in the church of ye sayd college, Fyve. Whereof it is thoughte sufficient to contynew – one.

Accordingly, four of the five bells were taken and the lead stripped off the roofs of the chancel and side-aisles, and these parts were left to fall into ruin. Moreover, in 1553 the Dean and two of the canons were committed to the Fleet Prison for taking down lead off the roof – the Dean had to be freed almost immediately "being dangerously sick of the gout". In 1572 the tower started to collapse, and the following year two sides came down, crashing onto the western end of the church, which was reduced to rubble.

In 1581 the parishioners set about rebuilding the nave and blocked off the chapels above the quire. What remained was four of the eight bays of the nave, the crossing and the first of the four bays of the chancel. The transepts were cut off level with the side walls of the church. Fragments of the east end, including the arch to the sanctum sanctorum, the tiny octagonal chancel, remain standing isolated from the body of the church. A new steeple was built in 1581 at the north-west corner of the truncated fabric. On either side of the remains of the chancel stand fragments of two side-chapels. In all, the church, which was heavily restored in the nineteenth century, is like a Victorian stone box containing a part of the interior of a much larger, twelfth-century, church.

The lofty north-west tower was seized by the besiegers in the Civil War, and they raised cannon into the tower with tackle.

Because of its height the tower was an excellent point from which to fire over the walls, and Ralph Richardson, one of the Sheriffs, was killed by a shot from there. Perhaps because of the fracture of the walls during these attacks, the steeple became dangerous and eventually started to disintegrate in April 1881. Great cracks appeared in the eastern and northern sides, and at ten o'clock on the night of the 14th there was a massive crash and tinkling of bells. The citizens rushed to the churchyard and could see in the moonlight that the two sides had collapsed, demolishing the thirteenth-century north porch in their fall. Surprisingly, the entire peal of bells held in position and were all rescued from the ruin in the following days. The steeple was partly dismantled and remains today an interesting ruin.

The organ, which was installed in the church in October 1838, was originally in Westminster Abbey and was the one used at Queen Victoria's coronation; it was brought to Chester by barge. There are several interesting memorials in St John's, including the altar tomb of Diana, widow of Sir George Warburton of Arley, who died in 1693. In the true manner of that period, the tomb is decorated with a skeleton and has a long inscription to Diana "who survived her husband seventeen years in an unmarried state, with true mourning, fasting and prayers".

On the west wall of the north aisle are five handsome marble coats-of-arms. Several mediaeval tombstones have been dug up in the churchyard, including a fine incised slab depicting Agnes de Ridlegh, wife of the then Sheriff of Chester, who died in 1347. There is an interesting mediaeval fresco on the pillar at the end of the north aisle by the chancel arch, showing the church with St John the Baptist beside it, and various animals, including stags and an elephant and 'castle'.

In the ruins of the east end of the church, high in a wall, is a black oak coffin, in which have been painted the words "Dust to Dust". The coffin was discovered in 1813 during repairs to the chancel, built up in a part of the wall being pulled down a little to the north of its present position, and it was fixed here at that date, to be out of the way of passers-by. The inscription is a nineteenth-century addition.

Until the sixteenth century the precincts of St John's were surrounded by a stone wall, with a gatehouse at the north-west corner. Within this area was a surprising diversity of buildings, some of which survived to the nineteenth century.

Thomas de Quincey, 'the opium-eater', relates how, when he ran away from Manchester Grammar School in July 1802, he went to his mother's house a building called 'The Priory', which had once been owned by Sir Robert Cotton, the antiquary. The house, adjoining the south transept on the east side, had been converted from a cottage on this site by Sir Robert, who is today chiefly famous for his collection of (Cottonian) manuscripts, now in the British Museum. He was a close friend of Ben Jonson, who is said to have visited him here.

This brick edifice contained part of the picturesque stone ruins of the church. The main entrance was through a Norman window; the kitchen was the chapter house, or the "chamber of the church's priests", probably on the site of the ancient college buildings, adjoining the quire on the south.

Near to the east end of the church was a chapel dedicated to St Anne. Another chapel, of St James, stood close to the south-west corner of the surviving fabric and after the Dissolution was used as a granary. Associated with this chapel were two hermits' cells, south of the chapel and on the edge of the cliff which then formed the south side of the precincts above the Dee.

Giraldus records the tradition that King Harold Godwinson, far from having been killed at the Battle of Hastings, escaped to Chester, where he recuperated and lived out his life as a hermit in St James's Chapel:

> Of kyng Haralde
> Poudre there hit is halde

There is certainly some evidence that Harold's widow, Queen Ealdgyth, retired to Chester after the battle under the protection of her brothers, Earl Edwin of Mercia and Earl Morcar of the North. The Welsh chronicle *Brut y Tywysogion* records that after the kalends of May in 1332 King Harold's body was discovered in St John's "with his crown and his robes and his leather hose and his golden spurs, as entire and as well odoured as on the day when they were buried".

The 'Anchorite's Cell', a pretty sandstone mediaeval building restored in the nineteenth century still stands, above the Groves and next to the croquet-lawn below St John's Church. The modern house called 'The Hermitage' incorporates masonry from the ruins of the old church. Within the precincts there were also houses for petty canons and vicars choral. Before the siege of Chester a house here was used as a hall by the Cholmondeleys of Cholmondeley, but most of these buildings were swept away in the general destruction of 1645.

Against the north wall of the church stood the house used as a hall by the Company of Woollen and Linen Weavers. Adjoining the north porch was another small house in which a school was conducted in the seventeenth century by Jonathan Rutter. He was brought before the Vicar General in 1683 for teaching without licence and was excommunicated, but the school continued here into the eighteenth century.

On the west side of the precinct was the Dean's house, and below it the ancient palace of the Bishops of Lichfield. When Bishop William Jacobson was appointed to the see of Chester in 1865, he had a new mansion built close to the original site, called 'the Dee Side Palace', to make way for which the houses of the Archdeacon and Chancellor were demolished. The palace, now used by the YMCA, is a large brick building of no great interest, conveniently placed close to the river and the Groves.

Further west is the Dee House, or St John's House, a large brick school in which in 1853 was founded the Ursuline Convent, then occupied by the Faithful Companions of Jesus. This building was previously St Peter's Vicarage and had been badly damaged by a gale on 6th January 1839, which brought down a large chimney-stack. The vicar's nephew would have been killed by the collapse but for the providential fall of a beam across the bed in which he lay sleeping.

It was remarked when the house was built that there were more bricks in the foundation than in the superstructure. The convent was extended in 1867, and further building work in 1929 revealed an ancient curved wall with buttresses. Further stretches of this outer wall of the Roman amphitheatre were found near Newgate, and in 1960 a general excavation of the site exposed the northern half of the oval; this has been preserved in situ.

Although the amphitheatre was used mainly for training the troops, it would certainly have witnessed the bloody gladiatorial contests and animal combats which gave the Romans such delight. The seating was sufficient for about seven thousand spectators, and the theatre was about 100 yards in length.

Close to the northern entrance a lovely small altar was found with this inscription:

DEAE NEMESI
SEXT . MARCI
ANVS V S . EX VISV

("Dedicated to the goddess Nemesis by Sextus Marcianus, after a dream.")

About half the area remains buried in the grounds of the old convent school. The excavations revealed that the stone structure, dating from about AD 80, replaced one of timber. The excavated amphitheatre has been left exposed to view, and a copy of the altar placed in the 'Nemeseum' on the north. On the east side are fragments of columns from an official box above. The ruins are not impressive, nor has the restoration been sympathetic, but the amphitheatre makes an excellent addition to the city's sights and is well worth a visit.

The city wall from Newgate to the south-east corner is part of the mediaeval fabric and directly overlooks the amphitheatre, the foundations of the square south-east angle-tower of the Roman fort by the Newgate, and the Roman Garden. This last is a strip of land between the charming Souter's Lane (leading down to the Groves) and the walls, where various Roman relics, a hypocaust and shafts from large columns, have been re-erected.

The north bank of the Dee from the city walls to the east is called 'the Groves', a wide leafy avenue along the side of the river by the landing-stages and a bandstand. There are terraces along the side of the Dee, and the Groves are very popular in the summer, when the river is crowded with launches, little motor-boats and rowing-boats, swimmers and canoes.

The Groves, with the avenue of limes, was laid out in 1725 by an apothecary, Charles Croughton, then Swordbearer of Chester. Part of what is now the Grosvenor Park was the Lower Bowling Green, and there were already ornamental gardens along the river-bank. Much of the land had been waste until about 1610 when William, Earl of Derby, built a house here and set out gardens and the bowling-green. After the death of his wife in 1627, Earl William, Lord of Man and the Isles, retired to the house here; he died in 1642.

The Dee was already a popular resort, and not just for boating. In 1564, when the river froze over, the citizens played football on it; on 27th January 1600 it froze again, "and certain of the citizens went to walk thereon, not remembering to keep holy the sabbath-day, so that among divers that hardly escaped, three young men fell through the ice, and were drowned."

In October 1645, during the siege, while the Old Dee Bridge remained in the hands of the defenders, the Parliamentarians constructed a floating bridge upriver. At midnight on 25th November, while five hundred cavalry and two hundred foot-soldiers made an attack from one of the gates, the citizens set afloat on the incoming tide

> two boats . . . filled with gorse, tallow, pitch, powder, and other combustible matter, and underneath them, and upon the sides of the boat in a frame of wood about twenty pieces of carbine barrels scarce full length and others pocket pistol length charged with powder and carbine bullets. The one of these came within six yards of the bridge and there fired. . . . A soldier stept in, cast off the gorse and took the frame and brought [it] up with some six or seven of the pieces not discharged. The other boat gave fire over against my lord's bowling alley, and fired all the gorse and boat itself.

Undismayed by this lack of success, the defenders prepared another fire-boat, but the Roundheads put a chain across the river. Prince Maurice placed a boat on each side of the Dee and fastened ropes between them, on which he stretched a taut canvas, so firm that three men could walk abreast on it, it was reported.

On Whit Monday, 1st June 1691, a rowing-boat on the river was overturned, following some sort of panic on board. In full view of the shore, the holiday-makers, mainly young women, were pitched into the river, and ten of them were drowned. Local tradition is that the boat overturned because the girls scrambled for an apple thrown to them by one of the watermen.

The admiralty of the Dee extended from a stone called 'Arnold's Eye' below Handbridge to the Hilbre Islands off West Kirby. However, the jurisdiction of the Port included the whole of the Flintshire coast as far as the mouth of the Clwyd (beyond Rhyl), and the Comptroller of the Great Port of Chester had jurisdiction over all the coast of North Wales as far as Barmouth in Merionethshire, and the whole Lancashire coast. Liverpool was considered a creek of the port of Chester.

Until relatively recent times the Dee was a clean river and "aboundeth in all manner of fish, especially salmons and trouts". The mediaeval fishermen in the city were formed into a company, the Drawers of Dee, responsible for depicting Noah and the Flood in the Mystery Plays. They had exclusive rights to fish from the Old Dee Bridge down to Bruereshalgh and Blacon pool and gained the right to fish from a stank called 'the King's Pool of Dee' and the Royal Salmon Cage on the Causeway. There were several lawsuits about the relative claims to the river of various interested parties: in 1700 it was complained that the stakes and salmon-nets across the river at Blacon were blocking access by boat, besides preventing the salmon from coming further upstream.

From the amphitheatre, St John's Street runs north to Foregate Street, the main street leading east from Eastgate. The suburbs of Chester first extended themselves in the Middle Ages in this direction, and the Foregate is now almost an integral part of the city centre, so that the Eastgate itself is the centrepiece of the town. In about 1615 William Webb wrote: "The Foregate-street is that which begins at your going forth of the Eastgate, and so reacheth directly east, in a fair continued street, to another gate of stone called the Bars; without which the liberties of the city disperse themselves into the several ways that give passages into many countries." The Bars was a strong stone gate with a single arch flanked by two massive round towers, straddling the main road, the Roman Watling Street, to the north-east. There was a cross here, which was pulled down, as being 'Papist', in 1583. In 1608 "by reason of the Continewall passage of Cartes and horses through the same", a postern gate was constructed through the Bars for pedestrians. In 1687 James II was received there on his visit to Chester. The gateway was demolished in 1770, but the stretch of road where it stood, between Foregate Street and Boughton, is still called 'the Bars'.

Foregate suffered from a major fire in 1492 and, although fortified by outworks before the siege, was broken into by the attackers and almost razed to the ground.

Close to the Eastgate was Parry's Coach Factory, which shares with the Dee Mills the distinction of having been burned down on three occasions at the beginning of the nineteenth century (in 1805, 1811 and 1823).

On the south side of the street is a big oppressive half-timbered building of 1895 over a colonnade immediately adjoining the gate, called 'Old Bank Buildings', with carved wooden brackets of human and animal figures. Adjoining is the brick Old Bank (now Lloyd's), with an ugly Classical façade of buff stone, with four columns. On the corner of St John's Street is Blossoms Hotel, of

1896 (by Thomas Lockwood, who designed the Old Bank Buildings), replacing the Georgian brick inn of that name. The Blossoms Inn dates back to the seventeenth century. Along St John's Street there is a pretty five-storey Victorian brick frontage. The Snooty Fox Bar, with an amusing inn-sign, is in the basement. Immediately to the south is the little black-and-white-over-brick three-storey 'Marlborough Arms'.

The Union Hall was constructed in 1809 for tradesmen in Chester for the fairs. It is a large three-storey brick building around a small yard, supported on the inside by iron columns. The hall is partly demolished, partly boarded up; it is reached by a passage from the street. Across Foregate Street was the Commercial Hall, built in 1815. The Union Hall was used for the display of cutlery from Sheffield, Yorkshire woollens and Birmingham ware, and the Commercial Hall was used by retailers. In a later transformation, the Union Hall housed the Grosvenor St John's School, which was afterwards moved to the building in Vicar's Lane now called 'The British Heritage Centre'.

Both halls were built by a local man, Thomas Lunt, and he erected the Commercial Hall in just five weeks. He invented a wheelless train, driven by pulleys turned by loops of rope driven by stationary engines. Lunt, who was a prominent Quaker, also dreamed of reopening Chester as a port by the construction of a ship-canal from Dawpool near Parkgate – and this several decades before the Manchester Ship Canal was built.

On the south side of the street is Ye Olde Royal Oak Hotel of 1601, rebuilt in 1920 – a three-storey structure of black-and-white over brick. On the north side is a stretch of colonnade by the corner with Queen Street, next to the interesting half-timbered Penny Lane Records. Across the road Shapes Hair Design is in a timber building standing on wooden legs over the pavement, claiming the date 1571. The two-storey house has a crooked little lattice window overlooking the street. The rebuilt 'Old Queen's Head' on the north is a mock-Tudor magpie construction with a one-bay colonnade, marked 1508.

Queen Street was constructed in 1777, leading to the line of the canal. The Roman Catholic chapel of St Werburgh here, built in 1799 (originally with a Doric porch), is now a school. In the nineteenth century going to see the crib at St Werburgh's was one of the Christmas pleasures of the Anglican population. Nearby was the old Calvinist (Congregational) Church, built seven years earlier, also in a Classical style; it was demolished in 1978. Wesleyans were meeting in Chester from about 1750, and in 1765 they built the Octagon Chapel, on the north side of Foregate Street near the Bars. John Wesley preached there in 1776. The Wesleyans moved in 1811 to their new church in St John's Street.

In Frodsham Street (the old Cow or Coole Lane), running parallel with Queen Street closer to the walls, the Society of Friends established their meeting-house, the oldest Dissenting chapel in the city, at which William Penn preached. James II is recorded as having come to hear him there on one occasion, during his visit in August 1687 when Penn was among his retinue. The old meeting-house has been demolished and replaced with a plain and ugly edifice of dark brick and concrete on pillars over the Fads Homecare Centre. Across the road is a small new shopping precinct, Mercia Square, which has a higher level leading onto the city walls.

Cow Lane led to a rise not far from the north-east corner of the city walls called 'Henwalds Low'. Traces of a Roman road leading in the same general direction from Eastgate have been found on the west side of Frodsham Street, together with an alabaster figure of Fortune.

A new Roman Catholic church was constructed on Grosvenor Park Road in 1875 and dedicated to St Werburgh. In June 1877 the first Roman Catholic ordination at Chester since the Reformation was held there. The church is a large towerless building of white stone with a very awkward west end and entrance porch. It was designed to have a 200-foot spire, but this was alas abandoned as too ambitious.

Foregate Street overlies the eastern approach to the Roman fort, and there is ample evidence that in Roman times there was a substantial Romano-British settlement outside the walls in these suburbs. In 1653 an altar was discovered at the Greyhound Inn on the south side of the street, with this inscription:

I . O . M , TANARO
(L. BRVTTIVS.) GALER
PRAESENS (. CL)VNIA
PRI . LEG . XX V V
COMMODO . ET .
LATERANO . COS
V . S . L . M

("To Jupiter Tanarus, best and greatest, Lucius Bruttius, *praesens* the Galerian, from Clunia [in Hispania Tarraconensis], *princeps* of the 20th Legion Valeria Victrix, willingly and deservedly fulfilled his vow in the consulship of Commodus and Lateranus [AD 154].") The altar is now at the Ashmolean Museum in Oxford. Interest in the Roman relics found in the city started to be formalized only in the seventeenth century, and this is the earliest known find to have survived.

Not far from Queen Street is the site of the Justing Croft, which was used for many of the citizens' recreations, not only jousting. It is thought that the city butts were located there; these consisted of several pairs of mounds, about a hundred paces apart, before which the targets were set up. The archers would shoot, with long bows, at one target, then walk to the far end, recover their arrows and shoot at the other. The city records have several references to the Butts, at which all but clergy and judges were obliged to practise by statutes of Edward IV and Henry VIII. In 1562 it was ordered "that no p'son Shall Speake any Braggynge words to an other, as to say 'yf thow darr Shoote with me, or darr bett with me', w'ch woords be often tymes occasion of Inconvenience." Citizens were forbidden to shoot at night; they were obliged to practise every Sunday and holiday after divine service, on pain of a halfpenny per day omitted. Close at hand was Cock Fight Hill, providing another source of amusement for the men of Chester.

The first railway in Cheshire was opened in 1837, crossing the county from Warrington towards Birmingham. Three years later another line was put through, connecting Birkenhead with the Birmingham line at Crewe and passing through Chester. The first stone of the line to Crewe was laid on 20th August 1838 near the Hoole Lane Bridge. The workmen were regaled with beer and ale in a field nearby, while the directors, entertained by a band, "partook of a cold Collation" in two marquees erected for the occasion. The first train to arrive at Chester was on 12th September 1840, ten carriages pulled by the steam-locomotive *Wirral*.

In 1846 a line was completed to Saltney, from which the railway was extended to Bangor, Mold and Ruabon. In 1850 Chester was connected directly with Warrington, and in 1874 another line was built, from a station outside the walls near Northgate to Northwich. This line was extended west to Hawarden Bridge in 1890.

Moreover, in July 1879 a horse-drawn tram-service was started from the railway station to Saltney, and tramlines passed through the historic streets of the city centre. Electric trams were introduced at the turn of the century, beneath overhead power-lines, but they were abandoned in favour of motorbuses in 1930.

The present magnificent Chester General Station was built in 1848, to replace the two small stations then being used for the lines. The stretch of the line to Birkenhead was held by a different company from that to Crewe, and for some years no agreement could be reached for them to work in concert, and the line between the stations lay unused. Unfortunately, the site selected for the new station was already occupied by a flourishing nursery-garden, some flower-gardens and a row of very pretty cottages, near Flookersbrook, including one belonging to a shoemaker, who contested the compulsory-purchase order and refused to hand over his property. The railway company settled the issue by main force, sending in a gang of fifty men to demolish the cottage: "In less than half an hour every window and door was broken; every slate, and every trace even of a roof; Ten minutes more sufficed to make the whole thing a wreck, and by three o'clock not a vestige of the mansion was anywhere distinguishable." What compensation was awarded to the shoemaker was largely consumed by the costs of the litigation.

In the early days the railways had a rustic air. The clerk at the old Northgate station, when required to compute the fare for a cow and calf, could find the tariff for the cow in his guide but nothing for calves: at last it was classed as a 'child in arms' and travelled free. The manager of the Crewe line had great difficulty in getting permission to start a goods service on the line with a single wagon a day because it was thought that the traffic would not warrant it.

The General Station has a large and imposing brick façade of two storeys, with stone ornaments and Italianate turrets. Northgate Station was closed in 1969 when the Manchester service was transferred to the General Station. Thomas Hughes, in his *Stranger's Handbook to Chester* of 1856 facetiously described the Refreshment Rooms:

The noble range of Refreshment Rooms presided over with efficient zeal and attention by Mr Hobday, and his select corps of experienced assistants. If after your late journey, you feel any of the cravings of the inner man – if dinner *à la mode* lies uppermost in your thoughts – if you would enjoy an invigorating cup of coffee, unimpeachable pastry, a good glass of ale, or a fragrant cigar, take a turn in the Refreshment Rooms and the utmost wish of your soul will be incontinently gratified.

South-east of the station is the Lead Works, opened in 1801, with the 150-foot round brick shot-tower still standing, next to the canal. In the nineteenth century there was another lead-works in the city, in Commonhall Street.

Charles Dickens stayed at the Queen's Hotel by the General Station in 1867; he described it as looking like "an ornament on an immense twelfth cake baked for 1847":

I am now going to the fire to try and warm myself, but have not the least expectation of succeeding. The sitting-room has two large windows in it, down to the ground and facing due east. The adjoining bedroom (mine) has also two large windows in it, down to the ground and facing due east. The very large doors are opposite the large windows, and I feel as if I were something to eat in a pantry.

Beyond the Bars is the suburb of Boughton, which grew from a little hamlet within the bounds of the city. Part of this was called 'Spital Boughton' after the leper hospital of St Giles, founded by Earl Randle Blundeville in about 1200. A letter of Charles I survives, in which he orders that the brethren of the hospital should not be pestered for murage.

After a skirmish at Great Boughton between the Royalists and a party of Roundheads from Christleton in 1643, in which 140 of the King's men were killed, the garrison of the city came out and pulled the chapel down and burned down Boughton to clear the ground of cover. The site was granted to the Corporation by Charles II and continued in use as a graveyard. The precise location is at The Mount, near Barrel Well Hill, overlooking the bend of the Dee.

The chronicler of St Werburgh's Abbey says that in 1170 Earl Hugh Cyveliok slew a great multitude of Welshmen at Baldert's Gate and that one of the mounds of the hospital of the infirm outside the city was made from their skulls.

The public gallows and whipping-post were at Spital Boughton. Before the Reformation it was the custom for the crowd along the route from the city to put pennies into a little bag held out by the felon, and these alms would be used to pay for Masses to be said for his soul.

It was there that George Marsh, the only person martyred in Cheshire under Queen Mary, was burned at the stake, in 1555. Marsh was arraigned for professing the Gospel and was found guilty of heresy and taken out to the gallows hill, above the river, on 24th April. His feet shackled, he was led out by the sheriffs "with their officers and a great number of poor simple barbers with rusty bills and poleaxes". Marsh turned to the crowd, but a sheriff said, "George Marsh, we must have no sermonizing now." When the stake was ready, he was offered a pardon by the Vice-Chamberlain on condition that he recant, which he refused. John Cowper of Overleigh, one of the two sheriffs in that year, took matters into his own hands and attempted to rescue Marsh, but he was held off by Robert Amery, the other sheriff. Cowper fled across the bridge at Holt into Wales, where he hid until Queen Mary's death, and his family lost a great deal of their property in consequence. The sheriffs' officers had great difficulty in lighting the fire and keeping it going, but Marsh suffered the agonies with great patience.

On 8th September 1589 a woman was burned there for poisoning her husband, and another for a similar offence in 1608. In October 1762 Mary Heald of Mere near Knutsford was convicted at the Assizes of having killed her husband, Samuel, by administering arsenic to him in a "mess of fleetings". Mary put her mark to a confession which states that she was born in Alderley and that her family had become Quakers. 'Uneasiness' grew between her and her husband, whom she accordingly poisoned. She was kept in the Castle dungeon until the following April, the gaolers augmenting their income by exhibiting her to the curious. She was brought out on Saturday 23rd April and delivered over to the City Sheriffs at Gloverstone for execution. Mary Heald was burned at the stake in the time-honoured way at Boughton, on the north side of the main road, opposite the gallows, but as a concession to liberal thinking she was strangled before the fire was lit.

Some of the punishments inflicted by the city and county authorities for minor offences seem barbaric today. In September 1776, for instance, Mary Scott alias Brown was convicted at the Michaelmas Quarter Sessions for stealing two pieces of printed cotton and had her hand branded for the offence. The last public execution at the Boughton gallows was on 9th May 1801. After bull-baiting was banned from the city in 1803, it continued for about thirty years on Boughton Heath. The whipping-post stood close to the gallows but fell into disuse at the same period.

The public executions were often not short of lynchings. When three malefactors were taken to Boughton on one occasion, due to be hung at noon, one of them, called Clare, escaped and ran through the crowd, jumping down into the River Dee. Unable to swim, unable to return to land, he was drowned, but the body was pulled out of the water by the enraged populace, taken to the gallows and solemnly hanged. The bodies were loaded into a cart and taken back to the gaol for burial amid drunken rejoicing. The driver of the cart was so intoxicated that he ran one wheel onto the ramp by St Michael's up to Bridge Street Row, and the vehicle overturned, spilling the corpses onto the street. At an earlier period the bodies were left on the gallows, or taken off to appropriate vantage-points to remain as a public witness that justice had been done.

In 1771 a sailor called John Chapman was convicted of robbing a certain Martha Hewitt. The gaol was surrounded by an angry crowd of his shipmates; as he was led out in irons, the gaoler handed him a Bible, which he threw into their midst, and they tore it to pieces. A local clergyman stepped into the cart, advising him to behave in a more seemly manner, and was butted in the stomach and tumbled out of the cart for his trouble. Chapman leaped from the cart and tried to escape but was retrieved and tied down with ropes. At the gallows he continued struggling, refusing to pray or listen to the prayers for him; indeed, the hangman had great difficulty in getting the rope round Chapman's neck, and Chapman managed to bite the hangman's thumb through to the bone. Despite his struggles and the efforts of the crowd, he was secured and hanged.

5

SAINT PETER the APOSTLE
Rows, Pentice and High Cross

AT the centre of the ancient city is the High Cross, where the four main mediaeval streets meet – Eastgate Street, Bridge Street, Watergate Street and Northgate Street. The central area here, of about 500 yards square, formed the parish of Saint Peter. The church stands on the corner of Northgate Street with Watergate Street, overlooking the Cross, on part of the site of the central Roman building, the *principia*. This was once part of the crowded town centre – in 1801 there were 171 houses in this parish containing 810 inhabitants; most of the premises are now shops and offices.

All four main streets retain for a little of their length parts of the mediaeval Rows, a unique feature of the city, for which it is particularly famous. These are walk-ways along the first floor of the houses, which are cut back by a full bay, the second floors being supported on pillars. William Webb, in about 1615, described them:

> Though there be towards the street fair rooms, both for shops and dwelling houses, to which there is rather a descent, than an equal height with the floor or pavement of the street: Yet the principal dwelling-houses and shops for the chiefest trades are mounted a storey higher: and before the doors and entries, a continued row on either side the street, for people to pass to and fro all along the said houses, out of all annoyance of rain, or other foul weather, with stairs conveniently built, and neatly maintained, to step down out of these rows into the open streets, almost at every second house; and the said rows built over the head, with such of the chambers and rooms, for the most part are the best rooms in every of their said houses.

The Rows today extend for a short distance from the Cross on the four main streets. The best length is from the Cross to St Michael's Church along the east side of Bridge Street. Traces of

122

the Rows can be found in the older buildings elsewhere in the town, particularly in Lower Bridge Street.

During the great Victorian restorations, the Rows received ample attention, and the quaint junction at the corner of Bridge Street and Eastgate Street, with an oriel in the second storey surmounted by a pretty tiled timber cupola, and above a timber arch and a broad flight of stone steps to the street, was designed by Thomas Lockwood in 1888 for the Grosvenors of Eaton. Across the street, on the corner of Bridge Street with Watergate Street, Lockwood produced a similar timber confection with typical Eaton-estate diapered brickwork and sandstone dressings.

The first specific references to the Rows date from the early-fourteenth century, and since such a system could not be produced piecemeal, it is most likely that they were constructed when the town was rebuilt after the great fire of 1278. There are shops both at ground level and along the first-floor Rows, but the Rows also continue through private houses. The street levels have risen, and the floors of the ground-floor shops are now usually several steps down from the street and are sometimes called crypts, but below many of the shops there do exist mediaeval stone crypts, some of which were rediscovered during construction of cellars in the nineteenth century. The Rows were originally much more cramped than the present versions, and there was a general prejudice in the city that they were unhealthy to live in.

The courts of the sheriffs of Chester were held in the Pentice or Appentice (being built onto the side of St Peter's as an *appenticium*, appendage). Webb recorded that the Mayor

> remaineth most part of the day at a place called the Pentice; which is a place built for the purpose at the high cross, under St Peter's church, and in the middle of the city, in such a sort, that a man may stand therein, and see into the markets, or four principal streets of the city. There sit also (in a room adjoining) the clerks for his courts; where all actions are entered, and recognizances made, and such like. [The sheriffs] on the workdays, go in fair long gowns, welted with velvet, and white staves in their hands; but they have violet and scarlet for festival days.

The Pentice, the north side of which was demolished in about 1780, the remainder in March 1806, was a long timber building flanking the south wall of the church, with a great gallery from a wooden tower at the corner of Northgate Street to a chamber over the church porch. The north side of the Pentice was built in 1499, and in 1574 it was enlarged and the Sheriffs' Court removed to the Common Hall.

In 1617 the city prepared a sumptuous banquet in the Pentice for King James I, during his visit to Cheshire. The Mayor's rhyming oration on receiving the King, or rather a contemporary satire, said:

> When yesterday the post did tideings bringe
> That I sholde see you here (our royall kinge),
> For my part into an ague I did falle,
> And greatelie gloppened were my brethren all.
>
> We went about to muster upp our forces,
> To meet you at Botone; but we wanted horses.
> Our foote cloathes also by ratts and mice offended,
> In soe short space cold not be patched and mended.
>
> The streets as you doe pass on either hand
> Are sweetlie flored wth gravell and wth sand;
> The conduit at ye Crosse if you marke well,
> Is newlie painted, you may know by th'smell.

And he mentions the Pentice:

> The place aginst it is the place where I
> Doe sit in all my pompe and dignitie,
> While I doe justice, be itt right or wronge,
> To the rich or poore, or old or younge.
>
> St Peter's Church, where I am often seene,
> Stands neare unto itt, it's but a leape betweene.

The churchwardens of Holy Trinity strewed rushes and sand in front of the church ready for the King. The Mayor and aldermen met His Majesty on a scaffold by the Pentice draped in green, and the Mayor presented him with a "fair standing cup with a cover double-gilt, and therein an hundred Jacobins in gold".

In 1642 Charles I was also entertained there and presented with £200 by the Corporation, who also gave £100 to his son, Prince Charles. In 1687 his younger son, James II, was "splendidly entertained at the Pentice, where he was seated under a canopy of crimson velvet prepared for the occasion".

There were three annual fairs in Chester: on the last Thursday in February (the Horn and Hoof Fair), at Midsummer and at Michaelmas. On these occasions a carved oaken glove was hung from a pole in the front of the Pentice, indicating that while the glove was shown, the normal restrictions on non-freemen from exhibiting their goods in the city was lifted. The glove was hung out for a fortnight after the fair, at the end of which the Leavelookers combed the city evicting strangers.

After the Pentice was demolished, the glove was put out on a pole from the roof of St Peter's Church, over the site of the Cross, from fourteen days before each fair to the fourteenth day afterwards. The glove was last hung there in 1836. The clerk of St Peter's, Peter Catheral, was given the glove, and it passed to a man called Wilkinson, who sold it for two pints of ale at the sign of the Boot. It was acquired by the Mayer Museum in Liverpool, where it was destroyed during bombing in the last war.

A fair for three days at the Feast of St Werburgh (21st June, i.e. the three days before Midsummer) was granted by Earl Hugh Lupus to St Werburgh's Abbey. The jurisdiction over the fairs passed, on the Dissolution, to the Sheriffs. There were two Sheriffs: the King's Sheriff was elected by the court of aldermen, the Earl's Sheriff by popular acclamation. On Easter Monday the two sheriffs, with respective teams drawn from the Mayor, Recorder, aldermen and gentry of the city, had an archery match for the Sheriff's Breakfast, a meal of calves' heads and bacon. The winners paid 11d each towards the breakfast, the losers 4d.

The gable tenants held their lands by the duty of providing 'watch and ward' on the battlements, and they were summoned annually to appear before the Mayor and Sheriffs. By the sixteenth century the court had become the start of a round of banquets, on the three first nights of Christmas, at the houses of the Mayor and the two Sheriffs, the watch still being kept, not against marauding Welshmen but "to keepe the cittie from danger of fire, theeves, dronknes, and unmeete meetings, and drinkeinges in the nightes".

First the gable tenants (who held by Thewewaiche) were marshalled and led to the four gates preceded by pipe and banner, and the gates were locked for the night. The Corporation went round the city in triumph, with torches and fireworks, and the Recorder made an oration. New freemen were sworn in at the Pentice, appearing with halberd and helmet, with which they swore to defend City and Crown.

In front of the Pentice porch, and by the south door of St Peter's Church, stood a large square socket-stone on a four-step stone plinth. Into this socket fitted the shaft of the High Cross, a sandstone pillar which has recently been re-erected on the old site. The head of the Cross was a very decorative affair, embellished with large panels on which were carved saints and bishops. Beneath the panels were angels' heads and above were smaller carved panels. On top of the Cross head was a floriated cross on an orb. This assemblage was painted and gilded and formed the centrepiece of the city. William Webb, about 1615, wrote: "The High-Cross, for the beauty and situation, a special part of the comely splendor of the city, and boasteth itself with the shew of four or five of the churches, cross-conduit, and greatest traded shops, very seemly to all beholders." During the fairs bargains were settled at the cross. Plays were staged there, and proclamations read. The cross was regularly re-gilded.

In 1539 the Corporation tried to tackle the problem of unemployment with "An Order about Idle Begars, and other Poore of ye Citty". It was decreed that "all man' of Idle p'sons, being able to laboure . . . shall eu'y work day in the morning, in the tyme of Wynter at vj of the clocke, and in tyme of Somer at iiij of the clocke, Resorte and cou' unto the high Crose . . . and ther to offer them Selues to be hyryd to Labour." Stocks were to be set up in every ward, and anyone caught begging was to be put in them "ther to Remayne by the Space of a day and a nyght". It was a general rule in Chester until the nineteenth century for labourers during harvest-time to gather at the Cross on Sundays to be hired for the following week.

The conduit, which brought fresh water into the city, was altered in 1582 by "an ingenious workman, whereas before it came of its own accord only unto Mr Brerewood's house, near unto Chapel-gate", so that it came right to the Cross, forming a public fountain called 'the Cross Conduit', taken down in 1805. At times of public celebration a cask was put into the conduit to make it run with wine.

In 1592, when 2,200 infantry and a thousand cavalry arrived in the city on the way to Ireland, "the mayor had much ado to keep the soldiers quiet, and caused a gibbet to be set up at the high cross, whereon three soldiers had like to have been hanged." In 1599 there were so many soldiers in the city that they were billeted in surrounding villages: "The souldiers daiely fightinge caused the Cittizens to rise often, the Jebbett set up at the Hie Crosse; manye runawaye souldiers broughte againe and had theire ears neyld to logges of woode at the Hie Crosse."

Bull-baiting was a common sport in the city, despite attempts by Puritan mayors to put an end to it (their opposition was not so much to the suffering of the bulls as to the enjoyment of the spectators). There was a ring, the Bull Ring, at the Cross, to which the bulls were tethered. Henry Hardware, who was Mayor in 1599 and altered the Midsummer Shows and the Sheriffs' Breakfast, forbidding plays, bear-baiting and bull-baiting, had the Bull Ring removed, but other mayors spent their money promoting these activities for the delight of the populace. We have this record from 1619:

> A Bull-baiting at the High Cross according unto ancient custom for the Mayor's farewell, 2nd October where a contention fell out betwixt the Butchers and Bakers about their dogs; they fell to blows and would not be pacified, so that Mr Mayor seeing they would not stint their brawling, he in his own person went out of the Pentice down to them but they little regarded him like rude unbroken fellows, were in the end parted, and after committed to prison and punished. Mr Mayor smote freely amongst them and with a blow he broke his white staff and the crier Knowsley brake his mace and so the brawl was ended. After this the Butchers and Bakers knowing they had offended the Magistrate brought forth another bull upon the 5th October next ensuing to the bull ring, and there made very fair play in the presence of Mr Mayor and his brethren and Sir Thomas Savage with other Knights and Gents there present who Mr Mayor had that day dined at his house.

Sir Thomas sent the Butchers and Bakers 20 shillings to drink and be friends.

The Mayor and Corporation watched the bull-baiting from a special balcony, supported on oak pillars with carved floral capitals, painted and gilded, on the west side of St Peter's porch. The town crier would declare, "The Right Worshipful the Mayor doth strictly charge and command that all persons should behave themselves orderly, and that they keep forty feet off the Bull ring, upon Pain of Fine and Imprisonment."

Bull baiting at the Cross was finally brought to an end in 1803 under the powers of the new Police Act, and the balcony was taken down in 1806.

In 1603 the Cross was regilded. Three years later "a stranger did dance and vault upon a rope, which was fastened a great height above the ground, overthwart the street at the High Cross, which did seem strange to the beholders." In 1637 four portraits of

William Prynne, the Puritan pamphleteer, were burned at the Cross. Ten years later, after the surrender of the city to Parliament, the Cross was pulled down and broken. It had previously been accidentally knocked down in the dark on at least two occasions.

The absence of the stone pillar did not make the Cross less important to city life. In 1649 Charles II was formally proclaimed a traitor there. Under the Commonwealth, with the dismantling of the bishoprics and the transfer of church records into the control of the laity, marriages were performed by Justices of the Peace, and banns were read at the High Cross. On 9th January 1793 Thomas Paine, the American writer and supporter of independence, was burned in effigy there.

In the early-nineteenth century the Cross was frequented by Jacky Huxley, the Grosvenors' domestic fool, dressed in their livery:

His legs and clogs swathed in straw or hay-bands, a Grosvenor cockade in his old slouched hat, and a small toy fiddle in his hand, he would stand for hours each day at the Cross, chattering away with the sedan-chairmen, or with the porters and vent-peg makers who used to then crowd the thoroughfare; occasionally tuning his old sham Cremona, and singing some simple ditty for the enjoyment of his companions.

The surviving fragments of the old cross were discovered in 1804 buried in St Peter's Church porch but were carried off to become part of a rockery at Netherleigh House. They were rescued by the Corporation and have recently been re-erected at the High Cross on a new three-step plinth, and once again attract passers-by as a focus for the city. The shaft is also new-cut, supporting the battered old head with its six empty niches, above which the stone ball of the orb is supported by conical stonework. A stone with a set of smaller niches now supports the base of the shaft.

The pillory, whipping-post and stocks stood opposite and immediately in view of the Pentice. Miscreants sentenced by the mayor were removed on the spot to their punishment. The pillory, in which offenders were to be mocked, derided and made a common spectacle, was on the corner of the Bridge Street and Eastgate Street Rows, with the occupant facing Bridge Street.

In 1663 an Irishman was consigned to the pillory for several hours for speaking treason, and lost his ears. Women were also exposed to public abuse there: the Corporation accounts record 12 shillings paid to twelve constables to attend while a certain Mary Axson stood in the pillory in April 1771. The device was last used in 1800, when a bricklayer called Steele was exhibited in it during Race Week and was severely pelted by the mob. A few days later the Corporation decided to pull the pillory and stocks down "to improve the turn at the end of Bridge Street".

There were whipping-posts at the Cross and in the suburb of Boughton, but often a person was publicly whipped through the city. In 1778 Thomas Griffith, who had broken down a canal-railing, was whipped from the Northgate to Cow Lane Bridge. In April 1789 Richard Hicks, John Morgan and Sarah Hankins, stripped to the waist, were publicly whipped in a cart from the City Gaol to the Bridge. Two hours later Sarah was apprehended stealing a cloak.

St Peter's Church was held after the Norman Conquest by Robert de Rodelent (Rhuddlan), one of the new Cheshire barons created by Hugh Lupus. It is described in Domesday Book, in 1086: "The land in which is the temple of St Peter, which Robert de Rodeland claimed for *teinland*, as the earl has established, never appertained to a manor outside the city, but to the borough and was always in the custom of the king and earl, as of the other burgesses." In 1081 Robert gave the church to the Abbey of St Ebrulf of Utica in Normandy, from which it was later granted back to St Werburgh's Abbey.

The present church was built of local sandstone in the fourteenth century, with side-aisles separated from the nave by three pointed arches. An outer aisle was added on the north of the church about 1500, called 'the New Aisle', making the church ground-plan almost a perfect square. The west tower is square and directly faces Bridge Street. When the Pentice was removed in 1803, the south side of the church was refaced, as a Latin inscription on the outer wall records. There have been several restorations.

The tower now has a small pyramidal roof with a weathervane, but there was formerly a tall octagonal stone spire rising to about 130 feet. In 1489 the steeple was pointed, and the Rector, Thomas Bolton, and his friends celebrated the completion of the work by eating a goose on the very top, throwing morsels of the feast into the four streets below.

Two years later, two days after Christmas 1491, a storm brought down some of the masonry from the pinnacles, killing a child of one of the town's mercers, Tudor ap Thomas, who lived in Bridge Street. Poor Tudor's wife, Margaret, was killed at eleven o'clock at night on 7th December 1517 by falling backwards from the top stair in their house, striking her head on the stone at the bottom.

In 1580 the top 54 feet of the steeple was dismantled and rebuilt, and in 1612 "the jacks were set up at St Peter's church, and the quarters were made to strike upon the clock, at the cost of Mr Robert Amory, who died 21st September following." The curfew was rung from St Peter's each evening, except Sunday, at eight o'clock.

In 1762 the spire was partly rebuilt again by a mason from Liverpool. On 18th August a cordwainer called William Wright wagered with his friends for a quart of ale that he could climb to the top of the spire, but a plank of the scaffolding gave way, and he fell down onto the roof of the body of the church and was killed. On 23rd February 1783 the spire was damaged by lightning and was dismantled.

St Peter's is a small church, divided by pillars into the four aisles and with two internal galleries on the north and south walls; the west gallery was removed in 1886. Some faded wall-painting has been preserved on the north pillar of the tower. There are many monuments to citizens buried there: by the entrance is a mutilated brass to "Mr Henry Bennett Marchant one of the Covncell of this Cittie" who died in 1654; on the east wall, north of the altar, is a monument to William Wall of Helsby who died in 1598: it is decorated with his bust, and his arms and crest (a black bear's head with a golden muzzle); William was Mayor in 1586. There is also a brass of about 1460, from which the inscription is missing, depicting a local merchant. There was a great alabaster monument erected in the church in 1602 to William Offley of Chester, who had, by two wives, twenty-six children; but this sarcophagus and its effigies were probably destroyed after the siege. The images in the church were removed at the Reformation; in 1559 it was noted that "Mistres Dutton kepith secreatlye a Rode, too pictures and a masse boke" from St Peter's. The church records date from 1535 and are kept at the Cheshire Record Office. The churchyard is now a small paved area with passages to Watergate Street and Northgate Street.

St Peter's had a special relationship with the Corporation, who built a private pew there in 1611 and paid towards the upkeep of the bells, which were used on public occasions. In the seventeenth century the council appointed a City Lecturer, who preached there every Sunday with the Corporation in attendance, and the church was very crowded at such times.

The headquarters of the Roman fortress were in the *principia*, a large complex of buildings at the intersection of the *via principalis* (Eastgate Street and Watergate Street) with the *via praetoria* (Bridge Street). St Peter's and the part of Northgate Street adjoining stand on the south-east corner of the *principia*.

The *principia* extended northwards for over 300 feet, and almost as far west as Goss Street. It was apparently first built in timber but on the general rebuilding of Deva in the second century was reconstructed as a large and magnificent colonnaded headquarters building of stone, with the south front (facing the Cross) built up on a ramp to give a level floor-plan and a more imposing façade. The south door of St Peter's Church is some feet above the level of the street.

The buildings were arranged with 'cloisters' around a central quadrangle. The east, west and south sides housed the offices of the staff, while the north side was the *basilica principiorum*, in which were preserved the legionary standards and the treasury, *aerarium*; as we have already seen, the remains of the strong-room and of foundations from the *principia* can be seen in place in the Forum Precinct and Shoemakers' Row.

On the north side of Eastgate Street, east of St Peter's, sections of lead water-pipes with the Agricolan inscription of AD 79 were discovered. A little to the north, at the back of Chester House on the lower passage from Northgate Street through to St Werburgh Street, black-and-white mosaic pavement and a paving of herringbone tiles were found in 1865. However, it is in St Michael's parish to the south that further substantial Roman remains can still be seen.

6

ST MICHAEL the ARCHANGEL
Roman Remains, Bridge Street and Wolf Gate

THE substantial Roman remains in Chester were well known in
the Middle Ages. Higden wrote in the fourteenth century, in his
Polychronicon: "In this citee beeth weies vnder erthe, with vawtes
of stoonwerk, wonderliche i-wrought, thre chambres workes,
greet stoones i-graued with olde men names there ynne."
Hoveden and Giraldus Cambrensis mentioned the huge stones and
the passageways underground, and in the twelfth and thirteenth
centuries there must have been quite impressive evidence of the
Roman occupation. The underground passages were not a fantasy:
some were part of the ancient drainage-system of large stone
conduits taking water from the streets to the river. When the Old
Lamb Row, close to St Michael's Church, was pulled down in
1821, one of these passages was discovered.

As late as the seventeenth century we have William Webb
commenting:

> There remains only in these late ages, some pavements of four-square
> chequerwork stones . . . . I gather from daily reports that many of the
> citizens that have occasion to dig either in their houses, gardens,
> backsides, orchards, or in the streets of the city, meeting with great
> and huge foundations of stone; and those, for the most part, artificially
> hewn and fastened together.

There are few places in the city where Roman remains can now
be seen in their original position. There is Roman stonework in the
north wall and the quay wall, and we have the footings of a part of
the *principia*, and the amphitheatre. In Bridge Street, not far from
the High Cross, on the east side, below the entrance to St
Michael's Arcade, is the site commonly called 'the Roman Baths'.

At the back of the shops here an altar was discovered, with the
inscription:

DEAE M(I)
NERVA(E)
FVRIV(S)
FORTV
NATVS
MAG. P(R)
V . (S)

("To the goddess Minerva, Furius Fortunatus, senior master, has fulfilled his vow.")

When St Michael's Arcade or Row was constructed, the remains of a Roman exercise-hall were found. The columns were re-erected in the Roman Garden; some mosaic flooring is preserved beneath the Arcade, and at the shop below in Bridge Street the hypocaust can be seen. Another hypocaust can be seen at 'Miss Selfridge' in Northgate Street, and one has been reconstructed in the Roman Garden.

Bridge Street itself lies directly upon the Roman *via praetoria*, the main southern street of the fortress. St Michael's Church stands by the site of the Roman south gate, the *porta praetoria*, of which foundations were discovered at the west end of the church during excavations in 1886 and 1908.

From the High Cross to St Michael's Church there is a high wide Row lined with shops and balconies to the street. St Michael's Arcade, the arm of the shopping precinct which extends to Bridge Street Row, is the best part of this commercial warren. There is a lovely light tiled central square under a glass roof; the walls are decorated with Baroque ornamental scrolls and figures.

St Michael's Church is recorded from the twelfth century. In common with most of the ancient city churches, it has been abandoned for worship, and it was reopened in 1975 as the Chester Heritage Centre, where self-congratulatory slide-shows and exhibitions are presented by the Corporation.

The church is a very pretty structure, built in 1850 of pleasing ochre sandstone. The square tower is above the end of the Rows, which descend to the street there by a flight of stone steps. The ornamental detail of the tower is restrained and very effective. The roundels for clockfaces are now blank; the top of the tower is crenellated with eight crocketed pinnacles and a little weather-vane.

The interior of the church is virtually devoid of monuments. At the rebuilding, the roof of the chancel (rebuilt in 1496) and the octagonal pillars of the north aisle (with capitals ornamented with quatrefoils) were incorporated in the new fabric; the archway of the west door was re-erected in the Grosvenor Park.

In the seventeenth century a half-timbered gable, similar to those of many of the houses in the street, was supported on wooden pillars over the end of the Rows; a covered flight of steps led to the room above. At that time there was a little bell-turret over the west end of the church. Inside was a wooden gallery over the west door.

Before the Reformation the church was held by Norton Priory near Runcorn, by gift of the Baron of Halton. The registers, surviving from 1581 (with other records from 1560), are now at the Cheshire Record Office. The parish extended from the walls south of Newgate across to Bridge Street, including a few buildings on the far side of the latter. These are still marked with iron plates with the raised letters S.Ml.P'. The parish went as far north as St Michael's Arcade, and south beyond Unity Passage. The ancient Ward of St Michael's consisted of the east side of Bridge Street from the High Cross to Pepper Street, and the north side of Pepper Street. South of Pepper Street was Beastmarket Ward, which extended as far as Castle Street and St Olave's Street.

In 1745, when the city was preparing to resist Bonnie Prince Charlie, the main guard was posted in Bridge Street, at the corner of Commonhall Street. Thirty years later, in 1775, there was a highway robbery in Bridge Street, when a coach was held up at pistol-point.

St Michael's Arcade opens onto Bridge Street at the site of an old coaching-inn, 'The Feathers', a fine antique building with an open gallery and a quaint oak staircase, demolished in 1863. 'The Feathers' (so named from the plume of feathers of the Prince of Wales) was the inn from which the mail-coaches, which travelled the turnpikes free of toll, were sent to London and Holyhead. The coaches carried travellers as well as letters and packets, including parcels of bank-notes; the mail-guards, who were given free uniform, waistcoat and hat, were paid half a guinea a week, which they supplemented by begging from the passengers. They took the coach as far as Hinckley in Leicestershire, where the London guards took over. The guards carried a blunderbuss to ward off highwaymen.

Adam Martindale, the Puritan incumbent of Rostherne, was confined at 'The Feathers' under arrest and was forced to pay 8d a meal. The Duke of Monmouth stayed there in 1683. At the back of the inn a new cockpit was constructed in about 1810; there were regular fights both there and at 'The Royal' (now the Grosvenor Hotel) each Race Week.

The altar to Minerva was found on the site of another ancient inn, 'The Blue Posts'.

It is said that Dr Cole, Dean of St Paul's, who was sent to Ireland in 1558 on a commission for Queen Mary to enforce Catholicism, stayed at 'The Blue Posts'. The landlady, Bess Mottershead, had a Protestant brother, John Edmunds, living in Dublin, and, fearing for his safety, she substituted a pack of playing cards (the Knave of Clubs uppermost) for the Dean's commission. By the time the trick was discovered and Cole had returned to England, Queen Mary was dead. Bess Mottershead, the story concludes, received a pension of £40 a year from Queen Elizabeth.

The old rectory is thought to have been the pretty, delicate timbered house (above 'The Lunch Box') in Bridge Street Row to the south. Inside there is some original carved panelling. Compare this with the great brash five-storey aggressive black-and-white group over the entrance to St Michael's Row, or the amusing mock-seventeenth-century Art Gallery of Sherratt & Co to the south. This has stained glass in the gable window, a bucolic figure of Charles I and eight carved panels with Biblical scenes and the inscription: ". TO . GOD . MY . KING . AND . MY . COUNTRY."

The Dutch Houses, on the west of the street, were built after the siege and are quite distinctive, with twisted baluster decoration and three crowded gables. The group was restored recently: some woodwork is bare, the plasterwork painted cream, the balusters maroon. The house adjoins Thomas Lockwood's magnificent gross tall 'The Plane Tree' of about 1873, a mountainous timber house towering above the five-storey Dutch Houses, and with an oriel on its third storey supporting a balcony, supporting a projecting archway in a high dormer gable capped with a little pinnacle.

At the corner of Cuppin Street with Lower Bridge Street is 'The Falcon', derelict, propped up with wooden buttresses. The first storey has two gables and a long window-band over a row of quatrefoils. A flight of stone steps leads to the sandstone entrance arch, blocked in with brickwork. 'The Falcon', said to date from 1626, was originally the town residence of the Grosvenors of Eaton but overlies a thirteenth-century crypt. The house was built with the Row passing through the front; the brick infill can easily be seen running up against the older sandstone on the north wall.

South of 'The Falcon' is Bridge House, a handsome six-bay Georgian mansion, now the Oddfellows' Hall, with original staircase and oak panelling. From the traffic-lights by St Michael's Church and 'The Falcon', Pepper Street runs east towards the city walls, where there is a gate called 'Wolf Gate' or 'Wolfeld Gate':

Pepur Stret
Goith oute of Brugge stret Apon the Southe syde of the churche of Saynte Michell, & putteth ouer Flesshemongers Lane to Wolfelde yate in the walles . . . the whych yate some tyme had a Hollo grate wyth a Brugge for [horse and man]. . . . This yate was Clossyd vp and fordonne for so muche as a yonge man in the Somer season toke a mayres Doughter and Bere hair out of pepur strete, as she was playnge at the Baule Amongst other maydens, & yond wyth Hur A Waye. And after, He maryed the same mayde.

This gave rise to the Cheshire saying, "When the daughter is stolen, shut the Pepper Gate," which has much the same meaning as shutting the stable door when the horse has bolted.

The gate had a shield of Hugh Lupus, a white wolf's head on blue, over the archway, and this presumably gave it its name; 'Wolfeld', on the other hand, may be derived from the Old English girl's name Wulfhild, or the Norse Ulfaldi. It was called 'Newgate' from an early period and was rebuilt in 1608 and again in the late 1760s, in much the present form, a plain sandstone arch, which remained, after the replacement of the four main gates on Classical lines, the last survivor of the early city gates. There was a square tower there in the sixteenth century. The great new archway built in 1938 over the gap made in the walls to the south for the inner ring-road, giving traffic better access to the already congested city centre, is now called 'Newgate'.

The Wolf Gate was a major target for the Parliamentary forces during the siege. On Michaelmas Day 1645,

The besiegers made a breach in the walls near to the Newgate, by the battery of 150 cannon shot, and at midnight made a sharp assault on the breach. They likewise attempted to mount the walls with scaling ladders, but some officers and several soldiers were hauled in over the walls, some of the ladders too were dragged over, and many of the assistants thrown down and killed, and the rest forced to give over the attack.

Next to the gate was the city cockpit, last used in the nineteenth century. In the 1960s remains of the baths building of the Roman fortress were discovered north of Pepper Street. An altar was found, naming Titus Pomponius Mamilianus Rufus Antistianus Funisalunus Vettonianus, legate of the 20th Legion. Although Roman remains may be expected in any excavation in the city area, it should be remembered that the greater part of the fortress was given over to repetitive barrack blocks, and (for all that researchers have been happy to hypothesize the location of all the elements of the fortress on the basis of the plans of other legionary forts) the location of other buildings has generally been elusive. It so happened that the 1960s saw the completion of the inner ring-road and the sinking of foundations for several new major building-developments, and archaeologists suddenly had a glut of sites to try to record, and many areas could not be adequately investigated. Publication of satisfactory reports on several of these sites is still awaited.

There were almshouses on Pepper Street, founded by William Jones of the Middle Temple in 1658, for four men and six women at least fifty-three years old, each given a room and bedroom and one shilling a week – "all antient inhabitants of Chester; such as frequent the church on Sundays and holydays, and that hold no opinions contrary to the doctrine and discipline of the Church of England . . . and are not guilty of any gross sin, as adultery, fornication, drunkenness, swearing, railing or the like".

On the east side of Lower Bridge Street, below the corner with Pepper Street, is the Tudor House, dated 1503 but perhaps from 1603, a three-storey black-and-white house decorated with ogee braces. The Tudor House now contains the Oriel Fine Art Galleries. The building was recessed at the front for the Rows, but the gap was built up in Georgian times with the present first storey. A pseudo-antique plaque on the front reads: "THIS TUDOR HOUSE WAS BUILT ABOUT 1503 AD IN YE REIGN HENRY VII".

Pepper Street has been widened and devastated as part of the inner ring-road, which winds through here in a constricted form from in front of the Castle to Foregate Street via St John's Church. 'The Red Lion' near the south-west corner of Pepper Street, dated 1642, occupied part of the site of Windsor House, a modern office-block of dark red brick. The lion on the tower of the multi-storey car-park further to the east came from a brewery there demolished during the road-widening. In 1875 a battered altar was found at the corner of Newgate Street (which now survives in only truncated form as the back entrance to the shopping precincts) with Pepper Street:

DEO
MARTI
CONSERV
...TVS
......

("To the god Mars, the Preserver, . . . tus . . . . ." – nothing else remains.)

7

ST OLAVE, KING and MARTYR
Lower Bridge Street, Bridge Place and the Wishing Steps

WHO was St Olave? St Olave, King and Martyr, whose feast is celebrated on 29th July, is better known as King Olaf Haroldson of Norway, slain at the Battle of Stiklestad in 1030, in conflict with King Cnut (Canute) of England and Denmark. After his death the devout and ascetic Olaf became the centre of a nationalistic Christian cult in Norway, and in the eleventh century several churches in England were dedicated to him.

St Olave's tiny church had a tiny parish, 600 feet long, from Lower Bridge Street to the east wall, and at most only 400 feet wide, from above St Olave Street to the bottom of Duke Street (the ancient Clarton Lane): the parish did not provide an adequate living for its rectors. The civil area, St Olave's Ward, contained St Olave Street and the east side of Lower Bridge Street below it and across the river into Handbridge.

The church is recorded from about 1110, when it was granted to St Werburgh's Abbey. The present fabric, although heavily restored in 1859, is essentially that of the mediaeval chapel. In the seventeenth century there was a wooden bellcote over the west end. Even in its present state, used as a reading-room, it gives a better idea of the mediaeval city churches than can be gained from any of the others.

The church has had a history of being closed. In 1394 the parish was united with St Mary-super-Montem. It revived in the fifteenth century until 1628, when the parish was thrown in with St Michael's. The rectory buildings below the church fell into ruins and were not rebuilt. In 1666 the churchwardens reported "That in the time of the late warrs the silver boule and cover given by Dannat to the Church were by longe hydinge in obscure and moyst places to preserve them, from the hands of sacrilegious persons soe canckred that they were altogether useless, soe that they brake in peeces."

St Olave's was given a curacy in 1744 and continued until 1839 and reunification with St Michael's. The registers, which survive from 1611, are in the Cheshire Record Office. Inside the doorway of the church is an inscribed stone:

AD 1744
This Curacy of St
Olave was Augmen
ted with Lands
Purchased for 400£
Whereof were
Given by Queen
Ann's Bounty 200£
Collected by Thomas
Mather Esqr. 100
Part of Mrs Barons
Legacy 100

The small churchyard, enclosed by ornamental iron railings, is now overgrown, with fragments of sandstone and patches of cobbles and concrete among the weeds.

The rector of St Olave's from 1772 to 1816 was Thomas Crane, who was also for a time a master of the King's School. On one occasion, when a brass was being disturbed during work in the Cathedral, he observed that it was in fact a palimpsest, with a seventeenth-century inscription relating to the Verney family on the reverse. In consequence of his copying the inscription and sending the details to Earl Verney, the latter made him his private chaplain. A copy of the brass is now on the south wall of the Cathedral; it is to Mary Lloyd, who died in 1684, daughter of Sir Edmund Verney of Buckinghamshire, "G'T STANDERED BEARER TO HIS MAIESTIE K. CHARLES THE 1'ST, WHO DYED IN THE BEDD OF HONOVR IN THE BATTLE OF EDGE HILL".

Mr Crane's motto was *Qui corvos pascit pascere potest grues* ("He who feeds the crows can feed the cranes"). He is recorded as a very tall man, who lived with his eccentric spinster sister in Lower Bridge Street in a state of poverty induced by the meagre income of St Olave's. It is said that when they laid the table, they did so for three, in case the Devil should chance to join them. When Bishop Blomfield remarked, conversationally, "Well, Mr Crane, this is your living?", Crane replied, "Yes, my lord, only it is my starving." A churchwarden butted in to complain that the cocks and hens crowed during divine service, and what should they do about it? – to which the Bishop replied "Cut off their heads."

Thomas Crane published a small history of Chester and some notes on Eccleston. St Olave's parish lay outside the area of the Roman fortress, below the Roman walls. Close to the church inurned burials of the first century were discovered in about 1884.

Talbot House, formerly the Albion Hotel, stands near the church. The Duke of Wellington stayed there on 27th December 1820 for a banquet at the Exchange, during a visit to Combermere Abbey. He went over to the Castle, but when he attempted to get back to his rooms, "the crowd was so dense that the endeavours of the soldiers was found impracticable: whereupon the Duke mounted one of the Mail Coaches, and drove down Castle-street to the Hotel." There was an assembly-room in the Albion, a great range of stabling, and gardens and a bowling-green at the back. The four-storey 'Talbot', built in 1715 as the Park House, is part of a group of Georgian houses along this side of Lower Bridge Street, with No. 51 adjoining, and Bridge Place, a fine eighteenth-century terrace, at the bottom. Bridge Place makes a pleasant nook close to Bridgegate, with a row of limes and a little stretch of cobbles by the pavement.

Duke Street runs along from Lower Bridge Street to the walls; on the corner is 'The Cross Keys', a large terracotta and stone public house. Duke Street itself is virtually devoid of any feature of interest. In 1851 a Roman winged statue, about two feet tall, was unearthed there, and is now in the Grosvenor Museum.

The east wall is on a higher level than the south, and at the south-east corner there are six flights of three stone steps, of 1785, from the one to the other. These are called 'the Wishing Steps'. At the top is a stone inscribed:

O   So far goeth the Parish   S. M P
S. P.   of St. mareys

for this is the boundary between St Olave's parish ("S. O P.") and St Mary's, within the walls. The theory of the Wishing Steps is to make a wish at the bottom of the steps and then run to the top, down again and up again without drawing breath, in which case the wish should be fulfilled, "even to the half of the kingdom".

Nearby a flight of steps called 'the Groves Steps' or 'Recorder's Steps' leads down to the Groves. This was originally enjoyed by the inhabitants of St John's parish as a private right of way to

houses on Deeside (including that of the Recorder Roger Comber-
bach, who died in 1719). The steps were built about 1720 and
rebuilt in 1808. The plaque by the steps is nineteenth century and
inaccurate:

> RECORDERS STEPS
> Erected by the Corporation of this City
> AD 1700
> For the Convenience of
> ROGER COMBERBACH. Recorder.

To the west is a plaque in the outside of the wall recording the
laying and planting-out of the embankment in 1880–81 by
Charles Brown, the Mayor.

It is only a small distance along the walls to the far end of St
Olave's, marked by iron plates on the wall of the Nine Houses, on
Park Street below. Six of the nine seventeenth-century houses
survive, bisected by the boundary with St Michael's. To the north
is a large black-and-white house of 1881 with the inscription,
"THE : FEAR : OF : THE : LORD : IS : A : FOUNTAIN : OF :
LIFE :".

8

THE CASTLE
Great Hall, Exchequer and Gloverstone

THERE was probably a fortification in this prominent position in the south-west corner of the mediaeval walls when they were constructed in 907. Ordericus Vitalis says that William the Conqueror had the castle built in 1069, and the first written references to it are from the Norman period.

There were upper and lower wards surrounded by a high embattled stone curtain-wall. The Castle was on a natural knoll, rendered more precipitate by a deep ditch below the walls. The wall of the lower bailey was built in about 1251. The main gateway, to the lower ward, was not far from the present *propylaeum* (main entrance) to the Castle, but it was a large stone gatehouse formed by two arches between two massive round stone towers and defended with a drawbridge. In the centre of the lower bailey was the well; on the west a square tower on the curtain wall; on the east the Great Hall, or Hugh Lupus's Hall, a large, long stone building to which, at a later period, was added a small central cupola.

The Great Hall was demolished in 1790; the site is close to the present Military Museum. There was a single large sandstone hall, which the smaller Exchequer building adjoined, at right angles, on the south. The hall had two crenellated square turrets with large lattice windows facing the lower bailey, and a wide entrance with a Tudor arch into the more southern of these. An external staircase led up to a door above this entrance, and it is thought that this turret was Maysham's Tower, where the ancient rolls of the earldom were kept. This frontage and the cupola on the roof were added in a reconstruction in 1578.

At a later date the palatine court and the Assizes were held in the Great Hall, and the records of the earldom were stored there. Until 1581 the shire hall had stood outside and adjoining the castle walls, and lay "vncovered and in ruyn", but in that year it was removed to Northgate Street and was transferred here after the siege.

A bridge led to the upper ward, through another gatehouse over a second drawbridge. The upper ward had at least four square embattled towers along the wall, with arrowloops and crenellations. In this inner stronghold was a Norman tower, supported on a single stone arch, called 'Julius Caesar's Tower'.

The earl had a garden and an orchard within the Castle walls, and in the fourteenth century a keeper was paid 3d a day to maintain them. The Castle remained in active use as a fortified position throughout the Middle Ages, and the ministers' accounts are full of details of its provisioning and repairs. In 1303–4, for instance, the following items were purchased for use there:

1 hogshead of wine
1 corselet
2 cuirasses
3 old iron skullcaps
1 winder for a crossbow
1 wooden crossbow on two feet
6 crossbows on single feet
1,000 arrows

By the sixteenth century the Castle's main importance was as the administrative centre, but the defences were falling into dilapidation. On 30th November 1585 the Castle bridge collapsed, killing two horses and some cattle crossing it at the same moment as a load of coal.

In 1649, after the siege, Royalists imprisoned in the Castle plotted to seize the fortress and garrison it against their captors. The plan was discovered, and two of those involved were executed by firing-squad in the Cornmarket. On 4th November 1655 Parliament decided to break down the fortifications to render the Castle untenable, and it remained in this ruined state until the eighteenth century.

The whole of the Castle, except the walls of the upper bailey and Julius Caesar's Tower, was demolished in 1790. The tower continued in use for a while as the powder-magazine; the Castle as a whole held a huge armoury at this period, of no less than thirty thousand weapons. The tower was then cleared and refaced, destroying its picturesque crumbling appearance. When the foundations of the tower were excavated in 1837, one of the

Water Tower spur arch

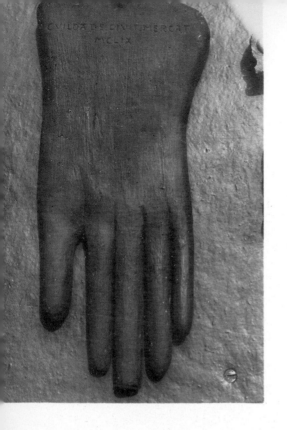

The Wooden Glove

(Below) Bridgegate

Entrance to St Michael's Arcade

Eastgate Street

Recorder's Steps

Water Tower

(Opposite) Constabulary Headquarters

Stanley Place

(Below) A house in Park Street

THE : FEAR : OF : THE : LORD : IS : A : FOUNTAIN : OF : LIFE :

DENTAL SURGERY

corners was found to rest on an arch thought to be of Roman construction.

The small plain upper chamber, which has a vaulted and groined stone roof supported on slender pillars, was the chapel of St Mary-infra-Castrum. James II heard Mass there on this visit to Chester on 28th August 1687. At that time the chapel was decorated with nine coats-of-arms, probably of castle or county officials. In 1831 a fragment of incised Roman tombstone was found in a wall near the south-east angle of the tower.

The Castle was an extra-parochial area. When the city was elevated into a county in 1506, the Castle was excluded, remaining part of the shire. The Great Hall, 99 feet long by 45 feet broad, with a high open roof "supported by woodwork, in a bold style, carved; and placed on the sides, resting on stout brackets", was built about 1251. The Earls of Chester held their Parliaments in the Exchequer; there were two seats at the top end, under Gothic arches, one for the earl, the other for the abbot of St Werburgh's, with eight seats on the right-hand side of the hall for the eight barons. A well-known early woodcut shows, on the other hand, four barons facing four abbots of the earldom.

Here the earls held their high courts of parliament, with chancery, exchequer and courts of pleas of the county "distinct and separate from the crown of England": "No inhabitant of the said county palatine, by the liberties, laws, and usages of the same county palatine ought to be called or compelled, by any writ or process, to appear or answer any matter or cause out of the said county palatine, but only in causes of treason and error." There was also a special liberty in Cheshire that a debtor could come to the Exchequer and solemnly swear that he would pay his debts as soon as he was able, and the Chancellor would issue a writ of protection for him against molestation by his creditors.

In 1649, after Charles II had been declared a traitor at the High Cross, the authorities removed his coat-of-arms from the Shire Hall, and those of the Earls of Chester from the Exchequer, which had for some time been used as the Custom House for the port.

In September 1785 the first balloon to be flown from Chester was launched from the Castle Yard, advertised with a couple of booms from a six-pound cannon. The Aerial Navigation was effected with steam; the balloon landed after a voyage of 108 minutes 12 miles away, near Frodsham.

The new buildings at the Castle were designed by Thomas Harrison and took about twenty-eight years to complete; Harrison was commissioned in 1785. The castle area was extended considerably, taking in the sites of several houses and a chemical works and two skinneries adjoining. Facing Grosvenor Street is the *propylaeum*, a grand entrance of Manley stone with massive Doric columns and lodges. When the last pillar was erected, in August 1813, the colonel of the Royal Denbighshire Militia placed coins and a brass plate in a cavity at the base, commemorating Wellington's victory at Vittoria two months before.

Across the pediment was painted the inscription "BRITAIN TRIVMPHANT", which after the Battle of Waterloo was adorned with laurels and illuminated. Directly facing the gateway across the Castle Yard is the pillared frontage of the Shire Hall. The whole of the building is of stone. The centre, the old County Hall proper, where the Crown Court is now held, is of a rather greyer stone, with a large pediment supported by twelve large columns. The first column of this portico was erected amid public celebration on 2nd October 1797. Coins were placed in a Wedgwood urn, encased in lead, under the base of the column.

The pillars, rough-cut, weighing about 15 tons each, were brought from the quarry eight miles away, on a six-wheeled carriage drawn by sixteen horses. A further ten columns support the semi-circular Shire Hall, forming a colonnade.

Until the reign of George IV Cheshire retained a measure of palatine status, in that the Assizes were conducted by their own judges, the Chief Justice and Puisne Judge, independent of Westminster. The notorious Judge George Jeffreys was born at Acton Park near Wrexham and became Chief Justice at Chester. Henry Booth, Lord Delamere, his contemporary, records that Judge Jeffreys misused his powers here in his arbitrary and boorish conduct in this office:

I must say [he] behaved himself more like a Jack Pudding than with that gravity that beseems a Judge. He was mighty witty upon the prisoners at the bar. He was very full of his joaks upon people that came to give evidence, not suffering them to declare what they had to say in their own way and method, – but would interrupt them because they behaved themselves with more gravity than he . . . it is said he was every night drinking till two o'clock or beyond that time; and that he went to his Chamber drunk . . . in the mornings he appeared with the symptoms of a man that overnight had taken a large cup.

Assizes were held twice yearly. The records of the Grand Jury for 4th March 1748 state: "There is no Bill of any sort brought before this Jury, nor any Business of any kind whatever, save Eat, Drink, Smoke, and be Jolly." At the opening of the Assizes there was a solemn procession, called 'the Judges' Entry', from the city boundary at Saltney, with the Sheriffs, horsemen, footmen and coaches.

In front of the portico is a fine bronze statue of Queen Victoria in imperial robes holding orb and sceptre, on a stone pedestal decorated with finely-carved coats-of-arms. To the right was the Prothonotary's office, which held the records of the county dating from the thirteenth century, before they were transferred to the Public Record Office in London in 1854. The County Record Office (which is also the Diocesan Record Office) is today in the east wing of the building, in what was the Debtors' Prison, and although the main mediaeval county records remain in London, this is now the repository for most major classes of document, private, public and ecclesiastical, for the shire.

The Debtors' Prison was described in the eighteenth century by Thomas Pennant:

> Their daily confinement is in a little yard, surrounded on all sides by lofty buildings, impervious to the air excepting from above, and ever unvisited by the purifying rays of the sun. Their nocturnal apartments are in cells, seven feet and a half by three and a half, ranged on one side of a subterraneous dungeon, in each of which are often lodged three or four persons. The whole is rendered more (wholesomely) horrible by being pitched over three or four times in the year. The scanty air of their straight prison yard is to travel through three passages to arrive at them, through the window of an adjacent room, through a grate in the floor of the said room into the dungeon, and finally through the dungeon, through a little grate above the door of each of their kennels.

The debtors were allowed six pounds of bread a week; they had a chaplain, who read prayers each Sunday, Wednesday and Friday and delivered one sermon each week.

On the left of the Castle Yard is the handsome Georgian block built to house the Exchequer and part of the Barracks. The building is now the Military Museum, in which are displayed various trophies and relics of the Cheshire Regiment. In 1858 new Militia Barracks were erected next to the Esplanade (now the south end of Nicholas Street) opposite St Bridget's Church, but these have been demolished, and opposite the *propylaeum*, close to the site of St Mary's Nunnery, has been built the eight-storey headquarters of the County Constabulary. This directly overlooks the Roodee and offers to the Castle a blank wall decorated with a concrete hieroglyphic relief.

The shire gaol was in the ancient northern gatehouse of the Castle. It is recorded from 1237–8 and was rebuilt 1292–3. At that period, apart from common felons, there were numerous Welsh and Scottish prisoners-of-war and hostages from the successive border campaigns. Prisoners-of-war were held separately from the felons; the Scots were housed in their own chamber with a trapdoor. In all there were four 'gaols' in the Castle, each provided with a pair of stocks, and some prisoners were manacled or held with bolts and fetters, collars and chains.

Richard II was held there on his fateful journey back to London and death at the order of Henry Bolingbroke. The prison was in the two great towers of the main gatehouse. Information was extracted from lesser offenders by starving them and by 'pressing' their chests with weights; some executions were carried out by pressing to death.

The prison was also used after the Reformation for the imprisonment of recusants – that is, persons refusing to attend the Church of England, mainly Roman Catholics. Discipline in confining the recusants was lax: they were allowed "to goe and ryde abroade at their pleasures". In 1581, however, it was decided to remove them to the New Fleet prison in Manchester, "for that the inhabitants of Manchester were found to be generally well affected in religion; and that the Castle of Chester stood too near unto the sea coast." Nevertheless, Chester continued to be used to hold Papist dissenters. In 1577 the prisoners included Richard Sutton and John Colpage "two olde preistes, verie wilfull and obstinate". In 1588 a Welsh Catholic priest dressed in a white surplice managed to get into the gaol and conduct a Mass for the recusants. The gaoler was also the castle gatekeeper.

On 23rd April 1590, St George's Day, during the general celebrations on the Roodee below, the gaoler, John Taylor, attacked and killed one of the prisoners with a pitchfork. The man, John Hocknell of Prenton, had been taken there because he had claimed to have read a prophecy "Wherein he found the letter G, whereof he cold make noe construction except it shold be that Queene Marie had a son called George. Whereof the prophesie made mencion as though he shold goe to Constantinople and theire fyght and lose his lief against the Sarizens." Taylor was hanged for his actions.

In the eighteenth century a visitor to the common gaol found that a man who had attempted to escape "in addition to the heavy double irons on his legs, a strong iron belt round his waist, and a long collar round his neck, with a prong that went down his back" and had been shackled for two or three months in this way. The gaoler had been impressed by ways in which he had seen blacks restrained in the Leeward Islands and had had a pair of iron gloves made to use on his inmates. The Castle prison was closed on 13th September 1884, when the prisoners were removed to Knutsford.

When the Castle was rebuilt, the line of the city walls was moved further south and west than the mediaeval line, and in front of the County Hall, opened in 1957 by Elizabeth II, the walls peter out to become part of the pavement. The space which was enclosed by this extension was the industrial area called 'Skinner's Lane'. The new County Hall is a flat-roofed, four-storey structure with a central columned porch at the head of a flight of steps. Above the doorway is a small carved stone Cheshire coat-of-arms. The county has extensive administrative buildings here, in the Castle above and in other buildings in Chester.

At the top of Castle Street, north-east of the Castle, was a small area outside the jurisdiction of the city but in St Mary's Parish. There was a knot of houses here, at Gloverstone, supposed to have taken its name from a large white stone on the city boundary. In the seventeenth century Gloverstone was described as a village, and it is recorded earlier as a manor. In 1811 there were 122 people in thirty houses living there, but when the Castle was rebuilt, the site was cleared for a new section of barracks.

By a peculiarity of law and custom in Chester, criminals from the county gaol could not be executed there but had to be taken from the Castle by a little lane called Holme Street to Gloverstone and were there handed over by the Constable of the Castle to the Sheriffs of the city, accompanied by their bailiffs and the Town Clerk, on horseback, and the Constables. They took the prisoners by cart to the City Gaol, and the executions took place there or at Boughton.

The church of St Mary-super-Montem immediately adjoins the Castle on the east and probably originated as a chapel for the stronghold; the oratory of St Mary-infra-Castrum (commonly called St Mary-de-Castro) was supplied with priests by St Mary's.

9

ST MARY-super-MONTEM
Bridgegate, Dee Bridge and Handbridge

THE street leading south from High Cross to the Old Dee Bridge is Bridge Street, passing through the city walls by Bridgegate. The right to the sergeancy of the gate became divided into moieties at an early date; one half was acquired by the Earls of Shrewsbury, the other by the Rabys of Raby. The earls held a house with the gate on the east side of Bridge Street directly above the gate. This is now 'The Bear and Billet', a fine four-storey half-timbered house, dated 1664, with a single large gable. 'The bear and billet' was the crest of the Earls of Warwick, and there is no obvious reason why the sign was adopted for this house in the nineteenth century; it may have been adapted from the sign of the White Bear. The second and third storeys, which project slightly over the street, have typical continuous windowbands with latticework leading; the house vies with Bishop Lloyd's House as the best in the city.

The Roman south gate was further north, where St Michael's now stands; Bridgegate is in the mediaeval walls, which were substantially repaired in the eighteenth century. The Raby moiety of the gate had belonged to a certain Richard Bagoth, who sold it in 1270 "because I have not been able to keep up the service of the said gate in proper manner, and especially in time of war, because of my weakness and poverty". That was after the city had been threatened with siege by both the Welsh and the magnates.

The mediaeval gateway was a single pointed arch, defended with a portcullis, between two large embattled round towers. Upon this was built a three-storey square tower called 'Tyrer's Tower', containing a tank into which fresh water was piped from Boughton. William Webb says, about 1615:

This bridge-gate, being a fair strong building of itself, hath of late been more beautified by a seemly water-work of stone, built steeple-

150

wise by the ingenious industry and charge of a late worthy member of the city, John Terer, gent. and hath served ever since, to great use, for the conveying of the river water from the cistern, in the top of that work, the citizens houses in almost all the parts of the city, in pipes of lead and wood, to their no small contentment and commodity.

Later an octagonal water-tower was built on the western turret, and the rooms in the gatehouse were let out to merchants.

The mediaeval gateway was demolished in 1781 and replaced by the present simple ribbed-stone archway, although a little of the fabric of the old gateway can be traced in the wall to the east. There is now a single arch for traffic, flanked by two small arches for pedestrians. The walk along the wall over the bridge is protected by pretty stone balustrades. Inscriptions over the pedestrian arches record the demolition of the mediaeval fabric "having been long inconvenient" and the building of the new, naming the mayors, architect and murengers. On the outside of the gate are stone plaques decorated with fasces and the scales of Justice. On the east side of the gate, in the city wall, is a carving of the Prince of Wales's feathers, dated 1714.

On the west side of Lower Bridge Street, above 'The Bear and Billet', is a black-and-white two-gable house with a projecting upper storey, 'Ye Olde Edgar' (the King Edgar Tavern), on the corner of Shipgate Street. Higher up is Gamul House, set back and reached by a flight of steps, with the front door on the first floor. The house is of about 1700 and has some Jacobean furnishings. Above the Georgian doorway with a pediment are five little third-storey windows, three oval and two square. Charles I stayed with Sir Francis Gamul in his house, which stood on this spot, during the siege. Gamul Terrace leads along south to four later houses above the street. A few years earlier, when a vault was being dug under the house, Roman tiles were found marked with the name of the 20th Legion Valeria Victrix, and perhaps these were shown to the King during his stay.

The Shipgate, which was held by the sergeants of Bridgegate, was a simple sandstone arch at the foot of St Mary's Hill, west of Bridgegate. The street is now blocked off at the bottom by part of the County Hall, and the archway, which was taken down in April 1831, has been re-erected in the Grosvenor Park. Drawings of the ancient Shipgate show it as a pointed arch below a square tower, but the structure in the park is semi-circular. In the fourteenth century it was written: "Anendz this yate before the Bruge was mayde ther was A Ferrye bott that Brought bothe hors and man ou' Dee."

The Old Dee Bridge at the foot of Bridge Street was the ancient crossing of the river, carried on nine or ten sandstone arches. In the early Middle Ages the bridge was of timber; it is recorded as having collapsed in 1227, and its replacement was broken down and carried away by a high tide in 1297. The far end of the bridge was rebuilt in 1500. The stone structure, which perhaps dates from 1297 and was repaired 1347 – 51, proved resistant to inundations: on 16th January 1551 "in the night, there arose a mighty great wind, and the flood came to such a height that many timber trees were left by the ebb, on the top of Dee Bridge." In 1574 the bridge was in ruin and decay and was repaired again.

At that period there was a gateway at the Handbridge end of the bridge, with a small mill with a single waterwheel on the west. This outer gateway was built about 1400, out of the murage tax, and demolished in 1784. West of Bridgegate, at the foot of the city walls, was a little pointed archway from which the city drainage-system, the *cloaca*, emptied into the Dee. In the eighteenth century the underground network of tunnels was described as "perfect still, their outlets into the river under the City Walls are visible; and they say that they are so high that a man may walk upright their whole length". The bridge was widened in 1826; tolls were charged for passage until 1885. It remains a narrow roadway, governed by traffic lights. There are now seven salt-caked sandstone arches of varying patterns, the furthest rebuilt in 1500. The footings of the Handbridge gatehouse can still be traced in the stonework.

At the north end, below the bridge, were the ancient Dee Mills, said to have been built by Hugh Lupus, the first Norman earl, in the late-eleventh century. There is a weir across the river, called 'the Causey' or 'Causeway', which is also attributed to Hugh, who granted sixty fisheries above the weir to various of his dependants. Apart from these Stalls-in-Dee, he himself had the Earl's Pool, next to the Causeway. He granted the tithes of fish and of the mills to St Werburgh's Abbey.

There were two, and later three, waterwheels at the Mills, to which all grain in the city was taken to be ground. By 1600 there were eleven wheels, six used for grinding corn, two for raising water to the Bridgegate tower, and three for fulling cloth – that is, for beating new cloth to cleanse and thicken it. The flow of water to the mills was governed by the Causeway, so that when it was broken by a torrential current in February 1601, the mills were left dry and useless until the breach could be repaired three months later. There was litigation at the time to try to have the Causeway demolished, for it was blamed not only for the flooding of the water meadows upstream but also for the silting of the port below the city walls. The matter was taken before the Privy Council, who decided to uphold the *status quo*. The mills were owned by the Gamul family. (Thomas Gamul was at that time Recorder of the city.) Until the late-nineteenth century lampreys were caught on the Causeway and taken to the High Cross to be sold.

In their latter years the mills suffered three successive disastrous fires. The first started at about midnight on Saturday 26th September 1789, when the mills were completely destroyed. At about midnight on Saturday 6th March 1819, when the city was disturbed with political troubles, the mills were alight again. One person was killed, and only part of the shell of the mills remained standing; the rebuilding cost £40,000. While the Infirmary Annual Ball was being held at the Albion Hotel nearby, at 2 a.m. on 6th January 1847, the mills were alight again; one was entirely destroyed, and £4,000-worth of damage was done. The Corporation bought the mills in 1895, and there was another fire shortly afterwards; milling stopped in 1908, and the buildings were demolished in 1910.

The site is now occupied by a little anonymous stone hydro-electric power-station, built in 1913; the turbines were then the largest in the country, producing 1½ million units of electricity a year, at a quarter of the cost of the Steam Works which they replaced.

From near Bridgegate a lane called Shipgate Street leads west to the bottom of St Mary's Hill. On the corner are two attractive Georgian houses with steps up to the front doors. St Mary's Hill is one of the most pleasant backwaters of modern Chester. A leafy cobbled lane rises up to St Mary-super-Montem (St Mary's-on-the-Hill) with flights of stone steps by the churchyard wall. Only the extensions of the County Hall at the foot of the slope obtrude. At the top of the hill is the old brick rectory, built in a Tudor style in the 1830s. Against the north wall were found remains of a massive Roman wall.

St Mary's Church has a high square pinnacled tower with

prominent gargoyles. The church was rebuilt in 1665 and restored in the nineteenth century but is recorded from the early-twelfth century. The top 30 feet of the present tower was added in the Victorian restoration.

The churchyard is still separated by a deep ditch from the Castle, which is immediately to the west. On 8th October 1656 three witches hanged at the Michaelmas Assizes were buried in the corner of the churchyard by the castle ditch. These ladies were Ellen Beech and Anne Osbaston, both from Rainow near Macclesfield, and Anne Thornton of Eaton near Eccleston, each of whom was charged with having cast spells upon particular persons by which they had killed them.

In 1745, in preparation for the Jacobite invasion of Charles Stuart, the churchyard walls were dismantled, and several buildings nearby were taken down and their foundations levelled; part of the church tower was demolished. Unfortunately, St Mary's has closed for worship, and it has become an 'educational resource centre' with the usual 'audio-visual facilities' for visiting schoolchildren.

Entry is by the north-west door. In the porch are two quatre-foils containing pretty stained glass in memory of the Randle Holmes family, of whom more within. Most of the church monuments remain *in situ*. There is a fine oak ceiling, said to have come from Basingwerk Abbey at the Dissolution.

The east end of the south aisle was anciently the chapel of the Troutbeck family, lords of Dunham-on-the-Hill. On the east wall is a faded mediaeval wall-painting of the Crucifixion, with the Queen of Heaven above, and a bishop. The agreement for the building of the chapel in 1433 has survived. The mason, Thomas Betes, was paid £20 and a gown for the work, to be completed "with v faire and clenely wroght wyndowes, full of light; that is to say, on gable wyndow in the Est ende, with iiij lightes; and iij wyndowes on the South side, ichone of iij lightes; and on in the Weste ende, in the beste wise to be deviset: and iiij botras on the South side, with a grete arche in the Weste ende".

Sir William Troutbeck, Chamberlain of Chester, who ordered the chapel, had a painted monument there, with effigies of himself, in armour, and his wife in a blue gown and black surcoat, and the whole ornamented with coats-of-arms; painted glass in their memory was in the south window. Their great-grandson Adam and his wife Margaret were also represented here in effigy. The

Troutbecks acquired a moiety of the sergeancy of Bridgegate and Bridge Street and had property in Bridge Street and Foregate. In 1660 the roof of the chapel collapsed, destroying these monuments. By that time, the Troutbeck estates had descended to the Earls of Shrewsbury, and the south aisle, although rebuilt, is relatively devoid of memorials.

In the north aisle are several notable monuments, the largest being a tomb of members of the Gamul family of Bridge Street. A plaque on the east wall commemorates "EDMVND GAMVL SOMETIME MAIOR OF THIS CITIE" (in 1585) and his wives. The inscription is incomplete: a space has been left for his date of death (1616). The plaque is decorated with strapwork; beneath the inscription is a jawless skull. The top of the monument is decorated with the Gamul coat-of-arms with its quarterings; on left and right it is shown impaled with the arms of the two wives. The Gamul arms were three black mallets on a gold shield.

Below this is one of the sarcophagi, with the effigies of Edmund's son, Thomas Gamul, Recorder of the city, and of Alice his wife. Their arms are shown on the side of the tomb, flanking figures of their three dead children, with the survivor, Francis, who was knighted in 1644, kneeling pensive with his prayerbook open, at their feet: "*minimus natu, nomine Franciscus, puerulus optimae spei*". This boy became the man who entertained Charles I during the siege. Sir Francis lost his eldest son and his fortune for the Royalist cause and died in 1654 (when Charles II was still just a pretender in exile) but had been created a baronet in April 1644 by Charles I; he was said by the Roundheads to have actually struck and wounded during the siege fellow-citizens who suggested surrender.

Thomas, the father, is shown with neat pointed beard and moustache, his hands in prayer. The detail of his costume, with traces of the original paint, is crisp. Thomas and Alice wear ruffs; the folds of her flowing dress are shown in great detail. Their heads rest on tasselled cushions. Thomas died in 1613, three years before his father, when Francis was seven.

Nearby is a second sarcophagus, on which reclines, propped up on his elbow, head on hand, Philip Oldfield of Middlewich and Bradwall, who died in 1616. The spiked iron grate to protect the monument, complete with sprickets for candles, and little metal ensigns with the Oldfield arms, is intact. Along the front of the tomb kneel Philip's four sons, Thomas, Philip, Michael and

William, with their hands on their swords, and shields displaying the Oldfield arms (three silver crosses on a red bend [diagonal stripe] on gold), impaling the arms of their respective wives (Wettenhall, Somerford, Maynwaring and Leftwich). Behind them a crude blackline sketch of a skeleton mockingly imitates the father's reclining pose. At the head of the monument are statues of Philip's two daughters, Elizabeth, wife of John Wettenhall, and Margaret, wife of Peter Shakerley.

The window behind the Gamul monument is also a memorial to Philip's descendants, and nearby an interesting brass explains the preservation of the Gamul and Oldfield monuments after the siege:

> In Memy. of Leftwich Oldfield of Leftwich Hall in this county. He was a zealous Royalist during ye Civil Wars, &, incurred imprisonmt. & ye sequestrn. of his estate by his faithful adherence to ye Stuarts. On ye surrender of this City to ye parliamentary forces in Feby. 1646, sir Francis Gamul, and Leftwich Oldfield Procured an assurance that their respective family tombs in St Mary's church, shd. be preserved from injury, as ye property they most value ye result proved ye advantage of their forethought, as ye two tombs beneath are ye only Monuments of a like character in Chester wh. escaped demolition by ye Puritans.

This suggests that the Troutbeck monuments may already have been destroyed before the roof fell in. The church had been cleared of 'Romish' images in the sixteenth century; in 1559 it was reported that a certain Peter Fletcher "hathe certin ymages" from St Mary's "whiche he kepithe secreatlye". The parish registers survive from 1628, with other records from 1536, at the County Record Office, but a stone's throw away. In the churchyard is a sundial, dated 1739, set on the stump of the mediaeval cross, which was cut down in 1645.

There is also an important set of more modest memorials to the Holme family of Chester. First there is a board on a pillar in memory of Randle Holme (I), alderman and justice of the peace, sheriff in 1615, mayor in 1633 and deputy herald in Cheshire, Lancashire and the six counties of North Wales, who died in 1655, and of Elizabeth his wife. The Holme arms with quarterings are shown impaling Elizabeth's. Randle paid a fine of £10 for contempt for not receiving his knighthood at the coronation of Charles I.

The Holmes had two sons, William and Randle, of whom the

latter survived to become mayor in 1643. There is an elaborate Latin inscription to him on a curvaceous painted wooden memorial nearby, decorated with the Holme arms and quarterings, which traces his ancestry back to the reign of Edward I. Randle II married twice and died in 1659.

Then there is a stone memorial to Randle II's son Randle III, "gent. sewer in extraordinary to King Charles ye 2d, and deputy to ye Kings at arms", who died in 1699, and to his son Randle IV, deputy to Norroy King of Arms, who died in 1707. (The king's sewers were high-ranking officials who served the food at royal banquets and brought water and hand-towels for the guests; although by Randle III's time the office may have become a sinecure, it certainly released him from the obligation of appearing on juries.) The four Randle Holmes are very important to Cheshire historians, because their manuscript notes, including armorials and some extensive descriptions of monuments and transcripts of early deeds now lost, are preserved among the Harleian manuscripts in the British Museum.

At the top of St Mary's Hill is a street called Castle Street which was paved in 1568. Behind the Grosvenor Museum runs Bunce Street from Cuppin Street; "& out of the Sayde Cuppynges Lane goithe Bunse Lane, & it putteth Apon the castyll Lane". On the corner of Bunce Street with Grosvenor Street is 'The Saddle', a black-and-white-over-brick Victorian public house.

St Mary's parish included the south-west corner of the city, except for the Castle, as well as Handbridge across the Dee, and also the townships of Claverton, Marlston-cum-Lache, Little Mollington, Moston and Upton. St Mary's Ward was the west side of Handbridge and of Bridge Street below Castle Street, together with Castle Street itself.

Until 1831 the only main crossing of the Dee at Chester was by the Old Dee Bridge. In that year was completed the Grosvenor Bridge, opened by Princess (later Queen) Victoria and her mother the Duchess of Kent, on 16th October 1832. The royal party stayed at Eaton Hall, where they were lavishly entertained by the Grosvenors. The family had laid out a magnificent park on the left bank of the Dee, with vast private drives extending across the countryside in each direction. The Chester Approach extends for three miles from the Hall to Hough Green on the old turnpike to Denbigh and Wrexham which doglegged in to the Old Dee Bridge by Handbridge.

From Hough Green the Grosvenors drove through a direct route, Grosvenor Road, across the Grosvenor Bridge, continuing as Grosvenor Street, directly into the city. The present state of the whole south-west side of the city attests the power wielded by this single family in the nineteenth century. The Grosvenor Bridge is a handsome single arch, spanning 200 feet, flanked by two tall side-arches on either bank. When it was opened, the bridge was the largest single-span in the world. The architect's original stone model can be seen set in the grass bank below the city walls above Little Roodee.

In front of the Castle *propylaeum* is an equestrian statue to Stapleton Cotton, Viscount Combermere, listing his principal battles. (Field Marshal Combermere, 'the Cheshire Hero', died in 1865.) When Lords Combermere and Hill returned to Chester after Waterloo, they were given a splendid reception, on 15th August 1814. Driving to the city in an open carriage, they were met south of the river by the Mayor and Corporation and the bands of the merchant guilds. After a service of celebration, they were paraded in triumph through the city streets:

A dinner was given to about 200 persons. The table for their Lordships was placed on a platform: they sat under a crimson canopy; the Deputy Mayor in the centre; with Lord HILL on his left, and Lord COMBERMERE on his right. The canopy was elegantly formed and fitted up. At the top were placed a couple of sheathed sabres, with a dove in the centre, holding an olive branch in its mouth. At each corner was the figure of a French eagle inverted, and over them the triumphant flags of England. The armorial bearings of the Noble Lords were placed behind each of their chairs. The music gallery was decorated with laurel and flowers, and gilt ornaments, excellently executed. The front of the hotel was decorated with laurels, flowers, and the flags of England. The carriage in which the gallant Noblemen were conveyed was lined with crimson: at the back were the arms of each and the Prince's plume. The Bridge-gate was covered with laurels and flowers; along the top were the words – "Brave Warriors, welcome!" – "Salamanca – Almarez." – "Europe Liberated".

On the corner of Grosvenor Street is a pretty buff stone bank, with a small clock-tower, erected as a Savings Bank in 1853, now the Trustee Savings Bank. A Roman vase was found on the site. When Grosvenor Road was being laid out, during the digging of the sewers a terracotta mask was discovered, perhaps an actor's mask from the fortress theatre.

On the south side of Grosvenor Street is the Grosvenor Museum, the principal museum for both city and county. The Newstead Gallery is named after Professor Robert Newstead of Liverpool University, a curator of the museum, who collected together and printed details of numerous Roman finds, beside conducting excavations on several local sites. It contains Roman relics together with models and dioramas explaining the lay-out of the fort, with a lifesize model of a Roman Legionary, a perennial source of amusement and interest. Most of the Roman inscriptions found in the city are collected together here, and the best are displayed in the adjoining Roman Stones Gallery. A Georgian house on Castle Street has been converted into the Period House (reached through the main museum) where there are exhibitions of costume and vernacular objects, and several rooms set out as dispiriting period-pieces. On the first floor of the main museum is the Kingsley Gallery, with natural history material (chiefly stuffed animals), and on the second floor an art gallery.

In December 1950 labourers laying a trench for an electricity cable below the Castle Esplanade found, 18 inches below the surface, a heap of what they took to be milk tallies. When the niece of one of the workmen took some to school, a mistress recognized them as silver coins. In the event more than 450 silver coins of the tenth century, with seventy-four silver ingots, bars and pieces of silver wire, were found. More coins and silver may lie beneath the live electric cable there. The cache probably belonged to one of the pre-Conquest moneyers by the name of Heriger, eleven of whose coins were in the haul, which was discovered less than a hundred yards from the museum.

Grosvenor Road cuts across the Roodee, and the smaller area south of the bridge is called 'Little Roodee'. It is a large public car-park by the river, and the first sight of Chester for many visitors. In 1925 a human skull, thought to date from the Roman occupation, was found in the silt 11 feet below high-water-mark on the riverbank at this place.

Chester was the major obstacle to the north Welsh in any attempt to attack or raid Cheshire. The city was protected from Wales by the city walls and the Dee; the Dee was crossed only by the old bridge, protected on the far bank by a gatehouse. Outside it lay part of Chester, within the city liberties and St Mary's and St Bridget's parishes, but beyond the Dee, called Handbridge. When the Welsh attacked, they naturally first plundered and burned

Handbridge (which they called 'Treboeth', 'hot village') before attempting to storm the city. Since most of the men of Handbridge were Welsh, fishers on the Dee, the citizens could view such attacks with equanimity. No Welsh raid on the city has had any success within recorded English occupation.

The manor of Handbridge ('Brvgge') was held in the time of King Edward the Confessor by an Englishman called Leofwine. It was worth three shillings. After the Norman Conquest Handbridge, together with Redcliff (opposite St John's Church) and Leigh (Overleigh and Netherleigh) were all held by Hugh de Mara, to whose estates the Barons of Montalt (Mold) succeeded. By the nineteenth century the Grosvenors of Eaton were the principal proprietors. Although never incorporated, the people of Handbridge chose their own mayor.

Directly facing the south of the city across the Dee, Handbridge is an important part of the landscape, an attractive village running up a knoll on which stands the mock-mediaeval church of St Mary-without-the-Walls (built in 1887) with a handsome tower and tall stone spire. Along the river below are stakes where the boats of the salmon-fishers are moored. In fact, the view of Handbridge from Chester is much better than the view of Chester, with the flaccid staring frontage of the County Hall, from Handbridge.

ʼ The Roman crossing of the Dee was probably close to the Old Dee Bridge, and their approach to the fortress from Whitchurch to the south through Handbridge. Ironically, when the site for St Mary's graveyard was being cleared, seven Roman cremations were discovered. The road (Watling Street) probably closely followed the line of the present Eaton Road. At Heronbridge, just beyond the mediaeval city boundaries, the Romans had an industrial settlement in the second century.

There was an ancient chapel in Handbridge, perhaps not far from St Mary's, dedicated to St James, recorded in the fifteenth century but abandoned by the sixteenth. The house of the Earls of Chester stood in Handbridge, opposite Shipgate, but was in ruins by 1575.

In 1816 George Ormerod described Handbridge as "a populous suburb of Chester, consisting of narrow steep streets, built on a red rock, and almost exclusively inhabited by the lower orders". A few years later the American writer Washington Irving said: "I shall never forget the delight I felt on first seeing a May-pole. It was on the banks of the Dee, close by the picturesque old bridge

that stretches across the river from the quaint little city of
Chester." Curiously, this maypole, rather than being a symbol of
local gaiety and rustic antiquity, had only recently been set up on
the bank, in a bout of political rivalry between the Grosvenor and
Egerton factions.

Until 1807 there was one maypole in Handbridge, at the
junction of Overleigh Road with Eaton Road, close to where St
Mary's was built. In that year John Grey Egerton was elected MP,
and following the election there was strong party feeling in the
city. On May Day the Egerton faction erected their own maypole
close to the river, at the bottom of Sty Lane (later called Greenway
Street) and decked it in blue, the Egerton colour. (This was the
maypole seen by Washington Irving.) A little later fishermen of
the Grosvenor party erected a third maypole nearby, garlanded
with ribbons of yellow, the Grosvenor colour, but this was plainly
out of mere factiousness. The Grosvenor revels continued at the
ancient site, where the old pole was lowered and repainted in
yellow, blue and white diagonal stripes. The weathervane on the
top, a talbot (the Grosvenor crest) was regilded, and the
Handbridge 'Corporation' paraded the streets with the Grosvenor
Band holding the dog and the new garlands on high for public
approval. The pole was re-erected with solemnity, and to a tune
from a fiddle the first dances round the new pole were performed.

Above Handbridge the river makes a wide loop below
Boughton before turning south. The line of the river has shifted a
little to the east, and the Meadows, rough grassland and playing-
fields which were all water-meadows until the nineteenth
century, were once Earl's Eye, an island on the east side of the
current. In 1285 Edward I as Earl of Chester exchanged Earl's Eye
with Randle de Merton for his manor of Merton. Earl's Eye and
Queen's Park, a suburb created east of Handbridge in the last
century, were anciently part of St Bridget's parish.

The loop of the river beyond Roodee, now cut off from Curzon
Park by the railway line, was called 'Bruereshalgh' (heathy nook),
corrupted into 'Brewers Hall', which was held with the sergeancy
of Eastgate from the thirteenth century. The old hall was
demolished in the siege, and the site was used for firing cannon at
the city, but the place was later rebuilt as a farmhouse. The site is
now empty, and the river loop now forms Curzon Park Golf
Course.

The ancient manor of Leigh, held by the Barons of Halton, was split into Overleigh and Netherleigh, south-west and south of Handbridge. In about 1230 Overleigh was granted to the monks of Basingwerk Abbey, who built a chapel there, which survived to the fifteenth century. Overleigh Hall was destroyed during the siege and rebuilt in brick after the Restoration. The Grosvenors had the hall demolished in the 1830s while clearing the ground for their pompous lodge and gateway to the Chester Approach. The name is remembered in Overleigh Cemetery and School nearby. Netherleigh House stood close to Eaton Road; both areas are now part of the city suburbs.

Immediately opposite Little Roodee across the river is the Old Cemetery, opened in the late-eighteenth century, "and, in part, formed out of a stone-delf or quarry; it contains many monuments of considerable taste, and some of very elaborate ornamentation, and of a costly character. It is well planted with trees, and is a favourite place of resort."

Edgar's Field, close to the Old Dee Bridge below Handbridge, is a small quarry excavated by the Romans and now almost entirely overgrown and used as a playing-area and park. On the quarry wall can be seen the worn remains of a relief of Minerva, originally depicted holding a spear with her owl above her, under a crude pediment. The shrine is now protected (and disfigured) by iron railings. In 1923 the ground in front of the shrine was excavated, and traces of camp fires were found with rock waste and pottery from the second to fourth centuries. Much of the softer sandstone used by the Romans in the city will have been cut from there. In 1958 defacing the shrine became a popular recreation among some Chester youths: one boy wearing football boots was found with his leg through the railings kicking pieces off the figure; the owl, which is now just a lump on the rock, had been quite distinguishable until 1957.

10

ST MARTIN-of-the-ASH
Black Friars, White Friars, St Martin's-in-the-Fields

THE parish of St Martin extended from the west wall, south of Grey Friars, east as far as White Friars, and south to the Nunnery. This was once a crowded area of backstreets, many of which have disappeared, and the central area has been cut through by the inner ring-road, Nicholas Street.

The ancient Ward of St Martin extended further north to include the south side of Watergate Street from Watergate to High Cross. The church of St Martin's-of-the-Ash stood just outside the south-west corner of the Roman walls, at the west end of White Friars and Cuppin Street. The church is recorded from the thirteenth century, but there is a curious tradition that it was the most ancient church in the city, the one at which Christianity in Chester was founded.

It was a small building with no side-aisles, lit by lattice windows and with a little wooden bell-turret. On the south side was a small timber priest's room supported by brackets over the south door, with a flight of wooden steps to its entrance. The church was rebuilt in 1721 in brick with a large square tower with stone cornerstones and mouldings. There was a clock on the tower, and large round-headed windows in the side walls and the steeple; entry was by the west door under the tower.

John Wesley, whose evangelizing was supported by the rector of St Martin's, Nathaniel Lancaster, preached near the church on 21st June 1752; he described St Martin's Ash as "as eminent a part of the Town as Drury Lane is in London". Wesley started speaking on "We preach not ourselves but Christ Jesus the Lord", but since as many persons were waiting outside as could crowd in to hear him, he continued the sermon from the doorway; and three hours later a larger congregation had formed and he started again.

When Wesley returned to Chester on 3rd July, he discovered that, two nights before, a mob had pulled down the house where he had preached. His followers had appealed to the Mayor, but he refused to issue a warrant to arrest the rioters, who returned the following night and completed the demolition.

In succeeding months Wesley would preach to a large assembly in the open air at five o'clock on summer mornings at St Martin's Ash; his reception was almost entirely sympathetic. When Mr Sellers, a schoolmaster and lay-preacher friend of Wesley, rowed up from Chester to Sandycroft and to Hawarden to preach, he was met with obscenities, and had bad eggs thrown at him.

In 1842 the living of St Martin's was united with the more prosperous St Michael's, and for a period the church was used by a Welsh congregation. Welsh services commenced there in 1826 and continued into this century, although the church was closed from 1842 to 1869. The ancient monuments included a marble slab of 1647 to "Richard Mvncksfeeld, Bvtchar", decorated with an hour-glass, spade, mattock, skull and crossbones: "My glass is rvnn." The church records, at the Cheshire Record Office, do not date earlier than 1671.

By the time of the construction of the new inner ring-road in 1964, the congregation of St Martin's had shrunk considerably, and the church had suffered some vandalism. The last service was held in February; the church was closed, and two memorial windows were taken down and re-erected at St John Street Welsh Presbyterian church, where they may still be seen. There were anxious protests against the destruction of the church, but equally archaeologists were curious to see what might be uncovered of the corner of the Roman walls.

Before the bulldozers moved in, the burial-ground was cleared, and the remains, with the original gravestones, were removed to Blacon Cemetery. Then the archaeologists set about the site, locating the fortress wall, which had been extensively robbed for masonry in succeeding ages. They also found the north wall of the corner tower. The actual site of St Martin's Church now lies beneath the widened Nicholas Street, the four-lane inner ring-road.

The old St Nicholas Street was at one time called Blackfriars Lane. The Dominican, or predicant (preaching), order of friars, founded in 1216 by St Dominic, wore a white habit under a black cloak, from which they were called 'black friars', and it was for them that a house was established by the earl in Chester in St Martin's parish in the thirteenth century. Pipes were laid to bring in water from a spring, and the friars were exempted by royal charters from toll in the city and at the mills.

St Nicholas's Church, which was in ruins by the sixteenth century, stood next to the Blackfriars', at the end of St Nicholas Street. The friary was broken up in the early-sixteenth century, at the Dissolution. Part of the estates became the grounds of the Stanley Palace in Holy Trinity parish; another part, called 'Black Hall', was a half-timbered mansion with fine gardens, which became a residence of the Grosvenors of Eaton in the seventeenth century and was demolished in the early nineteenth century.

The old street running west from Nicholas Street called Walls Lane was named Black Friars in commemoration of the friary; this roughly marks the southern boundary of their estates, which extended northwards as far as Watergate Street.

The Carmelite Friars, who wore a dark brown habit with a white mantle. were established in Chester in 1279, north of the street still called White Friars, leading off from opposite St Michael's Church on Bridge Street. Their ground extended north to Commonhall Street. In 1400 the earl granted them freedom from tolls because they had so suffered from a Welsh raid and by the great murrain that "they could not serve God or live honestly without aid".

In about 1495 a spire was built on the friary church. After the Dissolution Richard Dutton esquire, who was mayor in 1567, held the White Friars. In that year "He kepte howse at the White Freeyers, and in all the twelue dayes of Christmas kepte open howse for meate and drynke, at meale time, for any that came. All the Christmas tyme was a Lo[rd] of Misrule." Richard also had White Friars Lane paved during his year of office. A map of Chester of about 1590 shows the friary church in ruins.

The lands were obtained by Sir Thomas Egerton, who pulled down the church and built a house on the site. On 21st July 1597 the spire was demolished:

"The White-freeres steeple, curiously wrought, was taken downe and a faire house built there: a great pitie that the steeple was put away, being a great ornament to the citie. This curious spire steeple might still have stood for grace to the city, had not private benefit, the devourer of antiquitie, pulled it down with the church, and erected a house for more commodity, which since hath been of little use, so that the city lost so goodly an ornament that tymes hereafter may more talk of it, being the only seamark for direction over the bar of Chester.

The house of the Egertons was destroyed in the eighteenth century, one of the last surviving parts being a chapel dismantled in 1795. Remains of the friary were discovered on the building of White Friars Cottage in 1884.

The street called White Friars lies upon the Roman street on the inside of the ramparts of the Roman city wall, which lay between what are now White Friars and Cuppin Street. The south-west corner being at St Martin's Ash, Weaver Street is on the Roman street inside the west wall.

Near the junction with Bridge Street, White Friars has some nice plain old three- and 3½-storey brick houses. No. 1 White Friars is a black-and-white house, dated 1658, with two gables on a projecting upper storey. Further up White Friars is an interesting three-storey terracotta house of 1885 called 'White Friars Lodge'.

The land between Black Friars and the Castle is Nuns' Gardens. Randle Gernon, the fourth Norman earl, granted crofts there to the nuns of Chester for the building of a church in honour of God and St Mary in remission of his sins and for the well-being of the souls of himself and his ancestors. The nunnery was free from tolls and was granted its own court, dignity and liberty. In 1358 Edward the Black Prince ordered that any of his officers of the city or the county interfering with the nuns' liberties should be fined £10 of silver. In 1394 Richard II granted them two oaks from Shotwick Park towards the repair of their house and church, and in 1400 Prince Henry (V) granted them ten loads of wood from Llwycyd for ever.

The nunnery itself was immediately north-west of the Castle walls, close to the site of the new County Police headquarters. The main buildings were of stone and dated from the twelfth and thirteenth centuries. The church, of four bays with thirteen altars, was on the north-east of the nunnery, with the cloisters on its south side, surrounding a quadrangle. South of the cloisters was a small chapel.

After 1537, when the nunnery and other religious houses were suppressed, the house was acquired by the Breretons of Handforth, who claimed the nuns' ancient freedom from rates and taxes. In the Civil War, when the city was being besieged by William Brereton, the house was destroyed by the citizens. However, a pointed archway still stood there in the nineteenth century, when it was removed to its present position, in Grosvenor Park: "Many of the bones of the nuns were discovered, and several beautiful fragments of windows and doorways, some of which were in the rich style of the fifteenth century and had been painted and gilt."

There was a detached part of St Martin's parish, extending from near the present Nicholas Street north of Princess Street across to the west walls, and including a segment of ground outside the walls down towards the Crane. This area was called 'St Martin's-in-the-Fields' and is largely occupied today by the Royal Infirmary and part of the inner ring-road. The latter overlies an old street here once called 'the Crofts' and later 'St Martin's-in-the-Fields'.

The Blue Girls School was set up there, in imitation of the Blue Coat School, in 1718, to teach poor girls the catechism and how to knit, sew and spin (including the yarn for their own clothing), for "it is evident to common Observation that the growth of Vice & Debauchery is greatly owing to the gross ignorance of the principles of the Christian Religion, especially among the poorer sort." At the end of their education, the girls were put out to service, complete with "A gown, and baze petty coat, two coifes, a pair of Shooes, a pair of Knitt Gloves, two Aprons, a pair of Leather bodice, and two suits of Pinners, a Bible and book of Common Prayer in octavo, a whole Duty of Man, and an Exposition of the Church Catechism". The school was later moved and in 1810 was settled at Vicar's Lane near St John's Church; the old school house was demolished in 1865, and the site was used for an extension to the Infirmary. The school itself was closed in 1940.

Dr Stratford, commissary of Richmond archdeaconry, left a bequest by which was founded, in 1755, a public hospital. Patients were first admitted on 11th March 1759; the hospital was formally opened on 18th March 1761. The building was erected close to the west wall of the city, in what was then open ground; it became the Royal Infirmary in 1914 and was extended in 1963 with the new out-patient and accident wing.

In 1783 separate fever-wards were constructed, according to the then novel idea of keeping such patients apart from other cases. This was the first hospital to adopt this principle, on the suggestion of Dr Haygarth, one of the consultants, who also in 1778 set up a society in the city to promote general inoculation against smallpox.

The hospital was constructed on an area which had been one of the main Roman cemeteries, below the west wall of the fortress. So many bones had been found in this space that it was commonly supposed to have been a plague-pit and was called 'the Plague Field'. In 1858 numerous graves, some constructed of roof-tiles, containing cremations and inhumations with various small grave-goods, were discovered, and a coin of the reign of Domitian (81–96) was found. During the First World War forty more burials were found nearby, including some of soldiers of the 20th Legion. Traces of the deceaseds' ironshod sandals were found in some cases, and six more coins, all of the second century.

The old main entrance of the Infirmary, with blue-painted pediment above columned portico, faces the west wall. On the façade are inscribed "INFIRMARY" and "Erected AD 1761". In front of the main door is a rough pillar of hexagonal stone blocks, a column of basalt from the Giants' Causeway.

11

ST BRIDGET the VIRGIN
Cuppin Street, Pierpoint Lane, Commonhall Street

ST BRIDGET'S parish lay between Bridge Street on the east, Cuppin Street on the south, Weaver Street on the west, and Commonhall Street on the north. The church of St Bridget or St Bride was on Bridge Street, immediately opposite St Michael's, at The Two Churches, on what is now an open area by the traffic-lights. The mediaeval building was a simple affair, with a large gable adjoining the tower, forming a shelter over the tower door. The body of the church was lit by round-headed windows in the side walls.

An oak pulpit, decorated with carvings of the Apostles, with their emblems, was installed in Elizabethan times and survived the iconoclasms of the Civil War. The church was badly damaged in the siege; in 1695 it was 'ruinate', and a brief was issued to gather funds for its repair; a new plain building of brick was erected.

In the south chancel was an inscription to Stephen Smith "esq., his majesty's customer of the port of Chester, controuler of the port of Dublyn, and eschaetor of the province of Munster, in the kingdom of Ireland". The inscription traced Stephen's ancestry back four generations and was ornamented with his arms.

On 24th May 1778 a certain George Harding, aged 106, married Catherine Woolnoth, eighty-three, in St Bridget's: "The Bridegroom served in the army 39 years, during the reigns of Queen Anne, George I and George II. This is his fifth wife and Mrs Woolnoth's fourth husband."

In February 1786 the churchyard was cleared to widen Bridge Street and White Friars Street, and the church was cased in stone. In 1829 Grosvenor Street was cut through the old street pattern from the new Grosvenor Bridge to St Michael's Church, and St Bridget's was demolished. As a sop to sentiment, an ornamental fountain was set up on the site, but it has long since been cleared away. The burials from the old church were dug up at night by the light of lanterns and transferred to graves in the new churchyard.

The stones and windows of the old church were taken to a Sandemanian Baptist chapel in Pepper Street, which later became a School of Art.

Behind the church site a public house called 'The King's Head' was built; this still stands on this corner, a grey-stuccoed building with two small gables and curving round to form the corner. St Bride's Cross probably stood close to here; in the pleas before the Mayor in the Common Hall on 12th June 1503 an assault is reported of Robert Goodman heuster upon Michael White tailor, at "le Seint Briddes Crosse" within the liberties of the city.

A new church was built next to Grosvenor Street, close to the Castle, at the angle with Nicholas Street. The first stone was laid 12th October 1827 by Bishop Charles Blomfield. This was "a plain oblong structure, with a neat, light, and airy interior, but with no architectural grace to recommend it. There is a gallery at the west end, a flat well painted roof, and it is adorned with a coloured east window, representing the Ascension." The church had an imposing west front with a single pediment upon inset Doric columns, above which was a cupola supported on Ionic pillars.

A memorial was erected in the far corner of the new churchyard to Matthew Henry (died 1714 and buried in the chancel of Holy Trinity), preacher of the Gospel to a large Dissenting congregation founded in Chester in 1687 and established in Trinity Street from 1700. This monument is an obelisk of pink granite decorated with a bronze medallion.

The new church was closed in 1892, when the parish united with St Michael's and the building was demolished. When the site was being cleared, some Roman coins, roof-tiles with the stamp of the 20th Legion and an uninscribed altar were discovered. When the roundabout near the Castle was constructed for the inner ring-road, the graveyard was partly removed, and the remains were re-interred at Blacon Cemetery, but the Matthew Henry memorial now stands in the grass in the middle of the roundabout, and several flat gravestones remain under the trees at the corner of Nicholas Street and Cuppin Street.

The Roman Catholic church of St Francis stands on the north side of Grosvenor Street, not far from the remains of St Bridget's. Work started on the site in 1862, but in December 1863, before completion, the building was half-destroyed by a gale. The congregation erected a temporary chapel in the ruins, until twelve years later the church was rebuilt.

It is a large, handsome building of pink and red sandstone with no tower, at an angle to the street. A new Franciscan friary is being constructed at the back; there has been a mission there since 1858.

In the fourteenth century the little streets running off from Bridge Street were described:

> In Brige stret vppon the west side is A Lane that is namyd of oulde tyme Normans Lane, and now yt is namyd the comenhall lane, and putteth vpon Alban lane, & vpon the same syde more Southe is a lane caulyd perpoyntz lane, that was the waye Su'tyme to the com'an haule; & more southerly this Lane ther is an other Lane caulyd Fustards Lane, and we now caule yt the Whyte Freres Lane, and it putteth vpon Sent Nycolas strete, & Beneyth yt vpon the Same syde is Cuppyng Lane, and it putteth vpon non Lane.

Commonhall Street runs off from Bridge Street to the west. On the corner is Sir Edward's Wine Bar, once the Grotto Inn, previously 'The Harp and Crown'. Commonhall Street, formerly Normans Lane and Moot Hall Lane, is thought to overlie one of the internal streets of the Roman fortress. Two column-bases found in 1899 under the Grotto Inn are now in the Grosvenor Museum. The building is an awkward erection with a bad mock-black-and-white third storey over the Rows.

No. 12 Bridge Street was the home of the distinguished city family of Cowper. It is a half-timbered house of about 1650, containing the city's principal bookshop, 'Bookland'. At the back of the shop on the ground floor, steps lead down to a remarkably good thirteenth-century vaulted crypt, lit by lancet windows in the west wall. Claude Crimes on the north corner of Pierpoint Lane is a fine three-storey Tudor-style wood building of 1897, ornamented with carved human and animal heads.

The Rows ('Scotch Row') extend down the west side of Bridge Street as far as Three Old Arches (in Owen Owen's department store), which takes its name from three plain stone arches, for which a date of 1274 is claimed.

Pierpoint Lane survived as a cobbled entry halfway from Commonhall Street to White Friars. A little bridge carries the Row across the opening to the entry. The name is a revival of the mediaeval form; by the nineteenth century it was a muddy passage called Dirty Lane. Forster's Lane is now White Friars, and Cupping Lane is Cuppin Street, leading off Grosvenor Street. The little stretch of Cuppin Street, where it joined Bridge Street, after

Grosvenor Street had chopped across, was called Little Cuppin Street, forming a passage by the north wall of 'The Falcon', but the buildings have been destroyed, further enlarging the open space by St Michael's.

Cuppin Street has few surviving buildings of either interest or antiquity. On the north side stood a public house called 'The Star', next to an entry called Star Court.

Until the Corporation moved to St Nicholas's Chapel in 1545, the Common Hall was held in a building in Commonhall Street, which thereafter was used by the city company of Smiths and Cutlers. The mayor's courts were crownmoot and portmoot, with jurisdiction over all persons within the city and its liberties, and on the Dee as far as the Red Stones beyond Hilbre Island, except in matters of treason and including sentence of death. The chapel of St Ursula the Virgin stood on the site of the old Common Hall; some of the painted window-glass survived in the building to the late-seventeenth century.

In 1532 the executors of the estate of Roger Smith founded the Hospital of St Ursula on the south side of the street, in front of Barker's Court, about half-way along the street, and incorporating part of the Common Hall site, for six aged persons, preferably freemen or their widows. A guild was established from which to maintain the poor of the hospital. In common with much of this side of the city, the site has been cleared and Commonhall Street widened.

12

THE HOLY and UNDIVIDED TRINITY
Grey Friars, Watergate and Roodee

HOLY TRINITY parish included the whole of Watergate Street and its side streets, with the Roodee outside the walls. The south side of Watergate Street lay in St Martin's Ward, the north side in Trinity Ward.

The church of Holy Trinity, recorded from about 1180, still stands on its original site, although no longer used for worship. Like all the Chester churches, it once stood in its own busy little parish of crowded houses, cottages and fields. In 1554 Ralph Jonson was accused of letting down a wall adjoining the churchyard "wherbie swyne come in and defile the same". Now most of the area is deserted after the mad scramble to flee the city in the rush-hour.

Holy Trinity is on the north side of Watergate Street, on the corner of Trinity Lane. Watergate Street overlies the Roman *via principalis*, and the church is next to the site of the Roman west gate, the *porta principalis dextra*. The church was held by the barony of Montalt, one of the nine Norman baronies, centred on the castle of Mold. A sketch of the church in the seventeenth century shows a building with a square tower decorated with elaborate castellations, turrets and an ornamental steeple with a weathercock. There was a little wooden porch over the tower door, and the body of the church had two aisles with a dormer window. A small chapel or vestry was attached on the north-east. The church records survive from 1633, with registers from 1656, at the Cheshire Record Office.

The sandstone spire was struck by lightning in 1760 and damaged again in 1769 and the year following; the top of the steeple was rebuilt three times in eight years. In the 1770 incident it was hit by a ball of fire during a thunderstorm. The spire was demolished in 1811, but when the church was rebuilt in 1869, in much its present form, a new stone steeple, the only one surviving within the walls, was built and remains a landmark for miles. When the weathercock was taken down in 1609, a bird's nest containing nine eggs was found in the belly of the cock, which was reckoned a minor prodigy at the time.

The old north aisle was called 'St Patrick's aisle'. In 1774 a new north aisle was built out to the west of this, and when the church was rebuilt in the 1860s, it was again extended to the west and a new north aisle added; the resulting ground-plan is rather unusual. The west end of the church now butts on the swathe of Nicholas Street inner ring-road. The square tower is at the south of the church, with crocketted corner pinnacles and the new tall stone spire. The general style of the church is a crisply-cut Victorian Gothic, a disappointing survival in an ancient city with few ancient churches.

The last of the ancient stained glass was destroyed during the Victorian rebuilding. Until the seventeenth century there was a rare representation of the coat-of-arms of Edward IV in the east window: "his arms are painted standing upon a Faulcon, within a Fetterlock, ensigned with a Crown, and supported with the Bull of Clare, and the Lyon of March."

A number of the Chester city guilds, which virtually fell into disuse in the eighteenth century, were revived in 1961. The church was fitted out as the Guildhall; the vestry now houses a small museum of their records and relics. Many of the old memorials there were destroyed long since. Still surviving, but buried under the flooring, is a monument with a recumbent effigy in armour and the inscription "Hic jacet Joannes de Whitmore, obiit 3 kal. Octob. A.D. 1374" and a marble tablet: "Here lies John Whitmore, esq. He was mayor of this city four years successively, King Edward the third then reigning."

From Watergate Street, Nicholas Street runs south towards the Castle. Nearby stood the ancient Franciscan friary founded about 1200. The Franciscans wore grey habits and cloaks, and were commonly referred to as 'grey friars'. After the Dissolution the friary was used as a house and was still standing, complete with the remains of the friary church and cloisters, until the seventeenth century. Pennant, the great traveller and antiquary, described the site as "in the yacht field near the place occupied by the new linen hall". He says that stained glass and painted tiles were occasionally found there.

One of the streets running west from Nicholas Street, and that part of the street under the city wall towards Watergate, was named 'Grey Friars', but the Linen Hall was on the north side of Watergate Street. Running north from Watergate Street opposite St Nicholas Street, and now also overlain by the ring-road, was Berward Street, described in the fourteenth century: "Berward street begenneth at the Graye freers yate, and putteth vpon Barne Lane; and out of this strete Ther went A Layne to sent Cedde churche, Called sent Chedde Layne, & from the Sayde church ther went a waye to the Waules called Dogge Lane." In commemoration of the old name the road south of the Infirmary has been named Bedward Row – although it will be observed that almost all these renamings were misplaced, adding to the confusion. Berward Street was later called Lower Street, and then Linen Hall Street, after the erection there of the new Linen Hall.

This was a quadrangle of sixty shops for the sale of Irish linen which, after the decline of the linen trade, were used for the sale of cheese. The Linen Hall was later fitted out as stables and is used during race-weeks. It was built in 1778, replacing an earlier Linen Hall built by the Dean and Chapter of the Cathedral between the latter and Northgate Street. In its heyday three to four million yards of linen were handled by the market there each year. The mediaeval linen-market was held in the Rows of Watergate Street itself.

The present Grey Friars Street was in the nineteenth century Smith's Walk. There was a ropewalk along the walls at this point. The city chamberlain had a house on the walk, which was struck by lightning during a terrible thunderstorm on 2nd August 1801, when a young woman was killed.

St Chad's Church was at the lower end of Princess Street and apparently fell into disuse in the sixteenth century. In 1662 it is described as "St Chad's chapel in ye field near Watergate, on ye N side now ruinated". The chapel stood on a street called Little Parson's Lane, at the foot of which was St Stephen's Cross, also mentioned in the mediaeval records. St Chad was the first bishop of the Diocese of Lichfield, of which Chester was a seat.

The western walls of the city, mediaeval in origin, overlook the Roodee on the west and the remains of the parishes of St Martin's, St Bridget's and Holy Trinity on the east. It is the least interesting stretch of the walls and no longer directly overlooks the Dee. For a considerable distance the walk is along nothing more than the pavement of the street. The walls were kept in general repair until the mid-eighteenth century, but then the full circuit was restored; the walk along Nun's Road rewards careful attention, because some of the mediaeval crenellation survives there.

In 1608 it was recorded that "a great part of the walls, between the Watergate and the New Tower, were repaired", but alas 1609 notes: "The walls, that were repaired the last year, fell down this year in the month of November." The same stretch of wall had fallen down in 1569 and was repaired with £10 levied as a fine on the Sheriffs for having fought one another in the city.

The west gate of the city, midway along the west wall, led to the Dee, and so was called 'the Watergate'. In 1615: "which gate is less than any of the other three, serving only for the passage to the Rood-eye, and to the bank of the river, where are brought into the city all such commodities of coal, fish, corn, and other things; which barks, and other small vessels, bring up so far upon the water of Dee." The gate was held, like the advowson of the parish, by the barons of Montalt and their descendants. It was a plain stone affair, without towers. In a plan of 1575 the river is shown flowing close to the *porta ad aquam*, with small boats moored by the gate. Timbers from what may have been the Roman wharf were found there in 1874.

The gate was walled up in 1745 as a part of the preparations for the arrival of Charles Stuart. On 3rd July 1788 work started on demolishing the old gate, which was replaced by the present bridge, a plain stone arch with a balustrade and an arch for pedestrians on the south side.

On the north is a little dry drinking-fountain dated 1857. The gate is governed by traffic-lights. There is the Georgian Grosvenor House on the north side of the street, and on the far side of the gate is Watergate Square, with the main entrance to the Roodee Racecourse. A small panel above the centre of the arch on the outside records the date of erection and the names of the mayors and murengers.

The street from Watergate to the High Cross is Watergate Street. These were the side-lanes in the fourteenth century:

"In Wat'gate Stret, Upon the northe Syde of the said strete next to the churche of Sent Peter is A Lane naymed goslane, and upon the same syde more westerlye next to the mansion place is a Lane named Gerrards Lane, & it puttythe vpon the p'sons Lane; & at the est ende of the trenite churche is a Lane naymed the trenite Lane, and upon the other syde Anendz that Lane is A Lane named Alban Lane, & it putteth vpon fosterds Lane."

We can still trace most of these streets. Goose Lane is now Goss Street; Gerrards Lane is Crook Street, Trinity Lane is Trinity Street; and Alban Lane is under the ring-road.

In 1579 Watergate Street, previously a muddy thoroughfare from the river, was paved as far down as the church. On the west side of the church, immediately adjoining it, was the Custom House, rebuilt in 1633, with a sundial above the street. The house was strategically placed between the city centre and the river. Before 1633 the Custom House was in the Castle, in the old Exchequer in the outer bailey.

In 1868 the Custom House was rebuilt in the south-west angle of Holy Trinity churchyard. Across the top is a stone balustrade and a frame with the royal coat-of-arms; the house is now used by an estate agents. In the 1860s, although most boats could not get further upstream than Mostyn, the city was handling £100,000-worth of goods a year.

A little further up the street, on the south side, is a Victorian black-and-white house (dated 1637) called 'Ye Olde Custom House Inn'. Higher up still stood the King's Fish Board, the market to which were taken "all fryshe fyshe Coming to the Citie to be soulde, As Samon, mylvell, Rey or enye other fyshe". The citizens had first choice of the fish: "Non but Cittizens to bye to ix of Clock; fishmongers to x; and after, Strangers; and so of all fish cominge by boots, vpon payne of Imprisonment."

Watergate Street has a good length of Rows, especially on the south side, extending beyond Bishop Lloyd's House, the finest surviving timber town house in Chester, of about 1615, restored in 1899. This is a large black-and-white building with two decorated gables, rising to four storeys. There is a flight of steps from the second storey, the Row level, to the street. The façade is richly decorated with carved timbering.

George Lloyd was Bishop of Chester from 1604. He died on 1st August 1615 at Thornton-le-Moors Rectory. James I called him the "Beauty of Holiness". The Bishop's daughter Anne first married Thomas Yale, grandfather of Governor Elihu Yale, from whom the American university takes its name. Her second husband was Theophilus Eaton of Stony Stratford, who in 1639 founded New Haven in America and was Governor there until his death in 1658.

The house is dated 1615, the year of George's death, but the evidence to connect him with the house is the arms of Lloyd (three white horses' heads on black) impaling those of the see of Sodor and Man on the frontage. There are eight carved panels above the Rows, showing Biblical scenes (such as Adam and Eve, and Abraham and Isaac), the badge of James I and an inscription:

FORMA DAT
ESSE . REI
INTVS . VTR
IN CVTE
AN. DOMINE 1615

("The form gives the essence of the matter, within or without, 1615.") Below the gable are twelve more panels with heraldic motifs, including a nice representation of a dog.

Closer to the High Cross is God's Providence House, dated 1652, with the inscription on a beam: ". GODS . PROVIDENCE : IS . MINE . INHERITANCE ." picked out in white. The painter has chosen to black over the words "RECONSTRUCTED 1862". The white rectangles formed by the timbering of the frontage are decorated with stucco patterns. The house is essentially a Victorian construction exhibiting ornamental timbers saved from its predecessor. The panels between the beam and the window of the original building were decorated with three upright anchors. Nearby is an imitation Tudor house ('The Mandarin Restaurant Ltd') with a similar inscription: ". IN . THE . LORD . IS . MY . STRENGTH ." To the west is an antique-shop in the Old Leche House, the only significant seventeenth-century building on this side, with a nice decorated fourth-storey gable. This was the town house of the Leches of Carden and dates from about 1600. The frontage of the lower three storeys is disappointing, but the Leche House does have a well-preserved interior with elaborate Jacobean plasterwork. There is a high great hall, with a large fireplace below the Leche arms.

The city has a long association with the family, descended from John Leche, surgeon (leech) to Edward III. In 1384 John le Leche and Richard le Leche were pardoned for having murdered a certain Thomas Deek in Eastgate Street, having laid in wait for him armed with lorine, plates, palettes and ketelhattes. It is thought that the Leche House was in the eighteenth century an inn called 'Ye Hand and Snake'.

Adjoining God's Providence House on the west is a group of Georgian houses above the Quellyn Roberts wine-shop. Steps lead down from the street into the shop, at the east end of which is a four-bay thirteenth-century stone crypt supported by octagonal pillars.

The north side of Watergate Street is rather disappointing, although the Rows stretch down to near Holy Trinity Church. The Deva Hotel, near St Peter's, has rambling interiors with a Tudor chimneypiece at the back on the second floor, dated 1509, with the arms of Henry VII.

The Assay Office (closed in 1962) was in Goss Street, an entry running north from Watergate Street next to St Peter's. Apart from official coining, there were occasional unofficial attempts. In 1446 Richard Oldom, a monk from St Werburgh's, was found to have issued £40-worth of false coins (nobles, half-nobles and farthings) in Liverpool. In 1587 a man was drawn, hung and quartered at Boughton for "clyppinge and quoyninge" of money; his quarters were hanged on the four main gates, and his head was stuck on a pole on the further Bridge Gate at Handbridge. In 1613 a tinker was drawn, hung and quartered for coining 2d pieces, and again the gates were embellished with his remains. In 1695 a Londoner called Joshua Horton set up a little private mint in Watergate Street, not far from the Assay Office, but the heat from his furnace attracted attention and he fled, together with an alderman's daughter.

Among the Roman remains found in Watergate Street are two altars, of which one has this dedication:

```
FORTVNAE . REDVCI .
. ESCVLAP . ET . SALVTI . EIVS
LIBERT . ET . FAMILIA
(T. PM)PONI . T . F . GAL . MAMILIAN(I)
RVFI . ANTISTIANI . FVNISVLAN(I)
VETTON(I)ANI . LEG . AUG .
D D
```

("To Fortune the Home-Bringer, to Aesculapius, and to Salus, the freedmen and slave-household of Titus Pomponius Mamilianus Rufus Antistianus Funisulanus Vettonianus, son of Titus, the Galerian, imperial legate, gave and dedicated this.")

The old Yacht Inn stood in the Yacht Field, close to the site of the Infirmary. The new Yacht Inn was built on the corner of

Watergate Street with Nicholas Street and was, in the nineteenth
century, "without exception, the most picturesque and curious of
all our Chester inns". Jonathan Swift stayed there during his visits
to Chester and scratched on a window:

> Rotten without and mould'ring within
> This place and its clergy are all near akin.

Also attributed to Swift is this verse about the yacht:

> My landlord is civil, But dear as the devil:
> Your pockets grow empty With nothing to tempt ye:
> The wine is so sour, 'Twill give you the scour:
> The beer and the ale are mingled with stale:
> The veal is such carrion, A dog would be weary on.
> All this I have felt, For I live on a smelt.

Below Holy Trinity Church, on the far side of the ring-road,
stands the Stanley Palace, a substantial timber house built on part
of the ancient estate of the Black Friars. Dated 1591, it is a three-
gable building, to which a further gable to the north and two
facing Watergate Street have been added by the Corporation,
which acquired the building in 1931. The house was in a narrow
entry, but the buildings opposite were demolished to present it to
the general gaze. It is now used by the English Speaking Union but
was the Chester residence of the Stanleys of Alderley. They
extended the house at the back in about 1700, and here can be seen
their arms and motto 'Sans Changer'.

Near the Linen Hall is a street called Stanley Place, close to the
site of an open space called Linen Hall Field where on 17th April
1779 the General Assembly of Quakers was held.

Stanley Place, built on the Yacht Field, was laid out in 1778 and
was for many decades an exclusive neighbourhood, a square of
elegant Georgian houses in "a most convenient, dry and healthy
situation, commanding a very pleasing prospect of the Flintshire
Hills and the River Dee". The two terraces remain; the house on
the south-west still has the Georgian porch for accommodating a
sedan-chair. Perhaps the inhabitants were dismayed when the new
City Gaol was built there in 1807.

Public hangings usually took place beyond the Barrs in
Boughton until the new gaol was built to replace the prison in the
Northgate. The new gaol was built of brick, close to the city walls
near Watergate. On the east side was the House of Correction; the

executions were held on the roof over the stone gateway. The first hangman, or Deputy Sheriff, there was Samuel Burrows, a local butcher. Hangings were public events, and barriers had to be erected in the road between the gaol and the city walls to hold back the assembled crowds.

On 3rd January 1823 this announcement appeared in the *Chester Chronicle*:

> Debtor's Room, City Gaol,
> Jan. 1st
> The Debtors in the City Gaol beg respectfully to return thanks to the Sheriffs for the very liberal treat they gave them of roast beef, plum pudding, and excellent ale, on Christmas Day: and if anything can enhance the value of the gift, it is the handsome manner in which Mr Sheriff Ducker ordered the distribution.

On Sunday night in the following May, Samuel Williams, a convict under sentence of transportation for breaking into a counting-house, broke out of the City Gaol. He was locked in his cell at nine in the evening. He smashed through a strong brick partition wall into the felons' dayroom. The heavy door was locked but, taking embers from the fire, he burned the corner of the door and squeezed through into the felons' yard. Attaching a brush to a hook, and these to a rope made of old linen, he made a grapple. Standing on the bars of a lower window, he hooked the bars of a higher grating with the grapple and lifted himself up to the roof of the chapel, from which he dropped down to the ground outside the north wall. He had been left in his cell manacled with irons on each leg, connected with a chain. The chain and one iron were left in the cell, but he had to effect his escape with the other iron still in place. Job Williams, his accomplice, had escaped the gaol three weeks earlier.

The gaol's governor, Horatio Nelson Tivy (forty-eight years of age, rather slender in person and of a dark complexion, a native of Cork), absconded in February 1853 with cash fraudulently appropriated to himself from the gaol accounts, and the property of several prisoners. He was thought to have made off for London, bound for Australia, having left his children in Chester unprovided-for.

The City Gaol was demolished by the Grosvenors in 1879, and in 1883 the Queen's School for girls was moved to new buildings there from Watergate Street. The school (taking its name from

Queen Victoria) has a fine ivied Tudor-style terracotta frontage facing the west walls.

On 5th November 1772 a puppet-show was held in Eaton's Room next door but three, below Bishop Lloyd's House in Watergate Street. The show was crowded with children. Tickets had been bought for the scholars in a small school in Mainwaring House across the street, but the master was unwell, and to their disappointment, the boys could not go. The main show was a puppet pantomime called *Harlequin Restored*. Tickets (pit 1s, gallery 6d) were sold at the door. Handbills had been posted: "Those who please to honour the Projector of these curious Performances with their Company will find a great deal to laugh at, and nothing to be sorry for."

Beneath the room was a vault used as the warehouse of a city grocer, including about a third of a ton of gunpowder. At the height of the performance, perhaps because of a Guy Fawkes Night firework, the stores were ignited, and almost instantly the gunpowder went off, wrecking the first storey of the house above. The explosion brought down the floor and the injured and dying spectators into the cellar. Rescuers were at first afraid to enter the ruins for fear of a further explosion; but a certain Joseph Hand, hearing the groans and screams of the wounded, declared "What is my life more than that of another man?" and leaped into the gaping ruins, soon joined by other helpers.

Nineteen bodies were found in the ruins. Gentlemen arriving on the scene insisted that all persons showing any sign of life must be taken immediately to the Infirmary. The thirteen city constables were drafted in to keep order amid the mounting hysteria as the labourers searched the wreck. In all, twenty-three people were killed and eighty-three injured, of whom fifty-three had to be treated at the Infirmary, and three died shortly afterwards.

Funeral sermons were preached in all the churches of the city; the bells were tolled, and Chester was thrown into mourning. The loss of his son and daughter were too much for one of the city merchants, who never recovered his sanity. The owner of the cellar fell into a fever caused by the shock, and died within a few days. £630 was collected in the city for the injured and the relatives of the dead.

When Mr Thomas Townshend of the Abbey Square was given the news, he asked "Was anyone of consequence injured?", and was thereafter stigmatized by the tag "Mr Consequence" for his apparent heartlessness. A Quaker called Thomas Brackenbury, seeing the accident as a divine warning against puppet-shows, issued a pamphlet called *The Explosion: or an Alarming Providential Check to Immorality.* The passage by Eaton's Room, leading back to Commonhall Street, was called Puppet Show Entry. Today this whole area has been replaced with a modern block of property in which a Row level has been retained, and there is no trace of Eaton's Room or the entry.

In the early Middle Ages the west wall of the city immediately overlooked the River Dee, which then flowed round the city on both south and west. Today the river runs in a great bow on the far side of a large open space next to the walls called 'the Roodee'. This originated as a muddy island ('ee' or 'eye') in the river, on which stood a stone cross, the Rood. The cross, the foot of a square-section stone pillar in a square socket-stone, still stands on the Roodee, which is now the city race-course, enclosing 65 acres of open, level grass. In the sixteenth century the Rood stood on a base of three or four steps, with a pillar at each corner.

The Roodee was deemed part of Holy Trinity parish, but it could not be tithed because it was land recovered from the sea. In 1636 "The maior caused the durt of many foule lanes in Chester to be carried to make a banke to enlarge the roodey, and let shipps in. It cost about 100£." An embankment was built along the far side of the ground to protect it from the river in 1710; in 1720 part of this cop was washed down, so it was rebuilt and faced with stone. By 1615 the Roodee was

a very delightfule meadow place, used for a cow pasture in the summertime; and all the year for a wholesome and pleasant walk by the side of the Dee, and for recreations of shooting, bowling and such other exercises as are performed at certain times by men; and by running horses in presence and view of the mayor of the city, and his brethren; with such other lords, knights, ladies, gentlemen, as please at these times, to accompany them for that view.

At the foot of the city wall by Nun's Road, close to the Roodee, is some substantial masonry thought to have been part of the Roman quay wall. Although only four or five courses of these sandstone blocks now show above the surface, the wall extends a further 15 feet in depth underground and had groin walls running off at right angles. The quay wall stands about 40 feet in front of the mediaeval city wall, and in the intervening space several

Roman burials have been discovered, with two silver *denarii* of the late-first century.

At the south end of the main grandstand by the city wall (built in 1839) was discovered, in 1874, a Roman tomb of about the year 90, containing two skeletons, one with a gold ring, beneath an inscribed gravestone, now in the Grosvenor Museum:

> D M
> FL . CALLIMOR
> PHI . VIX . ANI . XXXXII
> ET . SERAPIONI . VIX
> ANN . III . M . VI . THESA
> EVS . FRATRI ET FILIO
> F . C

("To the spirits of the departed, Flavius Callimorphus, aged forty-two, and to Serapion, aged three years six months. Thesaeus set this up to his brother and his brother's son.") Above the inscription is a representation of Callimorphus reclining on a couch, with Serapion sitting on his lap. An amphora stands on one side, and a capon on a three-legged table.

Each year in the Middle Ages the Shoemakers "upon Tuesday, commonly called Shrove Tuesday, or Goteddsday, on the after noone of the same day, at the crosse upon the rood Dee, before the mayor of the cittie did offer unto the company of Drapers an homage, a ball of leather, called a footeball, of the value of 3s 4d or thereabout," which football was played for by the Shoemakers and Saddlers to bring it to the house of the Mayor or of either of the Sheriffs: "Much harme was done, some in the great throunge fallinge into a traunce, some haveinge theire bodies brused and crushed, some theire armes, heads, legges broken, some otherwise maimed, and in peril of their liffe." In 1533 football was banned, and from 1539 the Shoemakers provided six silver arrowheads which were awarded as prizes for a foot-race. Similarly the custom of the Saddlers' providing a ball of silk or a ball of wood painted with flowers and arms to be fought for by the crowd was discontinued in favour of a horse-race for a silver bell. There had also been an old custom of city couples who had married outside the walls, and country couples who had married within the walls, presenting a ball of salt to the Drapers, and this was replaced with silver arrows, prizes for an archery match.

The Roodee was also used for various public and private

occasions. In 1441 the rival gaolers, from the Castle and the Northgate, settled their differences with a fist-fight there. Two years later a suspected case of felony was decided on the Roodee with a trial by combat between accused and accuser. The latter lost and was subsequently hanged.

In January 1791 a young man called Woodfin from Shotwick achieved a record of 61 yards in just seventeen hops on Roodee (he later managed 151 yards in forty-six hops on the saltmarsh nearby). The 'bearing of the bell' developed into the annual races, held on St George's Day. On the Saturday before the Races, they were announced in the streets of the city by a drummer and the Town Crier. The prizes, the bell and a silver bowl, were borne down to the Roodee in a great procession of the Mayor and Corporation and numerous allegorical figures, led in 1610 by "ij men in greene evies, set with worke upon their other habet, with black heare and black beards, very owgly to behould, and garlands upon their heads, with great clubbs in their hands, with firr works to scatter abroad, to maintain way for the rest of the Showe". From 1609 the prizes were three silver bells provided by the Mayor, to be held for a year for the honour, with the prize-money put in by the competitors. The winners gave 10 shillings to the prisoners in the Northgate. The race was "from the new tower to the netes, there torning to run up to the Watergate".

From 1623 a single silver bell was given as the prize, and the race was right round the Roodee, as at present. In the late-seventeenth century St George's Race was transferred from Chester to Farndon, upriver. Chester Town Crier nevertheless was paid 2s 6d to proclaim the races in the city, and he was the official Starter at Farndon.

After 1700 the race returned to the Roodee. In 1807 the Mayor and Corporation had their own stand erected at the city's expense, by which time St George's Plate was called 'the City Plate'. The race-course is today owned by the Corporation and has three meetings which attract huge crowds. The first of these is the successor to the St George's Race, a three-day event early in May, for the Chester Vase, the Cheshire Oaks, Chester Cup, Great Cheshire Handicap Stakes, Ormonde Stakes and the Dee Stakes. There are two days in early July and two days in early September.

The Roodee was the site of the Midsummer Shows. In 1563 "Upon the Sunday after Midsummer-day, the history of Enease and queen Dido was played in the Roods-Eye, . . . on which triumph there were made two forts, and shipping on the water, besides many horsemen well armed and appointed." The Midsummer Shows were already, in the sixteenth century, regarded as of great antiquity, greater than that of the Mystery Plays: "This Midsomer showe had divers thinges in it, which weare ofensive in anchant times (as Christe in stringes, men in women's apparell, with divells attendinge them, called cuppes, and cannes, with a divell in his shape ridinge there." In 1599, "The mayor caused the giants not to go in the Midsummer Watch or Show; also the Dragon and the naked Boys in the same shew not to go, nor the Devil for the Butchers, but a boy to ride as other companies."

On Midsummer Day the heads of the city companies processed with their banners before the Mayor, to do him homage, to St Oswald's Church; after the Restoration the ceremony was moved to 29th May, Oak Apple Day. Moreover, on Midsummer Eve there was the Watch procession, instituted about 1497. The Shows were suspended under the Commonwealth, but on the Restoration £45 9s 8d was spent in replacing the various figures of the pageant, including

For the four great giants, all to be made new, at 5£ a giant, the least that can be, in all 20£ . . . .
   For making new the dragon 5s, and for six naked boys to beat at it 6s
   For making a-new the elephant and castell, and Cupitt to look out of it, and two men to carry it 56s 8d
   For making a-new the four beasts for the leave-lookers called the Unicorn, the antelop, the flower de luce, and the camell, at 33s 4d a-piece.

The pageant normally consisted of four giants, one unicorn, a dromedary, a camel, a luce (wolf), a dragon, six hobby-horses and other figures. The accounts mention a pair of old sheets to cover the 'Father and Mother Giants' and one of the two others was the 'daughter'. Arsenic was put in the paste "to save the Giants from being eaten by rats – 1s 4d". The Merchant's Mount was a cardboard representation of a ship on an iron frame, which could be swivelled on a pivot by a handle turning a mechanism under the frame. In 1670 the shows were transferred to Whit Tuesday, and in 1677 abolished.

In 1539 the reforming mayor Henry Gee ordered:

Forasmooche as the wretched Lif of otiositie or Idlenes is the rote of all vic's, and engendreth slough, pou'tie, mys'ie, and other inconuenienc's as voluptuositie.

Children to be sett to Schole all week, & to Come to Church to here diuine seruice on holy days & Sundays; and afternoone to Shute on Roodey, or elswhere, for pinns or poynts.

All & eu'y the saide mayle chyldryn shall Resorte to the rode ee, or sum other conuenyent place, To shoute, And ther shall shote and ex'cise the craft of Shoutinge and artillarie duryng the Rest and Remynant of the Said holedaye for pynes or poynts, and none other thing.

All parents of children to buye them Bowes & Arrows to sute with on Roodee . . . .

On the north-west corner of the Roodee, next to the river, a House of Industry was built in 1757, a workhouse for the poor of the city. Tickets were given to beggars, which allowed them supper, a bath, a bed for the night and 6d in the morning. It was a large plain building of brick, to which was added an asylum for pauper lunatics and a schoolhouse. The buildings were replaced by a new workhouse at Hoole in the late-nineteenth century.

A little to the north were the Chester shipyards, which produced wooden vessels in the early years of the nineteenth century, at the Crane. New wharfs had been constructed there in the 1730s at the point where the canal joined the Dee. The road leading out of Watergate is called New Crane Street. There were two yards, which were superseded with the advent of larger ships, of iron, built at Liverpool and Birkenhead. *The Mersey*, a sloop of war, was launched at Cortney's shipyard at the Crane on 23rd March 1814. Ten years earlier the same yard produced a gun-brig called *The Defender*.

Between the Roodee and the Crane runs the railway line from Chester across the Dee towards Saltney Junction, and then to North Wales. The river was bridged and the line opened in 1846. On the evening of 24th May in the following year part of the bridge collapsed as the six o'clock train to Shrewsbury was crossing the river. The engine and tender reached the far side but several of the carriages fell the 50 feet into the Dee, killing four persons and injuring many more.

There were originally two gasworks, that of the Chester Gas Light Company behind new St Bridget's Church close to the city centre, the other of the Roodee Gas Company, on the west side of the railway viaduct. The companies were united in 1856 and a new works was built on the Roodee site in 1886. When the site was being cleared, various Roman remains, including a pile from a river wharf, four human skulls and a pig of lead and coins of the first century, were discovered 23 feet below the present ground level.

On Christmas Day 1836, during the packed afternoon service at the Cathedral, a singer was performing the solo portion of Handel's "For unto us a child is born". At the same moment Robert Jones, a clerk at the Gasworks, was taking a stroll by the river. In the Cathedral the gaslights were gradually becoming dimmer, and the congregation began to have difficulty following the texts. With a start of horror, Robert Jones, out by the Dee, realized that he had forgotten to turn up the valves for the oncoming evening. As the singer reached "For darkness shall cover the earth", the church fell into gloom. Robert Jones reached the tap, and the extra gas came surging through the pipes; as the words "Upon them a light hath shined" were uttered, the gas burst up again in great brilliance. In the Cathedral feelings of astonishment, suspicion and superstition mingled.

So let us leave the good people of Chester, the people who made the city, at that memorable moment in a happy Christmas celebration. The city motto is "*Antiqui colant antiquum dierum*", "Let the ancients look after the ancient of days": Chester, beautiful Chester, the city of memories.

INDEX

189